INTRODUCTION TO
CHRISTIAN WORSHIP

INTRODUCTION TO CHRISTIAN WORSHIP

Third Edition Revised and Expanded

JAMES F. WHITE

ABINGDON PRESS
Nashville

INTRODUCTION TO CHRISTIAN WORSHIP:
THIRD EDITION REVISED AND EXPANDED

Copyright © 1980, 1990, 2000 by Abingdon Press

This book is printed on acid-free paper.

Library of Congress Cataloging in Publication Data

White, James F.
   Introduction to Christian worship / James F. White.—3rd ed., rev. and expanded.
      p. cm.
   Includes bibliographical references and index.
   ISBN 0-687-09109-8 (alk. paper)
   1. Liturgics.   2. Public worship.   I. Title.
   BV176.3.W48 2001
   264—dc21

                                                                    00-063986

ISBN 13: 978-0-687-09109-6

12 13 14—18 17 16

To
Decherd H. Turner, Jr.
who has given his time
to help others write in theirs

CONTENTS

LIST OF DIAGRAMS

LIST OF PLATES

PREFACE

his book was originally written twenty years ago after I had taught Christian worship for two decades.. Now, as I approach the end of my ministry of classroom teaching, I marvel at how much more there is to teach. I am most grateful for the wide acceptance the book received in its two previous editions. But I am aware of how much has changed in the intervening years. Many things that were obvious and true twenty, or even ten, years ago are no longer so. Possibilities once dreamed of are now realities, and fresh dreams are in the air. So a new edition seems necessary.

When I started teaching, more than forty years ago, there were few people teaching Christian worship. Now I am surrounded by a multitude of accomplished scholars and teachers. This book tries to incorporate the collective scholarship of a generation of liturgical scholars as much as possible. It is the greatest joy of my life to have so many companions on this journey, and I hope this book will be of help to them in their teaching. I plan to spend the rest of my ministry doing what I can to strengthen the efforts of others teaching Christian worship.

Churches have changed drastically in the past decade. It is probably safe to say that the post–Vatican II era of liturgical revision has now ended with such monuments as the English *Methodist Worship Book*, the American Presbyterian *Book of Occasional Services*, and the Church of England *Common Worship* series (currently in progress).

But the ending of one era gives rise to another and already my former students are discussing the service books and priorities of another generation. I hope this book will help them teach a generation of students who will see yet further change. I am amazed at how much has changed in worship and church music in the past decade; I am confident that the rate of change will not slacken in the future but that the possibilities for the praise of God in Jesus Christ will expand yet further.

A major shift in our consciousness about what it means to be a worldwide church has occurred during the past decade. Translations of this book into Portuguese, Korean, Japanese, and Chinese are now either complete or in production. They have made me realize how thoroughly "North American" I am in all my assumptions. I hope my tone is more modest in this edition and that the book will not inhibit but encourage expressions of Christian worship in forms familiar to other cultures. After all, the West represents a minority of humanity but, at present, a majority of the world's Christians. Soon other cultures will be producing their own liturgical scholars. I have had the joy of teaching some of them in various graduate programs. They will go far in directions I cannot travel.

In these pages I have tried to present, as briefly as possible, what I regard as essential information in preparing one for the ministry of worship leadership. I have attempted to include all the data one really needs to know in planning, preparing for, and conducting Christian worship—except the details pertaining to one's own denominational service books or customs. The information in this book should be equally relevant to both lay members of worship committees and ministers or priests. They will, of course, need to complement these materials by familiarity with their own service books or customs.

Some teachers may find it useful to use my sourcebook, *Documents of Christian Worship* (Westminster John Knox, 1992), which has parallel chapters, in conjunction with this textbook. More detail can be found in my *Protestant Worship* (Westminster John Knox, 1989) and my *Roman Catholic Worship* (Paulist Press, 1995). My book *A Brief History of Christian Worship* (Abingdon, 1993) is an exclusively historical treatment of liturgical developments. And, of course, there are excellent books by other authors as well.

It is not easy to compress an entire discipline into the pages of a moderate size book. Almost every paragraph represents materials that could fill a book or several books. I have reduced books to paragraphs and chapters to sentences, allowing little space to qualify statements. This frustration has been alleviated slightly by listing related reading at the end of the book and in the notes. Many essential books, not repeated in the bibliography, are cited in various notes. I have had to concentrate on areas of widest interest and eliminate others. For example, a disproportionately small number of these pages represent worship in the Eastern Orthodox churches—a major segment of Christianity, but not of my readership.

Vocabulary is an important part of studying any discipline. I have placed about six hundred of the most significant terms, names, and dates in boldface type. The text tries to explicate these in the context they are employed. This edition includes a new chapter on church music in an attempt to remedy a major gap in previous editions. Other sections, such as that on sacramentality, in chapter 7 are new. Parts of chapter 1 have been thoroughly rewritten, and all other chapters and the bibliography have been updated. More diagrams appear in order to introduce as many teaching aids as possible. I am happy that the publishers have made possible the inclusion of a section of full-color illustrations.

Though much of the book is academic in nature, its aim, throughout, is in a pastoral direction for strengthening the worship of Christian communities. The text is predominantly descriptive in order to explain what has been and why, but many chapters have a normative conclusion on what ought to be and why. The descriptive sections provide backgrounds for the normative resolutions. Christian worship, like Christian ethics, is both a descriptive and a normative subject. Specific decisions have to be made locally in terms of people, places, and times, but they should be based on the experience of the whole Christian community throughout space and time. I have tried to portray the richness and variety in Christian worship.

It is my hope that this book will help Protestant readers in the West claim the first fifteen centuries of common heritage as their own history. I trust many Eastern Christians will recognize themselves in much of the material that focuses on the first Christian millennium. At the same time, I believe Roman Catholic readers will identify many practices from the last five centuries that have become a common heritage in recent decades. I believe the study of Christian worship is the best way to learn ecumenism.

I am most grateful to those whom I taught for more than four decades for the questions I have tried to answer. More than two thousand former students are now presiding over worship or teaching. I hope this book will strengthen their various ministries. In particular, I want to thank Shirley Luttio for her help in proof-reading and Cheryl Reed for computer work on my manuscript. Most of all, I thank my wife, Claire Duggan White, for putting up with me while I was thinking about the book and without me while I was writing it.

University of Notre Dame
January 23, 2000
James F. White

CHAPTER ONE

WHAT DO WE MEAN BY "CHRISTIAN WORSHIP"?

n order to speak intelligently about "Christian worship," one must first decide just what this term means. It is not an easy expression to define. Yet until one reflects on what is distinctive about authentic Christian worship, it is all too easy to confuse such worship with irrelevant accretions from present or past cultures in which Christians have worshiped.

First of all, "worship" itself is an exasperatingly difficult word to pin down. What distinguishes worship from other human activities, particularly those noted for their frequent repetition? Why is worship a different type of activity from daily chores or any habitual action? More specifically, how does worship differ from other recurring activities of the Christian community itself? What distinguishes worship from Christian education or works of charity, for instance? Is a "seeker service" meant to be worship?

And second, once we have made up our minds about what we mean by "worship," how do we determine what makes such worship "Christian"? Our culture is full of various types of worship. A variety of oriental religions have made their advent in many communities. Many practice worship but obviously it is not Christian. What distinctive marks make some worship "Christian"? For that matter, is all worship offered by the Christian community always "Christian"?

None of these are easy questions to resolve but they certainly need to be probed. And they are not simply speculative matters of theoretical interest alone. Defining what is distinctive about Christian worship is a vital practical tool for anyone who has responsibility for planning, preparing for, or leading Christian worship. The continuing appearance of new forms of worship has made this type of basic analysis even more crucial for those people charged with worship ministry. Such people are constantly involved in decision making as they serve the Christian community through worship leadership. The more practical the decision, the more necessary the theoretical foundations often become. Is a certain act, such as pledging one's allegiance to a national flag, appropriate in Christian worship? Or is that act out of place? Should other acts, such as celebrating the adoption of a child, which we have not customarily included in worship, find a place in the worship life of the church? Or is that not appropriate in Christian worship? Only if one has a working definition of "Christian worship" can one cope with such practical problems.

I shall explore three methods of clarifying just what we mean by "Christian worship." I have increasingly come to feel that the most adequate approach is a phenomenological one, which simply describes what Christians usually do when they come together for worship. Although this may seem the most simple and straightforward method, careful observation is essential if we are to understand the meanings of the structures or services Christians use over and over again for worship. Most of this book will concentrate on describing the development, theology, and use of actual structures or services.

It is helpful, second, to explore some definitions of greater abstraction that Christian thinkers have used to explain what they understand Christian worship to be. A third method examines some of the key words Christians choose most often (in various languages) to express what they experience as worship. These three methods should force us to reflect on what we ourselves mean when we speak of "Christian worship." In addition, we must consider some of the factors giving both diversity and constancy to Christian worship.

THE PHENOMENON OF CHRISTIAN WORSHIP

One of the best ways to determine what we mean by Christian worship is to describe the outward and visible forms of worship by Christians. This approach looks at the whole phenomenon of Christian worship as it might appear to a detached or alien observer trying to grasp what it is Christians do when they come together.

Christian worship belongs to a wide category of human behavior known as ritual and is the subject of the academic discipline of **ritual studies**. The term "ritual" is used in a variety of ways but seems to have certain abiding characteristics. First, it is behavior; second, by its very nature ritual is repetitive. Third, it is social activity and serves some communal function. George Worgul describes it succinctly: "as a repeated interpersonal behavior, ritual is purposeful."[1] It is of great interest to anthropologists, sociologists, and psychologists. Various kinds of ritual are necessary to the cohesive existence of any human community. Whether it is the celebration of a national holiday, the opening of a new highway, or a college football weekend, ritual plays a vital role in making a proper observance. Family rituals include birthday parties, anniversary celebrations, and visits from grandchildren.

Christian worship, as a repeated social behavior with definite purposes, is probably the most common form of ritual in many Western societies. We can analyze it as a whole because, despite all the different cultures and historical epochs in which it occurs, Christian worship has employed remarkably stable and permanent forms. We shall speak of these as **structures** (such as a calendar for organizing a year's worship) or as **services** (such as the Lord's Supper). Despite constant adaptation, these prove to be remarkably durable. One way to describe Christian worship is simply to list these chief structures and services. We do not need to go into great detail here since most of the book will discuss them much more thoroughly.

In the late twentieth century, liturgical scholars often speak of the essential structures and services collectively as an *ordo*, from the term used by the Russian Orthodox theologian, Alexander Schmemann. Gordon W. Lathrop, a Lutheran theologian, describes the *ordo* as a "core Christian pattern" of worship which he identifies as consisting of Sunday and the week, the service of word and table, praise and beseeching, teaching and bath, and the year and Pascha (Easter).[2] United Methodist theologian Don E. Saliers prefers to speak of a "canon" of basic structures "that have endured the test of time."[3] He adds the "pastoral offices" to the list.

While useful in identifying historically central items, the limitation of such categories is that they suggest that the *ordo* or canon is limited and, presumably, closed. This method ignores ecstatic worship which has been around for centuries (1 Cor. 14:6-19), in which Paul himself excelled (v. 18), and which may have been the most prevalent form of Christian worship at mid–first century and may again be predominant at mid–twenty-first century. It overlooks the richness of recent centuries in developing new functions for worship and creating new forms to fulfill them. For example, early Methodist worship in England took on a new missional function which demanded new services (watch nights) and new components in familiar services (hymnody).

With these cautions in mind, we shall immediately do what Schmemann, Lathrop, and Saliers suggest: list the chief components of the perennial structures and services as a means of defining Christian worship. Even within the New Testament, we see indications of a weekly structure of time. This structure was soon elaborated in various annual calendars for commemorating events in the memory of the Christian community: Christ's death and resurrection, for example, and memorials of various local martyrs. Eventually, daily schedules for public and private prayer were devised. Daily, weekly, and yearly schedules of time are still important components of Christian worship, and we shall survey the operation of these in chapter 2. For our present purpose, however, one thing we can say about Christian worship is that it is a type of worship that relies heavily on the structuring of time to help it fulfill its purposes.

Just as they have found it necessary to arrange time, Christians have always found it convenient to organize a space to shelter and enable their worship. Though various forms have been tried by different cultures over the centuries, the requirements in terms of space and furnishings have remained remarkably consistent. We turn to these in chapter 3.

In addition, since early times, Christians have found music a vital means of expression for their acts of worship. Music is the subject of chapter 4.

In ancient times and up through today, Christians have used a small number of basic services. The first of these is services of daily public prayer. Within the category of daily prayer, there are various forms, some of which are described in chapter 5.

A second type of service focuses on the reading and preaching of scripture and hence is often referred to as the "service of the word." It is familiar as the usual Protestant Sunday service; it also serves as the first portion of the eucharist or Lord's Supper. We shall examine the various forms of this type of service in chapter 6. It provides a constant order, which many Christians identify as their prime experience of what Christian worship is.

Virtually every Christian community has some means of distinguishing those who belong within its body from outsiders. In terms of forms of worship, this designation takes place in various services of Christian initiation. Baptism is the most widely known of these rites but catechesis, confirmation, first communion, and various forms of renewal, affirmation, or reaffirmation of the baptismal covenant are important parts of the ritual process too. Most Christian communities are currently rethinking their theology and practice for making one a Christian, which we shall discuss in chapter 8.

Since New Testament times, we have testimony of Christians gathering to celebrate what Paul calls "the Lord's supper" (1 Cor. 11:20). For many Christians, this is the archetypal form of Christian worship. Only a small minority avoid celebrating it in outward forms. In many churches, it is a weekly, or even daily, experience. Chapter 9 will deal with the forms and meaning of the Lord's Supper.

Finally, there are a variety of occasional services or pastoral rites common in one form or another to almost all worshiping Christian communities. Some of these mark steps in life's journey, which we may or may not repeat: services of forgiveness and reconciliation or services for healing and blessing the sick and dying. Others are one-time rites of passage such as weddings, ordinations, religious profession or commissioning, or funerals. Many of these are called for only as the occasion demands. Many of life's stages and experiences are common to all people, Christian or not. Occasional services to mark some of these journeys or passages have evolved into permanent types of Christian worship. We shall explore these in chapter 10.

Obviously, these basic structures and services do not cover all the possibilities in Christian worship, but they do describe the vast majority of instances of such worship. Various prayer meetings, sacred concerts, revivals, novenas, and a wide range of devotions may be added to them. But, for most Christians, all of these are clearly subsidiary to the items we have listed above and are, to a certain degree, dispensable. Accordingly, our discussion in this book will be chiefly concerned with the basic structures and services with only occasional mention of other possibilities.

Thus our first answer to the question, What is Christian worship? is simply to list and describe the basic forms Christian worship takes and to say these define it best. Nonetheless, we must also investigate other approaches.

DEFINITIONS OF CHRISTIAN WORSHIP

Our purpose in looking at the various ways different Christian thinkers have spoken about Christian worship is not to compare practices but to stimulate reflection. The best way to grasp the meaning of any term is to observe it in use rather than to give a simple definition. So we shall look over the shoulders of several Protestant, Orthodox, and Roman Catholic thinkers to see how they use the term. None of these varying uses of the term excludes the others. Frequently they overlap, but each application adds new insights and dimensions, thus complementing the rest. This effort to "say what we mean and to mean what we say" is a continuing one that is subject to revision as our understanding of Christian worship matures and deepens.

One of the most attractive definitions of Christian worship can be found in a sermon preached by Martin Luther at the dedication of the first church built for Protestant worship, Torgau Castle, in 1544. Luther says of Christian worship "that nothing else be done in it than that our dear Lord Himself talk (*rede*) to us through His holy word and that we, in turn, talk (*reden*) to him in prayer and song of praise."[4] A similar approach appears in the *Large Catechism* where Luther says that in worship the people "assemble to hear and discuss God's Word and then praise God with song and prayer."[5] Thus worship has a duality, revelation and response—both of them empowered by the Holy Spirit.

John Calvin had many negative things to say about idolatry and superstition in worship. But "God has given us a few ceremonies, not at all irksome, to show Christ present."[6] The ultimate purpose of Christian worship is union with God: "We are lifted up even to God by the exercises of religion. What is the design of the preaching of the Word, the sacraments, the holy assemblies, and the whole external government of the church, but that we may be united *(conjungant)* to God."[7]

Anglican Archbishop Thomas Cranmer found the end of the ceremonies of worship to be the "setting forth of God's honor or glory, and to the reducing of the people to a most perfect and godly living."[8] Worship, then, is directed to God's glory and to human rectitude. Cranmer is echoed in modern theologies that link worship to social justice.

The duality of revelation and response is echoed by Russian Orthodox theologian, George Florovsky: "Christian worship is the response of men [*sic*] to the Divine call, to the 'mighty deeds' of God, culminating in the redemptive act of Christ."[9] Florovsky is at pains to stress the corporate nature of this response to God's call: "Christian existence is essentially corporate; to be Christian means to be in the community, in the Church." It is in this community that God is active in worship as much as the worshipers themselves. As a response to God's work both in the past and in our midst, "Christian worship is primarily and essentially an act of praise and adoration, which also implies a thankful acknowledgement of God's embracing Love and redemptive loving-kindness."[10]

These ideas are reinforced by another Orthodox theologian, Nikos A. Nissiotis, who stresses the presence and the actions of the Trinity in worship. He states: "Worship is not primarily man's [*sic*] initiative but God's redeeming act in Christ through his Spirit."[11] Nissiotis stresses the "absolute priority of God and his act," which humans can only acknowledge. By the power of the Holy Spirit, the church as the Body of Christ can offer worship that is pleasing as an act both from and directed to the Trinity.

In Roman Catholic circles, it has been common to describe worship as "the glorification of God and the sanctification of humanity." This phrase comes from a landmark 1903 *motu proprio* on church music by Pope Pius X in which he spoke of worship as being for "the glory of God and the sanctification and edification of the faithful."[12] Pope Pius XII repeated this expression in his 1947 encyclical on worship, *Mediator Dei*. The same definition appears frequently in the 1963 Vatican II *Constitution on the Sacred Liturgy* which "in more than twenty places corrects the former definition of the liturgy and speaks first of the sanctification of man [*sic*] and then of the glorification of God."[13] That reversal of order presents this question: Which takes precedence, glorifying God or making people holy? Many of the debates about worship have revolved around that question, a question particularly pertinent for church musicians.

Should worship be the offering of our best talents and arts to God—even in forms unfamiliar or incomprehensible to people? Or should it be in familiar language and styles so that the meaning is grasped by all even though the result is less impressive artistically? Fortunately, these are false alternatives. Glorification and sanctification belong together. Irenaeus tells us the glory of God is a human fully alive. Nothing glorifies God more than a human being made holy; nothing is more likely to make a person holy than the desire to glorify God. Both the glorification of God and the sanctification of humans characterize Christian worship. Apparent tensions between them are superficial. Humans must be addressed in terms they can comprehend and must express their worship in forms that have integrity. Addressability and authenticity are both part of worship. Furthermore, artistically naive people have often created high art through their genuineness of expression.

In many churches it has also become normal to describe Christian worship as the **paschal mystery**. Much of the popularity of this term is due to the writings of Dom Odo Casel, O.S.B., a German Benedictine monk who died in 1948. The roots of the term are as old as the church. The paschal mystery is the risen Christ present and active in our worship. "Mystery" in this sense is God's self-disclosure of that which surpasses human understanding, of the revelation that was hitherto hidden. The "paschal" element is the central redemptive act of Christ in his life, ministry, suffering, death, resurrection, and ascension. We can speak of the paschal mystery as the Christian community sharing in Christ's redemptive acts as it worships.

Casel discusses the way that Christians live, "our own sacred history," through worship. As the church commemorates the events of salvation history, "Christ himself is present and acts through the church, his *ecclesia*, while she acts with him."[14] Thus these very acts of Christ again become present with all their power to save. What Christ has done in the past is again given to the worshiper to experience and appropriate in the present. It is a way of living with the Lord. The church presents what Christ has done through the worshiping congregation's reenactment of these events. The worshiper can thus reexperience them for his or her own salvation.

Each of these definitions is only a way station on the reader's own journey toward a personal understanding of Christian worship. One must remain open to discovering other definitions and coming to deeper understandings while continuing to experience and reflect upon what defines Christian worship.

KEY WORDS IN CHRISTIAN WORSHIP

Another useful way to clarify what we mean by "Christian worship" is to look at some of the key words that the Christian community has chosen to use when speaking about its worship. Often these words were originally secular but were chosen as the least inadequate means of expressing what the assembled community experienced in worship.

There is a rich variety of such words in past and current use. Each word and each language adds shades of meaning that complement the others. A quick survey of the most widely used words in several Western languages related to worship can show the realities being expressed.

The English language could well be envious of the German word *Gottesdienst*. Seven English words are needed to duplicate it: "God's service and our service to God." "God" is discernible but less familiar is *dienst*, which has no English cognate. Travelers will recognize it as the word identifying service stations in Germanic lands. **Service** is the nearest English equivalent and it is interesting that we, too, use this word for services of worship just as commonly as we use it for gas stations. "Service" means something done for others, whether we speak of a secretarial service, the Forest Service, or a catering service. It reflects work offered to the public even though usually for private profit. Ultimately it comes from the Latin word *servus*, a slave who was bound to serve others. The word **office** from the Latin *officium*, service or duty, is also used to mean a service of worship. *Gottesdienst* reflects a God who "emptied himself, taking the form of a slave" (Phil. 2:7) and our service to such a God.

There is only a slight difference between this concept and the one conveyed by our modern English word **liturgy**. Too often confused with smells and bells (ceremonial), "liturgy," like service, has a secular origin. It comes from the Greek *leitourgía*, composed from words for work *(érgon)* and people *(laós)*. In ancient Greece, a liturgy was a public work performed for the benefit of the city or state. Its principle was the same as the one for paying taxes, but it could involve donated service as well as taxes. Paul speaks of the Roman authorities literally as "liturgists *[leitourgoí]* of God" (Rom. 13:6) and of himself as "a liturgist *[leitourgòn]* of Christ Jesus to the Gentiles" (Rom. 15:16 literal trans.).

Liturgy, then, is a work performed by the people for the benefit of others. In other words, it is the quintessence of the priesthood of believers that the whole priestly community of Christians shares. To call a service "liturgical" is to indicate that it was conceived so that all worshipers take an active part in offering their worship together. This could apply equally to a Quaker service and to a Roman Catholic mass as long as the congregation participated fully in either one. But it could not describe a worship in which the congregation was merely a passive audience. In Eastern Orthodox churches, the word "liturgy" is used in the specific sense of the eucharist, but Western Christians use "liturgical" to apply to all forms of public worship of a participatory nature.

The concept of service, then, is fundamental in understanding worship. A different concept appears behind the word common in Latin and the Romance languages, a term reflected in our English word **cult**. In English, cult tends to suggest the bizarre or faddish, but it has an esteemed function in languages such as French and Italian. Its origin is the Latin *colere*, an agriculture term meaning to cultivate. Both the French *le culte*, and the Italian *il culto*, preserve this Latin word as the usual term for worship. It is a rich term, even richer than the English word "worship," for it catches the mutuality of responsibility between the farmer and the land or animals. If I do not feed and water my chickens, I know there will be no eggs; unless I weed my garden, there will be no vegetables. It is a relationship of mutual dependence, a lifelong engagement of caring for and looking after land or animals, a relationship that becomes almost part of the bone marrow of farmers, especially those whose families have farmed for generations on the same land. It is a relationship of giving and receiving, certainly not in equal measure, but the two are bound to each other. Unfortunately, the English language does not readily make the connection between cultivate and worship that is found in the Romance languages. Sometimes we find richer contents in the words of other languages such as the Italian *domenica* (Lord's day-Sunday), *Pasqua* (Passover-Easter), or *crisma* (Christ-anoint) than in their English equivalents.

Our English word **worship** also has secular roots. It comes from the Old English word *weorthscipe*—literally *weorth* (worthy) and *-scipe* (-ship)—and signifies attributing worth, or respect, to someone. It was and still is used to address various lord mayors in England. The Church of England wedding service, since 1549, has contained the wonderful pledge: "with my body I thee worship." The intention in this last case is to respect or esteem another being with one's body. Unfortunately, such frankness disturbs us and the term has vanished in American wedding services. Other English words such as "revere," "venerate," and "adore" derive ultimately from Latin words for fear, love, and pray.

The New Testament uses a variety of terms for worship; most of them words that also bear other meanings. One of the more common is *latreía*, often translated service or worship. In Romans 9:4 and Hebrews 9:1 and 9:6, it implies the Jewish worship in the temple, or it can mean any religious duty, as in John 16:2. In Romans 12:1, it is usually translated simply "worship"; it has a similar meaning in Philippians 3:3.

An important insight appears in the word *proskuneîn* which carries the explicit physical connotation of falling down to show obeisance or prostration. In the temptation narrative (Matt. 4:10; Luke 4:8), Jesus tells Satan: "It is written, 'worship [*proskunéseis*] the Lord your God and serve [*latreúseis*] only him.'" In another famous passage (John 4:23), Jesus tells the Samaritan woman that the time has come "when the true worshipers will worship the Father in spirit and truth." *Proskuneîn* in various forms is used repeatedly throughout this passage. In a less familiar passage (Rev. 5:14), the twenty-four elders "fell down and worshiped [*prosekúnesan*]." The physical reality of worship is underscored by this verb.

Two interesting words, *thusía* and *prosphorá*, are both translated as sacrifice or offering. *Thusía* is an important term in the New Testament and to the early fathers even though it was used in both pagan worship ("to demons," 1 Cor. 10:20) and Christian ("a living sacrifice," Rom. 12:1 or "sacrifice of praise," Heb. 13:15). *Prosphorá* is literally the act of offering or bearing before. It is a favorite term in 1 Clement—whether referring to Abraham's offering of Isaac or to those of the clergy or of Christ, "the high priest of our offerings" (36:1). Hebrews 10:10 speaks of "the offering of the body of Jesus Christ once for all." Both words play a significant, if controversial, role in the development of Christian eucharistic theology.

A much less prominent word in the New Testament literature is *threskeía*, which means religious service or cult (as in Acts 26:5; Col. 2:18; and James 1:26). *Sébein* signifies to worship (in Matt. 15:9; Mark 7:7; and Acts 18:3 and 19:27). In Acts, another use of the verb designates God-fearers, Gentiles who attend synagogue worship (13:50; 16:14; 17:4, 17; and 18:7). One other term from the New Testament has important uses to describe worship. *Homologeîn* has a variety of meanings: to confess sins (1 John 1:9), "if we confess our sins"; to declare or profess publicly (Rom. 10:9), "if you confess with your lips that Jesus is Lord"; or for the praise of God (Heb. 13:15), "the fruit of lips that confess his name."

These terms from other languages can expand the one-dimensional image of the English term "worship." All are worth pondering for insights into what others have experienced at various times and places. A few English words related to worship need some clarification.

We need to make a clear distinction between two kinds of worship: common worship and personal devotions. The clearest aspect of **common worship** is that it is the worship offered by the gathered congregation, the Christian assembly. The importance of meeting or coming together can hardly be overstated. At times, the Jewish term "synagogue" (coming together) was also used for the Christian assembly (James 2:2), but the chief term for the Christian assembly is the church, the *ekklesía*—those who are called out from the world. This word for the assemblage, congregating, meeting, convening, or gathering is used repeatedly throughout the New Testament for the local or universal church. One of the most easily overlooked aspects of common worship is that it begins with the gathering, in one place, of scattered Christians to be the church at worship. We usually treat the act of assembling as merely a mechanical necessity, but coming together in Christ's name is itself an important part of common worship. We assemble to meet God *and* to encounter our neighbors.

In contrast, **personal devotions** usually, but not always, occur apart from the physical presence of the rest of the Body of Christ. This is not to say they are not linked to the worship of other Christians. Indeed, personal devotions and common worship are both fully corporate since they share in the worship of the universal community of the Body of Christ. But the individual engaging in personal devotions can determine his or her own pace and contents, even while following a widely used structure. On the other hand, for common worship to be possible, there must be consensus on structure, words, and actions or chaos would ensue. These ground rules are not necessary in devotions where the individual sets the discipline. ("Devotion" comes from a Latin word for vow.)

The relationship between common worship and personal devotions is important. Although the subject of this book is common worship and little will be said about personal devotions, it should be clear that common worship and personal devotions depend on each other. The Anglican theologian Evelyn Underhill tells us:

[Common] and personal worship, though in practice one commonly tends to take precedence of the other, should complete, reinforce, and check each other. Only where this happens, indeed, do we find in its perfection the normal and balanced life of full Christian devotion. . . . No one soul—not even the greatest saint—can fully apprehend all that this has to reveal and demand of us, or perfectly achieve this balanced richness of response. That response must be the work of the whole Church; within which souls in their infinite variety each play a part, and give that part to the total life of the Body.[15]

Common worship needs to be supplemented by the individuality of personal devotions; personal devotions need the balance of common worship.

A widely used term in recent years is the word **celebration**. It is frequently used in secular contexts and seems to have developed a vagueness that makes it rather meaningless unless used with a specific object so that one knows what is being celebrated. If one speaks of celebration of the eucharist or celebration of Christmas, the content may be clear. Since the whole community celebrates worship, the leader should be referred to as **presider** not as celebrant.

Ritual is a tricky term since it means different things to different people. To many people, it often implies emptiness (hence "empty ritual"), a rut of meaningless repetitions. Liturgists use the term to mean a book of rites. For Roman Catholics, the word "ritual" refers to the manual of pastoral offices for baptisms, weddings, funerals, and so on. In the Methodist tradition, "ritual" has been used since 1848 for all the official services of the church, including the eucharist, the pastoral offices, and the ordinal. **Rites** are the actual words spoken or sung in a service of worship, though sometimes used for all aspects of a service. The term can also refer to those bodies, such as Eastern-rite Catholics, whose worship follows a distinctive pattern. Rites differ from actions or **ceremonial**, the actions done in worship. Ceremonial is usually indicated in service books by **rubrics**, or directions for carrying out the service. Rubrics are frequently printed in red as the name, derived from the Latin for red, indicates. Another essential element is the pattern for each service, one meaning of **ordo** or **order** (of worship). Order, rite, and rubrics—that is, pattern, words, and directions—are the basic components of most service books.

DIVERSITY IN EXPRESSION

Thus far, we have spoken of the common factors enabling us to speak of Christian worship in general terms. There is certainly enough basic unity that we can make many general statements and expect them to apply to most, if not all, of the forms of worship by Christian people. We need, however, to balance these general statements of **constancy** by considering the cultural and historical **diversity** that is also an important part of Christian worship. The constancy, as we have already seen, is enormous; the diversity is equally impressive. Christian worship is a fascinating mixture of constancy and diversity. We have practiced basically the same structures and services for two thousand years; people on the other side of town also practice them but in their own distinctive ways.

In recent years, we have become much more attuned to how important cultural and ethnic factors are in understanding Christian worship. A strong concern with the link between Christian **worship and justice** has emerged out of this. In a sense, this is nothing new for some Christians. Since the Quaker movement in the seventeenth century, there has been a strong awareness among the Friends that worship must not marginalize anyone because of sex, color, or even servitude. Indeed, the Quaker insistence on human equality derives directly from their understanding of what happens in the worshiping community. That means, of course, that women and slaves were expected to speak in worship—hitherto an exclusively white male prerogative.

The nineteenth-century Anglican theologian Frederick Denison Maurice advanced our thinking about worship and justice as did Percy Dearmer, William Temple, Walter Rauschenbusch, and Virgil Michel in the twentieth century. But it is only in recent years that large numbers of Christians have become sensitive to the injustice of worship forms that marginalize large segments of worshipers because of gender, age, race, or other human distinctions. The result has been efforts to change the language of liturgical texts and hymns where they have tended to make women invisible, to redo buildings that have excluded the handicapped, and to open new roles for those who were previously not welcome to serve in them.

Closely allied with the move to include all people in worship has been the effort to take seriously the cultural and ethnic diversity within the world church. This involves encouraging respect for the variety in and the gifts of differing peoples as legitimate expressions of Christian worship. The technical name for such a process is **inculturation**; the reality is the acceptance of diversity as one of God's gifts to humanity and a willingness to incorporate such variety in the forms of worship. Music is often one of the best indicators of diversity of cultural expression. How limited have we been in emphasizing European expressions of Christian praise when a whole world sings God's glory? New hymnals have tended more and more to reflect cultural diversity, but most of them still have a long way to go before they mirror the variety of people in even a single nation.

The concern for the embodiment of justice in worship has taken many forms, but all of these efforts share a common goal of stressing the individual worth of every worshiper. Where some are neglected or relegated to inferior status because of age, gender, handicap, race, or linguistic background, these injustices are being recognized and alleviated. But it is a slow process to become aware of discriminatory practices then try to find the most equitable ways of redressing them. The result is that Christian worship becomes more complex and more diverse as it tries to reflect a worldwide community. Thus, although what we have said about constancy remains valid, the cultural expressions of that constancy are becoming ever more diverse in the present.

Actually, diversity is nothing new in Christian worship, although regarding it in a positive way may be an important innovation. Even in the earliest liturgical texts, we see different ways of stating the same realities—whether in theological principles or human needs. The differences reflect the varieties of peoples and places. The differing liturgical books provide parallel routes to cover the same journey, but they vary in style and details, just as different peoples in various places differ in those areas that make them distinctive, such as the particularity of the native tongue of every tribe and nation. Liturgies are, most naturally, local, and as we see in diagram 1, a small number of cities, whose local rites won wider usage, have been particularly important in the history of Christian worship.

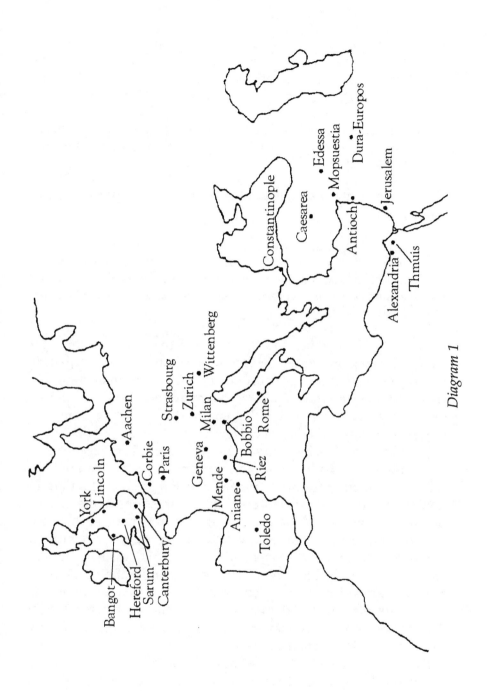

Diagram 1

Let us compare two passages with identical functions from the world's two most widely used liturgies. The first is from the pre–Vatican II Roman Catholic mass, the common preface of the eucharistic prayer:

Just it is indeed and fitting, right, and for our lasting good, that we should always and everywhere give thanks to thee, Lord, holy Father, almighty and eternal God, through Christ our Lord.

The second is the parallel passage from the liturgy of St. John Chrysostom:

It is fitting and right to sing to You, to bless You, to praise You, to give thanks to You, to worship You in every place of your dominion: for You are God, beyond description, beyond understanding, invisible, incomprehensible, always existing, always the same; You and your only-begotten Son and your Holy Spirit.

Both say the same thing, but the style and the spirit are quite different. The language of the first has been compared to the legalistic rhetoric of the Roman law court; the second, to the splendor of the court of the Byzantine emperors. Clearly we are dealing with two different styles of expression that emerged respectively from particular historical and cultural contexts.

Liturgical scholars have sorted out the various ancient eucharistic liturgies into distinct liturgical families. Like human families, they bear common features. Some may belong to the Alexandrian family, named for Mark, and place the intercessions in the middle of the opening part of the eucharistic prayer. Others, such as the Roman rite, use characteristic words to introduce the words of institution: "who the day before he suffered"; while other families, such as that named after John Chrysostom, prefer the phrase: "on the night on which He was delivered up." Just as one may recognize a person's sons and daughters or brothers and sisters by facial similarities, so too, one can learn to identify the liturgical family from which a certain text comes.

Different peoples and places around the Mediterranean world and in northern Europe gave their own linguistic characteristics to Christian worship. Some features disappeared, often because of the stereotyping that printing made available in the sixteenth century. But a wide variety still persists, particularly in Eastern Orthodoxy—and within Roman Catholicism, though isolated in places like Milan, Italy, or Toledo, Spain, or in the Eastern rite Catholic churches. In these disparate rites, we have frank acknowledgment of the true catholicity, that is, universality, of the church. What may seem to be curious and quaint survivals are actually the voices of different peoples and places, adding their own distinctive contribution to the praise of God.

It is common to identify **classical liturgical families** from various areas of the ancient world. Each of these families uses the same services of worship and the same types of service books but each shows individual peculiarities of style and expression. The relationships are shown in diagram 2.

It is easiest to go around the Mediterranean world counterclockwise for a quick enumeration of these families. We shall return to the question of distinguishing between families of rites in more detail in chapter 9. We know of ancient North African liturgies, but they have ceased to exist. The first surviving family we encounter is centered in **Alexandria**, Egypt, the most notable example known is that of Mark. It has Coptic and Ethiopian survivors today in Egypt and Ethiopia. **Western Syria** included the ecclesiastical centers of Jerusalem and Antioch. A liturgy, probably conflating those used in these cities, preserves the traditional name of James, first bishop of Jerusalem. The liturgical patterns of **Armenia** preserve many early features and probably derive ultimately from and belong to this western Syria family. **Eastern Syria** around Edessa was the early center of a most distinctive family, of which the prime example is the rite named for Sts. Addai and Mari. Caesarea in Asia Minor was the home of **St. Basil**, and the liturgy named after him (with an earlier Alexandrian version) derives from the western Syrian pattern. Also deriving from a western Syrian background is the so-called **Byzantine** liturgy or liturgy of **St. John Chrysostom**, fourth century patriarch of Constantinople. From Constantinople, it spread throughout much of the Byzantine Empire and Russia. Only the **Roman rite**, at one time known as the rite of Peter, is in wider use. It is the dominant rite of Roman Catholicism. A large and mysterious family, the **Non–Roman Western** comprises the

The Classical Liturgical Families
Sixth Century to Present

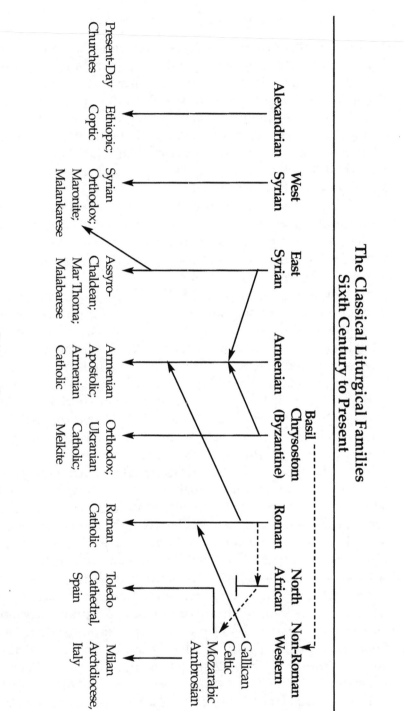

Diagram 2

remainder, with four branches on its family tree: the Milanese or Ambrosian, the Mozarabic, the Celtic, and the Gallican.

The persistence to this day of this diversity within the Orthodox and Roman Catholic worlds, despite occasional efforts at suppression and standardization, is a triumph for ethnic and national differences. It represents the ability of people to preserve expressions and thought patterns that are natural and dear to them.

Diversity characterized Protestant worship from the start. Almost all Protestant worship can be divided into **nine Protestant liturgical traditions**. These are not as easily distinguished on the basis of the texts of eucharistic liturgies as the Roman Catholic and Orthodox liturgical families are, although some Protestant traditions can be easily defined in terms of service books. Some groups, such as the Quakers, have no published rites. But we can speak of distinct liturgical traditions, that is, inherited habits and assumptions about worship passed on from generation to generation. In each case, though, certain dominant characteristics have enough coherence to enable us to distinguish a distinct tradition.[16]

It is not easy to differentiate these traditions geographically since they overlap considerably. Puritans, Anglicans, and Quakers lived side by side in seventeenth-century England, if not too happily. We can chart the nine traditions of Protestant worship in diagram 3. Horizontal lines show movement in relation to conserving (right) or rejecting (left) patterns from the medieval past. The more radical breaks from late medieval worship are indicated by groups in the left wing column; the more conservative reformation groups, in terms of preserving continuity, appear in the right wing, and the more moderate groups are shown in the center. Subsequent shifts are indicated by horizontal lines.

Lutheran worship, originating in Wittenberg, thrived in the Germanic and Scandinavian countries in the sixteenth century and has since spread throughout the world. **Reformed** worship had its genesis in Switzerland (Zurich and Geneva) and France (Strasbourg) but quickly spread throughout the Netherlands, France, Scotland, Hungary, and England. The **Anabaptists** began in Switzerland in the 1520s. **Anglican** worship, as its name soon indicates, was that of the national church of England and represented many of the political compromises necessary for a national

The Protestant Traditions of Worship
Sixteenth Century to Present

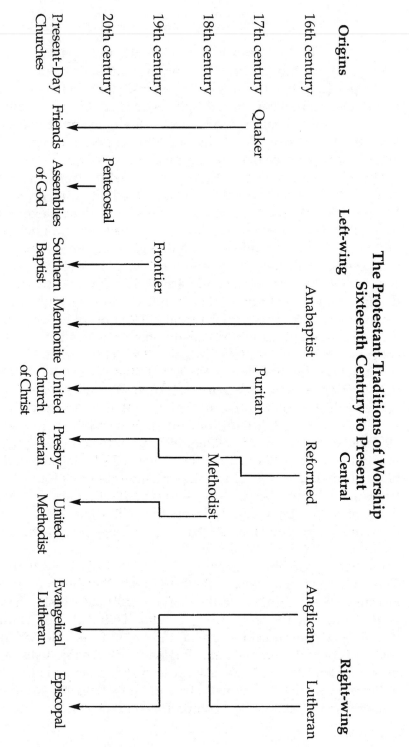

	Left-wing					Central			Right-wing
Origins									
16th century									
17th century	Quaker								
18th century									
19th century				Frontier		Puritan	Reformed	Anglican	Lutheran
20th century		Pentecostal					Methodist		
Present-Day Churches	Friends	Assemblies of God	Southern Baptist	Mennonite	United Church of Christ	Presby-terian	United Methodist	Evangelical Lutheran	Episcopal

Diagram 3

church. The **Puritan** (and separatist) tradition was a protest against compromises that seemed contrary to God's will as revealed in scripture.

The most radical tradition was the seventeenth-century **Quaker** movement. The Quakers' silent waiting on God without the aid of sermons, songs, or scriptures made a drastic break with the past. **Methodism**, in the eighteenth century, combined many strands, from both ancient and Reformation times, borrowing especially from the Anglican and Puritan traditions. The American frontier gave birth to another tradition, especially in developing forms of worship for the unchurched. This **Frontier** tradition is the dominant one in American Protestantism today and is especially conspicuous in television evangelism. In the twentieth century, America also gave birth to the **Pentecostal** tradition. Blacks and women were among the earliest leaders in fostering this tradition.

The coexistence of several traditions has allowed people to seek the forms of expression for worship that are most natural for them. In eighteenth-century England, those who felt too constrained by the *Book of Common Prayer* gravitated to services led extemporaneously in the Puritan tradition, and those who found such worship too clerical could find a different kind of freedom among the Quakers. Fervent hymnody and a warm sacramental life among early Methodists attracted others. Different people could match their diversities of expression by choosing the tradition that seemed most congenial to them. Yet, at the same time, a high degree of consistency existed through the generations within each tradition.

CONSTANCY IN FUNCTION

Much of the study of Christian worship revolves around studying the various service books that some churches use. Because the needs are so similar, certain types of service books recur in many different liturgical families and traditions. It is tempting, but dangerous, to identify worship with books. Books are indeed used for much, if not most, worship, and they are certainly the easiest evidence of worship to study and to analyze. But a large portion of worship is based on **spontaneity**, an elusive subject of inquiry. Various types of worship contain differing rates of both fixed formulas for word and action found in books and the spontaneity that ebbs and flows as the Spirit moves and cannot be found in print. Though little shall be said about spontaneity, it is nevertheless an important ingredient of worship in many Western churches today.

Where the charismatic movement has reached people, including classical Pentecostals and many African American churches, spontaneous exclamations are a vital part of worship. Quaker worship is spontaneity itself, though it exemplifies the need for a self-disciplined freedom if spontaneity is to bear its best fruit. Spontaneity is not just turning people loose for individual introspection or speaking. It is the use of the various gifts of individual people for the benefit of the gathered community. Paul's words on spontaneous worship immediately follow his chapter on love (1 Cor. 13) and aim at one purpose: building up the church (1 Cor. 14:26). What gifts Christians have received are given to be shared in community, not kept in isolation.

Early Christian worship seems to have involved some spontaneity. Most of it, however, had apparently disappeared by the late–fourth century only to spring up again in some of the Reformation traditions. Pentecostal worship in the twentieth century has stressed the unexpected possibilities of spontaneous worship. The absence of service books or printed bulletins in some churches does not ensure spontaneity by any means. In many congregations, repetition has firmly established a structured worship, which is followed with a high degree of predictability. On the other hand, traditions that use service books continue to allow for an increase in elements of spontaneity, especially in intercessions.

If we say little in this book about spontaneity in worship, it is not because it is unimportant but because it is so exasperatingly difficult to chronicle, since the evidence of it is so ephemeral. But it should be clear that worship and service books are by no means synonymous. Service books can only provide standard formulas. A healthy balance must remain between such formulas and the unwritten and unplanned elements that only spontaneity can provide.

With this caveat, let us look at what **service books** can tell us about constancy in Christian worship. Virtually all worship makes use of the Bible, which itself includes many portions written for cultic purposes. The Quakers are an exception to this statement, but widespread biblical literacy among Quakers makes up for their lack of actual reading from the Bible in public worship. Most Protestants and Roman Catholics also make use of a hymnal. In addition, worship in Roman Catholicism and several traditions of Protestantism frequently or always employ a service book. In short, one or more books are regarded as necessities for worship in most Christian traditions.

The books we shall survey are service books. They give a vivid glimpse of the constancy in Christian worship. Even though they vary among themselves, the contents have remarkable similarities. Despite differences in families and traditions, common needs and the application of similar resources to fill those needs are noticeable.

In the early church, a variety of books were used by several people performing ministries of worship leadership within a single service. Both laypeople and clergy had recognized ministries to perform, so they utilized books that contained the particular resources to enable them to take their distinct parts in worship. The idea of putting everything into one book, and placing that only in the hands of the clergy, is a medieval development that has little to recommend it. Currently there is a reversal of the single-book mentality and a return to various books for readers, commentators, song leaders, leaders of prayer, and priests or ministers. There are, after all, a variety of ministerial roles in leading worship, roles which can be shared among a number of people when appropriate books are available.

The invention of printing brought about a situation unknown before, the possibility of liturgical standardization. By the early sixteenth century, there were approximately two hundred versions of hand-copied mass books in use in European parishes and religious orders. Roman Catholics, as well as many Protestants, became convinced that liturgical uniformity was progress. So the first Anglican prayerbook of 1549 decreed that "from henceforth, all the whole realm shall have but one use." Effectively the same thing was done in standardizing the Roman Catholic books down to the last comma with the exceptions allowed only for a few dioceses and religious orders.[17] Such a standardizing tendency in Rome stifled service books written in Chinese in the seventeenth century and other adaptations to indigenous cultures that might have greatly strengthened the mission to China and drastically changed subsequent history.

Today, Protestants and Roman Catholics alike see standardization as a false goal. What may have been liberating in the sixteenth century seems stifling in the twentieth. In our time, many churches seek to undo the medieval clericalization that compressed all liturgical books into clerical documents and the sixteenth-century standardization that made all books identical whether for the clergy or the laity. A variety of ministries in various cultures demands a much more pluralistic approach to liturgical books. Already we see genuine liturgical pluralism with several alternative rites of equal authority made available within the same denomination's book or books. Thus the number of liturgical resources proliferates and only the typical ones can be mentioned.

The chief book for the structure of time is, of course, the **calendar**. Its brevity should not conceal its importance. It governs those elements that change from day to day, or from season to season, in daily public prayer and the eucharist and appears in breviaries and missals. Somewhat similar is the **martyrology**, a book of the deeds of the martyrs and other saints arranged by calendar according to the day of their death.

The services revolving around daily public prayer have entailed an entire collection of books, especially those services developed in monastic worship. Various types of books originally allowed different people to perform their individual functions. The most important was the **psalter**, with psalms and canticles arranged in a variety of ways in different editions. Some were structured according to the weekly recital of the psalms or to accord with feasts or for each hour service of the daily office. Musical portions appeared in the **antiphonary** and the **hymnal**. A **lectionary** eventually contained collections of the scripture readings.[18]

If this sounds complicated, that's because it was; but each person only had to master certain parts, found in the appropriate book. All this changed in time, though not until many centuries had passed.

Then efforts to collect this whole library of books into a single book, the **breviary**, began to succeed. The advent of the Franciscan and Dominican orders in the thirteenth century, orders which needed to be on the road constantly, brought about widespread use of the breviary from which an isolated individual could read all of the daily services. This was also encouraged by the necessities of life in the Roman curia. But the breviary represents a tremendous loss in the variety of ministries and in worship as a community. The 1971 _Liturgy of the Hours,_ which replaced the 1568 Roman breviary, seeks to return these services to both lay and clerical use.

The Reformation, in turn, compressed the breviary still further into Luther's two daily offices or those in the 1549 Anglican **Book of Common Prayer.** Psalter, calendar, lectionary, and morning and evening prayer shared space with other types of worship. These moves did make all types of worship available for the person in the pew, but it also resulted in a drastic reduction in the options provided.

The history of the books for initiation and the rites of passage is quite different. Originally, many of them occurred in the sacramentary, the priest's book for celebrating the eucharist and other sacraments. It contained all the appropriate prayers for various occasions and seasons. Baptism and confirmation, for example, occurred at the Easter vigil in the earliest books, and ordinations tended to come during Lent. In the course of time, baptism and other rites were weaned away from the sacramentaries, and separate books developed for the various offices. The revolution in the practice of penance, for example, led to the compilation of "penitentials" to guide the pastor and the penitent. "Benedictionals" are collections of various blessings of people and objects. In most traditions, some blessings are the prerogative only of bishops and others of priests. The latest Roman Catholic collection is the _Book of Blessings._

In time, these various rites of initiation and passage found their way into collections known variously as the _pastorale, manuale_ (handbook), _sacramentale, agenda,_ or _rituale._ Litanies, hymns, prayers and rubrics for processions found a place in the _processionale._ The Reformation churches usually incorporated many of these materials into a simple service book. For example, the _Sarum_

Manuale provided most of the *Book of Common Prayer* wedding service. Some churches still use the ancient terms as in the *Pastor's Manual* published by the Church of the Brethren in 1978. The *Rituale Romanum* of 1614 was, in effect, a collection of ten separate books: general rules, rites for baptism, penance, administration of the eucharist, ministration to the sick and dying, funerals, matrimony, blessings, processions, and exorcisms. Since Vatican II, most of these rites have been revised and published as separate books. At present, there is no single-volume Roman Catholic ritual.

Nowhere else has the constancy of Christian worship been quite so readily apparent as in the pastoral offices found in the ritual. American Methodists still get married with almost the same vows as fourteenth-century English Catholics made. The basic human needs the ritual ministers to are common: birth, marriage, sickness, and death. Along the way we need to be forgiven and to have God's blessing invoked on people and things about us.

The history of the rites that concern the bishop is similar. Prayers for ordinations originally occurred in the sacramentaries and **ordines** (collections of instruction). Gradually, the bishop's special rites became collected in a special volume, the **pontifical**. In the late–thirteenth century, Bishop William **Durandus** of Mende in southern France edited a pontifical which has shaped all subsequent Western ones. Within it were services for the blessing or consecration of various persons such as confirmation, tonsure, ordinations, the blessings of abbots, abbesses, the consecration of virgins, the coronation of kings and queens, and so on. In addition, there were rites for the blessing or consecration of such objects as churches, an altar-table, vessels, vestments, bells, cemeteries, and so forth. Finally there was an assortment of rites for excommunication, reconciliation of penitents, blessing of holy oils, processions, and such.

Some of this material pertaining to bishops, such as the ordination services, appears as the **ordinal** in Protestant service books. Many service books contain rites for confirmation and the blessing and consecration of various persons and objects such as offices for recognizing Sunday school teachers or for laying a cornerstone. The Roman Catholic pontifical has been revised since Vatican II. No Protestant parallel exists for a later collection, the *Caeremoniale* *episcoporum*, an A.D. 1600 compilation of rubrics and instructions on ceremonial for bishops. The current *Ceremonial of Bishops* was published in English in 1989.

The other principal collection of books is that dealing with the eucharist. We have already encountered the most important of these books, the **sacramentary**, which included prayers for the priest's use appropriate to various seasons and events. The term "sacramentary" has been revived in recent years for the comprehensive volume used at the altar-table in Roman Catholic churches though it does not include materials now found in the pontifical or ritual as did early sacramentaries. But there are other ministries at the eucharist besides that of the celebrant. A **lectionary,** or *comes*, provided the lector, subdeacon, or deacon with lists of the beginning and endings of lections read at mass. Eventually the lections were included in full.[19] Musicians depended on the *graduale* for sung portions of the eucharist.[20] What we call rubrics were recorded in early times in various *ordines*, which also dealt with services now found in the pontifical or ritual as well as the eucharist. Similar forces were at work here, too, as with the breviary, the ritual, and the pontifical. By the late medieval period, the clergy possessed all the books, as the lections, musical portions, and rubrics were placed together in the **missal** so one man could "say" mass by himself. Since the end of the tenth century, the missal has simply echoed the clerical monopoly of worship that had already occurred through a variety of other forces. Except for a few dioceses or religious orders, the sixteenth century standardized the missal. The ***Missale Romanum*** of 1570 remained scarcely changed (except for new feasts) for four hundred years until the Vatican II revision was published. Once again the lections have been relegated to a separate volume, the lectionary. Now others, besides the celebrant, are again encouraged to exercise ministerial functions at mass.

The contents of the missal proved no less essential to the Reformers. Most of them produced their own order of eucharist and incorporated it into their service books, sometimes accompanied by collects and lessons appropriate to the various days of the church year. Even on the American frontier, the Methodists preserved an irreducible minimum of fixed forms for the eucharist.

The contents of the missal are as universal as any in Christianity and provide a fascinating study of constancy.

Thus the contents of several of the liturgical books seem to witness to those constants of Christian worship for which we are looking. The Reformation merely took to its logical end the processes of compression and standardization already well under way in Roman Catholicism. Some of the Reformers managed to compress calendar, breviary, ritual, processional, pontifical, and missal into a single volume. For centuries, various Protestant martyrologies were widely used for devotional reading. People and clergy shared the same books. The results—whether in the *Book of Common Prayer*, the *Book of Common Order*, John Wesley's *Sunday Service*, or various others—are remarkably similar in their consensus in regard to the essentials of Christian worship. The latest liturgical books, currently *The United Methodist Book of Worship* (1992) and the Presbyterian *Book of Common Worship* (1993), serve the same functions (if in newer forms) of the books whose gradual evolution we have been tracing.

Of course, there are differences between books of the same type. The comparative study of rites is known as **liturgiology** and, in the last hundred years, has become a highly specialized science. But the striking fact that remains is the remarkable degree of constancy in agreement among these books from differing times and places about which deep human needs are reflected in, and addressed through, worship.

This quick survey of the phenomenon, definitions, and key words of Christian worship, along with the discussion of diversity and constancy in such worship, will, I hope, help the reader reflect on what he or she means by Christian worship. Further reading, more experiences of worship, and continuing reflection will help expand this understanding.

CHAPTER TWO

THE LANGUAGE OF TIME

T he calendar is the foundation for most of Christian worship except for the occasional rites of journey or passage. There is no better place to begin our investigation of the basic structures of Christian worship than with an introduction to the way Christians use time as a language through which to express their worship.

The centrality of time in Christian worship tells us a great deal both about Christianity itself and about Christian worship. It tells us that Christianity is a religion that takes time seriously. History is where God is made known. Without time, there is no knowledge of the Christian God. For it is through actual events in historical time that this God is revealed. God chooses to make the divine nature and will known through events that take place within the same calendar that measures the daily lives of ordinary women and men. God's self-disclosure takes place within the same course of time as political events: "In the days of King Herod of Judea" (Luke 1:5) or "This was . . . while Quirinius was governor of Syria" (Luke 2:2).

When we encounter religions in which time is illusory or insignificant, we realize just how crucial time is to Christian faith. Christianity talks not of salvation in general but of salvation accomplished by specific actions of God at definite times and places. It speaks of climactic events and a finale to time. In Christianity, the ultimate meanings of life are not revealed by universal and timeless statements but by concrete acts of God. In the fullness of time, God invades human history, assumes our flesh, and heals, teaches, and eats with sinners. There are specific temporal and spatial settings to it all: "At that time the festival of the Dedication took place in Jerusalem. It was winter, and Jesus was walking in the temple, in the portico of Solomon" (John 10:22-23). And when his work is done, Jesus is put to death on a specific day, related to the passover festival of that particular year, and rises on the third day. It is all part of the same time we inhabit—time that is measured by a spatial device, the calendar—the time in which we buy groceries, wash the car, and earn a living.

The centrality of time in Christianity is reflected in Christian worship. This worship, like the rest of life, is structured on recurring rhythms of the week, the day, and the year. In addition, there is a lifelong cycle. Far from trying to escape time, Christian worship uses time as one of its essential structures. Our present time is used to place us in contact with God's acts in time past and future. Salvation, as we experience it in worship, is a reality based on temporal events through which God is given to us. The use of time enables Christians to commemorate and experience again those very acts on which salvation is grounded.

Time is also a language of communication in our daily life (as when we are habitually late for unpleasant engagements). It is a form of communication used with significantly different meanings in differing cultures. (In some cultures, being late for an appointment is a token of respect to someone important, testifying that he or she is obviously a very busy person.) Christianity builds on the natural human sense of time as a conveyor of meaning by fluently speaking the language of time in its worship.

In order to understand how the structures of Christian worship speak through the use of time, we need to explore the past experiences of Christians who structured worship on the basis of time, the theological rationales for so doing, and how time functions in current practice. Through study of these historical, theological, and pastoral dimensions, we can grasp a functional understanding of how time provides the foundation for so much of Christian worship.

THE SHAPING OF CHRISTIAN TIME

The way we use our time is a good indication of what we consider to be of prime importance in life. We can always be counted on to find time for those things we consider most important though we may not always be willing to admit to others, or even to ourselves, what our real priorities are. Whether it is making money, political action, or family activities, we find the time for putting first those things that matter most to us. Time talks. When we give time to others, we are really giving ourselves to them. Not only does our use of time show what is important to us but it also indicates who or what is most significant to our lives. Time, then, is a definite representation of our priorities. We reveal what we value most by how we allocate this limited resource.

The same is true of the church. The church shows what is most important to its life by the way it uses time. Here again the use of time reveals priorities of faith and practice. One answer to What do Christians believe? could be, look at how they keep time! How have Christians kept time in the past?

The earliest portions of the New Testament are imbued with a sense of time as *kairós*, the right or proper time present in which God has accomplished a new dimension of reality: "The time is fulfilled, and the kingdom of God has come near" (Mark 1:15). Yet already within the New Testament itself, we see a tendency to look back, to recall past times in which things had happened. The **eschatological hope**, that is, the belief that the last times were at hand, seems to be slackening by the time Luke writes his Gospel and the writing of church history begins with the book of Acts. Even before the first century is done, remembering comes to be almost as important as anticipating.

The priorities of the early church's faith are disclosed by the way Christians of the second, third, and fourth centuries organized time. This was not systematic or planned; it was simply the church's spontaneous response to "the events that have been fulfilled among us" (Luke 1:1). The same type of response, the perpetuation of memories, also prompted the writing of the Gospels so that others might be able to follow these events "handed on to us by those who from the beginning were eyewitnesses and servants of the word" (Luke 1:2). The structuring of time was not quite so systematic as the evangelists' efforts "to write an orderly account" (Luke 1:3), but its influence has been almost as consistent in shaping Christian memories as it has been in the written

Gospels. Thus, for Christians, Easter is an annual event just as much as it is a written narrative. Christmas is far more a yearly occurrence than a nativity story.

What was the faith of the church of the first four centuries as witnessed to by the church's use of time? It was, above all else, faith in the resurrection of Jesus Christ. Second, it was trust in the abiding presence of the Holy Spirit, known and experienced in the holy church. And it was belief that witnessed to those signs by which God had become manifest in human flesh as Jesus Christ. This may not be a systematic summation of Christian belief; but it gives a clear indication of the heart of the faith of the early church, a faith revealed by how the church kept time.

There was even an implicitly trinitarian structure: belief in the Father made manifest, the Son risen, and the Holy Spirit indwelling the church. This, however, should not be pushed too far since it is more implicit than explicit. But the priorities are clear. The history of how the early church kept time may help us reconsider our priorities today in light of these precedents of the heroic age of Christianity.

The evidence begins not with the Christian year but with the **Christian week**, particularly with the testimony of **Sunday**. And the story really begins with the first day of creation, when "God said, 'Let there be light'; and there was light. . . . And there was evening and there was morning, the first day" (Gen. 1:3-5). The four Gospels are all careful to state that it was on the morning of the first day, that is, the day on which creation began and God "separated the light from the darkness," that the empty tomb was discovered.

In at least three places, the New Testament indicates a special time for worship—probably Sunday. Paul told the Christians in Corinth to set aside money for the collection on the first day of the week (1 Cor. 16:2). At Troas, after talking until midnight on Saturday, Paul broke bread (presumably the eucharist) and remained in conversation with Christians there until Sunday dawned (Acts 20:7 and 11). John tells us he "was in the spirit on the Lord's day" (Rev. 1:10). The term "Lord's day," had become a Christian term for the first day of the week by the early second century. **Ignatius**, Bishop of Antioch, wrote around A.D. 115 to the

Christians in Magnesia and spoke of those who "ceased to keep the [Jewish seventh day] Sabbath and lived by the Lord's Day, on which our life as well as theirs shone forth, thanks to Him and his death."[1]

The *Didache*, a church order written sometime in the late first or early second century, reminds Christians literally "on the Lord's day of the Lord come together, break bread and hold eucharist."[2] And even pagans noticed that "on an appointed day they [Christians] had been accustomed to meet before daybreak" though **Pliny**, the Roman administrator in Bithynia, who wrote those words about A.D. 112, hardly understood this to mean a meeting for the Lord's Supper.[3]

Another term appeared by the middle of the second century. Writing in Rome, the second-century apologist, **Justin Martyr** told his pagan audience about A.D. 155, that "we all hold this common gathering on Sunday since it is the first day, on which God transforming darkness and matter made the universe, and Jesus Christ our Savior rose from the dead on the same day."[4] Christians soon adopted the newly coined pagan term "Sunday" and compared Christ rising from the dead to the rising sun. Even today, the English and German languages speak of "Sunday" while French and Italian refer to the "Lord's Day." The *Epistle of Barnabas* called Sunday "an eighth day, that is the beginning of another world . . . in which Jesus also rose from the dead."[5] The themes of creation, both original and new, and light are important dimensions in the Christian celebration of Sunday as the day of the resurrection.

Sunday was a day of worship for Christians but not yet of rest. It was made such by the Emperor Constantine in A.D. 321, "All judges, city people, and craftsmen shall rest on the venerable day of the Sun. But countrymen may without hindrance attend to agriculture."[6]

The week had even more contour to it for the early church. Luke tells of the Pharisee who said: "I fast twice a week" (18:12). But the *Didache*, in all seriousness, told Christians: "Your fasts must not be identical with those of the hypocrites. They fast on Mondays and Thursdays; but you should fast on Wednesdays and Fridays."[7] Commemorative reasons had appeared for this by the time of writing of a late–fourth-century document, the *Apostolic Constitutions*

Early Documents and Writers on Christian Worship

	N. Africa	Egypt	Jerusalem	Syria	Asia Minor	Rome	Milan
1st Century				Didache		1 Clement	
2nd Century		Clement of Alexandria		Ignatius Barnabas	Pliny	Justin Martyr	
3rd Century	Tertullian Cyprian	Origen		Didascalia			
4th Century		Apostolic Church Order Canons of Hippolytus Sarapion	Cyril Egeria	Apostolic Constitutions Epitome Basil Chrysostom Theodore Testamentum Domini		Jerome Apostolic Tradition	
5th Century	Augustine					Ambros	
6th Century						Benedict Gretory I	Cassian (Marseilles)

Diagram 4

(probably in Syria), stated: "Fast . . . on the fourth day of the week, . . . Judas then promising to betray Him for money; and . . . on [Friday] because on that day the Lord suffered the death of the cross."[8] There is evidence that some early Christians also held a certain regard for Saturday as "the memorial of the creation" from which work God rested on the seventh day. **Tertullian**, an early third-century North African, tells us there were "some few who abstain from kneeling on the Sabbath." All these other days were inferior in importance to Sunday.

Sunday dominated all of the other days as the weekly anniversary of the resurrection. In the early church, Sunday also commemorated the Lord's passion and death, but it was, above all else, the day on which the Savior rose from the dead. Even today, Sunday takes precedence over most other observances. Every Sunday witnesses to the risen Lord. It is the Lord's Day, the day of the sun risen from darkness, the start of the new creation. Tertullian tells us Christians never knelt on Sunday, "the day of the Lord's resurrection." Sundays in Advent and Lent remain days of joy despite being penitential seasons. Each Sunday testifies to the resurrection. Every Sunday is a weekly little Easter but even more so every Easter is a yearly great Sunday. The primacy of Sunday and the resurrection is clear.

Even the ordinary **day** itself became a structure of praise for the early church. The *Didache* instructed Christians to pray the Lord's Prayer "three times a day." Late in the fourth century, Chrysostom urged each newly baptized Christian to begin the day's work with prayer for strength to do God's will and to end the day by rendering "an account to the Master of his whole day, and beg forgiveness for his falls."[9] Early in the Christian tradition, then, the Christian day led to a daily cycle of remembering Christ throughout one's daily labors in the midst of worldly concerns. (This will be discussed in more detail in chapter 5.)

Christians adopted the Jewish sense of the day as beginning at nightfall ("There was evening and there was morning, the first day." Gen. 1:5). Hence the **eve** of a festival (Christmas Eve, Easter Eve, and Halloween) is a part of the liturgical day that continues at daybreak and ends at sundown. Christians have made relatively little use of the month as a recurring cycle although Anglicans formerly used it as a basis for daily psalm readings and some Protestants currently observe monthly celebrations of the eucharist.

As the week and the day witnessed to Jesus Christ, so too, the **Christian year (liturgical year** or **church year)** became a structure that commemorated the Lord. Just as Sunday was the center of the week, so too, the **Pascha** (Passover-Easter) happenings was the focus of the year. The Pascha had been the center of the Jewish year as commemoration of deliverance from slavery; it was no less important for Christians. Paul deliberately took over the language of the Jewish **Feast of Unleavened Bread** (the Pascha):

Clean out the old yeast so that you may be a new batch, as you really are unleavened. For our paschal lamb, Christ, has been sacrificed. Therefore, let us celebrate the festival, not with the old yeast, the yeast of malice and evil, but with the unleavened bread of sincerity and truth. (1 Cor. 5:7-8)

This passage is the chief evidence for the keeping of Easter by the New Testament church. The old Jewish commemoration of deliverance was now made completely new in Jesus Christ. Slavery and redemption were rehearsed, but in the new sense of release from sin and death through Christ's actions.

The second-century and third-century church observed the Pascha with services signifying the making of new Christians through the acts of baptism, laying on of hands, anointing, and first communion. Just as the Pascha had commemorated escape from slavery by passage through the Red Sea, so Paul saw baptism as a burial with Christ in which "we have been buried with him by baptism into death, so that, just as Christ was raised from the dead . . . so we too might walk in newness of life" (Rom. 6:4-5). In the first three centuries, Christ's passion, death, and resurrection were commemorated together at the Pascha. Tertullian tells us that "the Passover affords a more than usually solemn day for baptism; when, withal, the Lord's passion in which we are baptized, was completed."[10] An early third-century document, *The Apostolic Tradition,* usually attributed to **Hippolytus,** tells us that those who were to be baptized fasted on Friday and Saturday, presumably before Easter, and then began an all-night vigil Saturday evening. At cockcrow, the hour of the resurrection on Easter morning, they were baptized beneath the waters and rose with Christ as from the dead.

Early in the fourth century, the church finally agreed that, unlike the Jewish Passover, which could come on any day of the week, the Pascha must always be celebrated on a Sunday. Previously, the **Quartodeciman** controversy had involved a long debate between those who kept Easter on a Sunday and those (the Quartodecimans) who followed the Jewish dating which often resulted in a weekday celebration. The resolution of this controversy clearly recognized the symbolic meaning of Sunday: "Never on any day other than the Lord's Day should the mystery of the Lord's resurrection from the dead be celebrated, . . . on that day alone we should observe the end of the Paschal fast."[11] Thus the weekly and yearly cycles of resurrection reinforced each other, but a small part of the Jewish roots of the Passover were lost.

In the course of the fourth century, the ancient unitive Pascha day which commemorated all the events of the last days of Jesus, including the crucifixion and resurrection, was divided into distinct commemorations (see diagram 5). The dissolution apparently first occurred in **Jerusalem** where time and space converged at the sites of Jesus' life and ministry. A need was felt to hold a separate commemoration for each event at the holy place where it had occurred in order to serve the throngs of pilgrims who were arriving from all over the world. Scripture was mined for evidence about the time and place of all the events of Christ's last week in Jerusalem. We have a good idea of what had developed by A.D. 383 as chronicled in the writings of a Spanish woman named **Egeria**. Her notes, apparently written down so she could give talks to friends at home, have survived and give us a clear picture of how late–fourth-century Jerusalem had developed its way of keeping time.

Egeria tells us that what we now call Passion Sunday or Palm Sunday, or the first day of Holy Week, was "the beginning of the Easter Week or, as they call it here, 'The Great Week.' . . . All the people go before him [the bishop] with psalms and antiphons, all the time repeating, 'Blessed is he that cometh in the name of the Lord.' "[12] There were minor services on the next three days, except on Wednesday the presbyter read about Judas' plot to betray Jesus and "the people groan and lament at this reading." On Thursday, after everyone had received communion, all "conduct the bishop to Gethsemane." And on Friday, services were held at Golgotha where fragments of the wood of the cross were venerated by all the people. They processed past the cross and kissed it.

By the end of the century, the historicizing process was complete, and Augustine stated as an accepted fact that "it is clear from the Gospel on what days the Lord was crucified and rested in the tomb and rose again" and that the church has "a requirement of retaining those same days."[13] The ancient unitive Pascha had been broken into separate commemorations: **Maundy** or **Holy Thursday, Good Friday, Holy Saturday,** and the **Easter Vigil** on the eve of Easter, along with **Passion** or **Palm Sunday** and the three lesser days of Holy Week. And this is how Christians have kept it ever since. This gives us **Holy Week** beginning with Passion or Palm Sunday, Monday, Tuesday, (Spy) Wednesday, Maundy or Holy Thursday, Good Friday, and Holy Saturday. The English term "Easter" comes from the Old English *eastre*, a pagan spring festival; Romance languages still use forms of "Pascha." Easter Day is the beginning of **Easter Week** during which new Christians receive instruction.

Closely connected with Easter are two seasons: Lent and the long Easter Season. The origins of Lent are controversial. It was customary to think that **Lent** originated as the final intensive period of preparation for those **catechumens** (converts under training) who had been set apart, after considerable preparation, to be baptized at the Easter Vigil. New evidence shows a possibly earlier stand, a post-Epiphany fast of forty days in Egypt, associated with Christ's forty days in the wilderness, which immediately follows the account of his baptism in the Synoptic Gospels.[14] At any rate, the **Council of Nicaea,** A.D. 325, first referred to Lent as "forty days" and made it immediately precede Easter. Around A.D. 350, Bishop Cyril of Jerusalem told those about to be baptized, "You have a long period of grace, forty days for repentance."[15] By Augustine's time, Lent, that "part of the year . . . adjoining . . . and touching on the Lord's passion," had become a time of preparation for all Christians, baptized or not. It begins on a day much later known as **Ash Wednesday** because of the **imposition of ashes** on the fore-

Divisions of the Early Unitive Commemorations

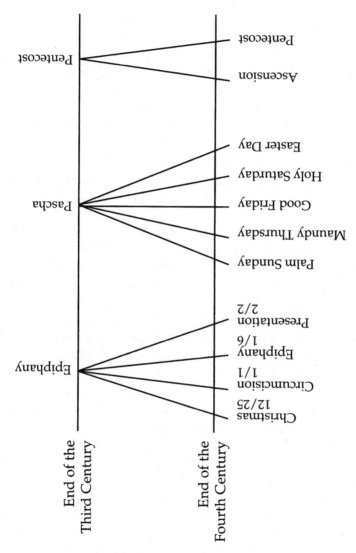

Diagram 5

heads of all Christians, a practice dating at least from the late–eleventh century. The Sundays in Lent are not counted as part of the forty days.

Far more important was the **Easter Season**, the fifty days extending the celebration of Easter through the Day of Pentecost. The great fifty days (originally called "the Pentecost") were at first far more important than the forty days of Lent. It is perplexing why modern Christians concentrate on Lent, the season of penance, rather than on Easter, the season of rejoicing. Augustine tells us: "These days after the Lord's resurrection form a period, not of labor, but of peace and joy. That is why there is no fasting and we pray standing, which is a sign of resurrection. This practice is observed at the altar on all Sundays, and the Alleluia is sung, to indicate that our future occupation is to be no other than the praise of God."[16] The resurrection is commemorated by a day each week—Sunday; a festival each year—Easter Day; and a season—the Easter Season. There can be no doubt about the centrality of the resurrection in the life and faith of the early Church.

The most significant development in the fourth-century calendar was the elaboration of Holy Week. Much of this elaboration occurred in Jerusalem, very likely under the leadership of **Cyril of Jerusalem**, bishop from A.D. 349 to 386. Egeria gives us a full report of what was being done in Jerusalem shortly before Cyril's death. Eventually, the Jerusalem practices became common throughout Christianity and represent some of the church's oldest liturgical treasures.

These rites employ the most dramatic forms used in Christian worship. Indeed, medieval drama sprang from Easter Day worship but eventually became too complicated to remain in the chancels. It was natural that Jerusalem should be the place where such dramatic rites developed, for the actual settings of the events leading up to and following Jesus' death and resurrection were at hand. Ever since Constantine had made Christianity respectable, pilgrims had been flocking to see those places for themselves. All that was needed for liturgical realism was to match the times and places mentioned in scripture with appropriate ceremonies. Jerusalem fused these together in the fourth century and has shaped Christian worship ever since. Revived in fuller form in 1955 under

Pius XII, the rites of Holy Week were reformed after Vatican II and now also appear in many Protestant service books.

The fully developed rites include on Passion or Palm Sunday an opening procession with palms and a dramatic reading (usually with several readers) of one of the passion narratives from the Gospels. Maundy Thursday begins in Roman Catholic and Anglican cathedrals with the **Chrism mass** in which the **three sacramental oils** used in parish churches during the year—olive oil for baptism, chrism (olive oil and balm) for confirmation, and olive oil for anointing of the sick—are consecrated. The unity of the priests of the diocese with their bishop is testified to by the presence of representative priests from the diocese at this service. The **Easter Triduum** (three days) extends from sunset on Maundy Thursday to sunset on Easter Day—the three most holy days of the Christian year. Maundy Thursday evening is marked in most churches by a eucharist commemorating both Christ's gift in giving this sacrament at this time and the events of his passion that followed. Often, **foot washing** is included (John 13:3-17), and at the conclusion of the service the **stripping of the church** may occur in which all textiles, crosses, and images are removed or covered until Easter eve.

Traditionally, the Lord's Supper is not celebrated on Good Friday or **Holy Saturday**, the Netherlands Reformed Church being an exception. The ancient Good Friday rite includes the service of the word with extensive intercessions, **veneration of the cross** (kneeling before it or kissing it), the singing of the **reproaches** (based on Lam. 1:12), and possibly, giving of communion with elements consecrated on Maundy Thursday. A seventeenth-century Hispanic rite from Peru, the **Three Hours** is based on the seven last words of Jesus from the cross. The service of **tenebrae** (darkness) may occur on any or all of the last three days of Holy Week with the reading of either psalms along with lessons or the passion narrative; in either case, the service includes the gradual extinguishing of candles on a special large candlestick.

Easter eve climaxes the whole year with the **Easter Vigil** as the church gathers in darkness to celebrate the resurrection. Traditionally, it includes kindling of new fire and lighting of a special large candle, the **paschal candle**, singing of the ancient *Exsultet*

("Rejoice, heavenly powers"), reading of nine lessons (mostly from the Old Testament), blessing of water for baptism or renewing of baptismal vows or both, and celebrating the Easter eucharist.

In ancient times, **Easter week** was devoted to instruction of the newly baptized about the meaning of the sacraments, the so-called **mystagogical catechesis**. Fourth-century collections of these catechetical lectures survive, attributed to Cyril of Jerusalem, Ambrose, John Chrysostom, and Theodore of Mopsuestia. These lectures are very important documents for recovering both the practices of various Christian centers and the differing interpretations they give to the sacraments. On the Sunday following Easter, the new Christians doffed their white robes as fully initiated and instructed members of the Body of Christ.

Second in importance in early centuries was the celebration of another event, the **Day of Pentecost**. Like the Pascha, it was also a Jewish feast: "You shall count until the day after the seventh sabbath, fifty days; then you shall present an offering of new grain to the LORD" (Lev. 23:16). Sometime during the first century A.D., the Day of Pentecost came to reflect, for Jews, the giving of the law at Mt. Sinai. Paul contrasts this with the giving of the Spirit: "Now if the ministry of death, chiseled in letters on stone tablets, came in glory . . . how much more will the ministry of the Spirit come in glory?" (2 Cor. 3:7-8). For Christians, the Day of Pentecost commemorated the birthday of the Church when, with the noise of a wind, tongues of flame rested on the disciples and they began to talk in other tongues (Acts 2:1-41). The book of Acts is a chronicle of the work of the Spirit-filled church in its earliest years.

The Day of Pentecost began as a unitive feast, too, originally including commemoration of the **Ascension**. Tertullian suggests that Christ had ascended into heaven at Pentecost.[17] And in the first half of the fourth century Eusebius speaks of "the august and holy solemnity of Pentecost [that is, the fifty days], which is distinguished by a period of seven weeks, and sealed with that one day on which the holy Scriptures attest the ascension of our common Savior into heaven, and the descent of the Holy Spirit."[18] In other words, for almost four centuries, the Day of Pentecost commemorated both the ascension of Christ and the descent of the Holy Spirit. By the end of the fourth century, these two commemorations had been separated. The *Apostolic Constitutions* describes forty days after Easter as the proper time to "celebrate the feast of the ascension of the Lord." Once again, the biblical witness has been historicized by being interpreted as a means of dating past events in time. In this case, Acts 1:3 and its mention of the "forty days" during which Jesus taught his disciples seems to have been the source of pinpointing the date of the ascension. Where there had previously been one feast, by the late–fourth century there were two: Ascension Day and the Day of Pentecost. Christ was in heaven and the Holy Spirit dwelled in the holy church on earth. It was a daily reality the church could experience, not an abstraction.

The third chief event in the calendar by the fourth century was **Epiphany**. Its origins are obscure; they were not Jewish but maybe Egyptian. The date may relate to the belief that Jesus was conceived on the date of his death, sometimes believed to be April 6, placing his birth on January 6. The Epiphany signified several things, all of which had to do with the beginnings of Jesus Christ's work of manifesting God. This feast referred to the birth of Christ (with which two Gospels begin), to the Magi (in the West), to the baptism of Jesus (with which the other Gospels begin), and to the first miracle of which John's Gospel says: "Jesus did this, the first of his signs in Cana of Galilee, and revealed his glory; and his disciples believed in him." The common theme of all these events is Jesus Christ manifesting God to humans. Appropriately, the early church often called this day "The Theophany" (manifestation of God) and some Eastern Orthodox churches still do. The prologue to the Fourth Gospel sets the theme: "It is God the only Son, who is close to the Father's heart, who has made him known" (1:18). Apparently, in some churches January 6 marked the beginning of the church year, symbolized by beginning the reading of one of the Gospels on this date.[19]

Epiphany underwent a split, probably beginning in Rome, during the first half of the fourth century. Our earliest mention (except among Donatist schismatics) of the new feast, **Christmas**, occurs in a Roman document from A.D. 354 that reflects usage of the feast about A.D. 336. It lists December 25 as *"natus Christus in Betleem Iudeae."* This date competed with a relatively new pagan festival of the Unconquered Sun as the sun begins to wax again at the winter solstice. (By the fourth century A.D., the Julian calendar was off by four days.) Gradually, the new festival of Christmas took over part of the commemorations of the Epiphany. Chrysostom told a congregation in Antioch on Christmas Day, A.D. 386: "This day . . . [which] has now been brought to us, not many years ago, has developed so quickly and borne such fruit."[20] The following Epiphany Day he explained: "For this is the day on which he was baptized, and made holy the nature of the waters. . . . Why then is this day called Epiphany? Because it was not when he was born that he became manifest to all, but when he was baptized; for up to this day he was unknown to the multitudes."[21]

The Epiphany, then, is older than Christmas and has a deeper meaning. For instead of simply being an anniversary of the birth of Christ, it testifies to the whole purpose of the incarnation: the manifestation of God in Jesus Christ, beginning both with his birth and with the beginning of his ministry (the baptism when he is proclaimed "My Son, the Beloved"). And the mighty signs and teachings, narrated in the Gospels as Jesus accomplished this manifestation, provide an opportunity in the Season after Epiphany (or Ordinary Time) for commemoration of those works and teachings of Jesus that led up to the final events in Jerusalem.

A council in Spain in A.D. 380 decreed that "From December 17 until the day of Epiphany which is January 6 no one is permitted to be absent from Church."[22] This is a precedent for the season of **Advent** at a time when Christmas itself was still unknown in Spain. By the fifth century, a forty-day season of preparation for the Epiphany was being practiced in parts of Gaul. (This paralleled Lent and began about when Advent now begins.) Rome eventually adopted a four-week Advent before Christmas.

A process similar to that which had splintered the Pascha into a series of commemorations also operated with Christmas. As a Jewish boy, Jesus would likely have been circumcised and named on the eighth day after his birth. Luke tells us: "After eight days had passed, it was time to circumcise the child; and he was called Jesus" (2:21). Accordingly, the commemoration on January 1 became known as the Feast of the **Circumcision** or the **Name of Jesus**. Roman Catholics now keep this as the **Solemnity of Mary, Mother of God**. Luke 2:22-40 gives the story of the **Presentation in**

the Temple (or **Purification** or **Candlemas**), an event which would have occurred February 2, forty days after his birth. It was discerned that the **Annunciation** mentioned in Luke 1:26-38 would have happened nine months before Christmas or March 25. Elizabeth was then six months pregnant and Mary's subsequent **Visitation** to Elizabeth (recorded in verses 39-56) was fixed at May 31 or just before the birth of John the Baptist, identified as June 24 (three months after the Annunciation). John's birth came at the summer solstice when the sun wanes until the birth of Christ: "He must increase, but I must decrease" (John 3:30). All these developments are combinations of Luke 1 and 2 and obstetrics.

The Christian year, especially the **temporal cycle** (movable dates and the Christmas cycle), was basically complete by the end of the fourth century. The subsequent history is that of the development of the **sanctoral cycle** (those fixed dates commemorating the deaths of saints aside from dates based on Christmas). These dates began early; the "Martyrdom of Polycarp" mentions commemoration of a second-century martyr. Basically such observances were commemorations of local heroes and heroines of the faith. Tertullian tells us, "As often as the anniversary comes round, we make offerings for the dead as birthday honors."[23] After all, one's birth into eternity (death) was far more important than his or her birth into time. The temporal cycle became increasingly obscured with commemorations of saints, especially after relics of saints began to be moved from place to place. The list of days of local saints was eventually supplemented with names of saints from other regions.

Few significant additions occurred after the fourth century. **Trinity Sunday**, the Sunday after the Day of Pentecost, was introduced about A.D. 1000. Unlike other feasts, it represents a theological doctrine unrelated to a historical event. In the West the ninth century saw the designation of November 1 as **All Saints Day**. It had earlier springtime precedents, but the Gallican placement of it in the harvest season was accepted by Rome about A.D. 835. By then, too, the **Assumption** of the Blessed Virgin Mary was kept throughout the West on August 15. In the thirteenth century, the Thursday after Trinity Sunday began to be observed as **Corpus Christi**. Later Roman Catholic developments were the mandatory observance of the **Immaculate Conception** on December 8 (eighteenth century), the **Sacred Heart** (nineteenth century), and **Christ the King** (twentieth century).

Let us recapitulate. John Chrysostom, in a sermon preached in A.D. 386, effectively sums up the liturgical year:

For if Christ had not been born into flesh, he would not have been baptized, which is the Theophany [Epiphany], he would not have been crucified [some texts add: and risen] which is the Pascha, he would not have sent down the spirit, which is the Pentecost.[24]

In the fourth century, the three great primitive feasts—the Epiphany, the Pascha, and the Day of Pentecost—had seen a split from these feasts of related days: Christmas, Good Friday, and Ascension, along with lesser days.

Gregory Dix interpreted these developments as a sign that the fourth-century church was becoming "reconciled to *time*" and was losing its fervent expectation of the end of time.[25] But this reconciliation to time was inevitable. People want to know, to visualize, to experience for themselves; this is a very normal human desire. Worship builds on our humanity. So what happened in the fourth century was that the church developed a more dramatic way of expressing the central realities Christians experienced—manifestation, resurrection, and the indwelling Spirit. Eschatological fervor had slackened long before the peace of the church under Constantine. But the imagination of Christians directed backward in time was no less fruitful and intensified their perception of the incarnation. The success of these fourth-century innovations is shown by their vivid presence among us today. Obviously they have rung true to both Christian faith and human experience.

All in all, the church year is a very satisfactory reflection of the life and faith of the early church and has remained in use with little change ever since. Modern efforts to systematize and tidy it up have never been very satisfactory. Granted the ancient church year leaves large gaps in time, especially after the Day of Pentecost. But its strength lies in its firm grasp of the core of the Christian experience and in its ability to reflect in a vivid way that Christ has made God manifest, that Christ has risen from the dead, and that Christ sent the Holy Spirit to dwell in the holy church.

The sixteenth-century reformers took various approaches to the calendar. **Martin Luther** (1483–1546) eliminated saints' days by seeking "to celebrate only on Lord's Days and on Festivals of the Lord, abrogating completely the festivals of all the saints. . . . We regard the festivals of the Purification [Presentation] and of the Annunciation as festivals of Christ, like the Epiphany and the Circumcision."[26] From the sanctoral cycle in its *Book of Common Prayer* (hereafter *BCP*), the Church of England retained propers to commemorate only those saints mentioned in the Bible and All Saints Day.

The Church of Scotland was more radical. Its 1560 *Book of Discipline* condemned all "feasts [as they term them] of apostles, martyrs, virgins, of Christmas, Circumcision, Epiphany, Purification, and other fond feasts of our Lady. Which things, because in God's scriptures they neither have commandment nor assurance, we judge utterly to be abolished from this realm; affirming further, that the obstinate maintainers and teachers of such abominations ought not to escape the punishment of the civil magistrate."[27] Eighty-five years later the *Westminster Directory* echoed the same sentiment, "Festival days, vulgarly called Holy Days, having no warrant in the Word of God, are not to be continued."[28] It did, however, urge days of "Public solemn fasting" or "of Public Thanksgiving" according as God's actions in present times indicated favor or judgment.

John Wesley, (1703–1791) always the pragmatist, abolished "most of the holy-days . . . as at present answering no valuable end."[29] His calendar included the four Sundays of Advent, Christmas Day, up to fifteen Sundays after Christmas, the Sunday before Easter, Good Friday, Easter Day, five Sundays after Easter, Ascension Day, Sunday after Ascension Day, Whitsunday, Trinity Sunday, and up to twenty-five Sundays after Trinity. Wesley's journals reveal a personal fondness for All Saints Day. Both Wesley's calendar and lections were soon lost among American Methodists.

Renewed interest in the church year among American Protestants occurred in the 1920s and 1930s, a period in which aesthetic approaches to worship tended to increase. An effort to rearrange the year was advanced in the form of a new season, **Kingdomtide**. It seems to have been promoted largely by Professor Fred Winslow Adams of Boston University School of Theology.

Kingdomtide originally appeared in a Federal Council of Churches publication, *The Christian Year*, published in 1937 and 1940. The first edition suggested observing Kingdomtide for the last six months of the church year; in 1940 this time was divided between Whitsuntide and Kingdomtide.[30] Today, United Methodists have the options of observing part of this time as Kingdomtide or entirely as the Season after Pentecost. A somewhat similar experiment was briefly tried by American Presbyterians. They experimented with a suggestion made in 1956 by Allan McArthur, a Scottish pastor, of having a season of "God the Father" in the fall.[31] After four years of trial use, this was abandoned.

Since Vatican II, a profound new interest in the calendar has emerged and a deep new appreciation has developed around how our lives as Christians are shaped and reflected by the way we keep time. The first landmark was the new ***Roman Calendar*** which went into effect among Roman Catholics on November 30, 1969, the first day of the liturgical year 1970. It is the fruit of the most careful review ever attempted of how Christians use time. Most of the new Roman Catholic reforms have since been adopted or adapted by major Protestant bodies in many parts of the world.

The most radical Roman Catholic change, that of treating the weeks after the Epiphany and those after the Day of Pentecost not as distinct seasons but only as parts of the "Season of the year" *(per annum)* or **Ordinary Time,** has not been adopted by most Protestants. Certainly, it is a realistic approach to those seasons having little distinctive character. Other changes, however, have been widely accepted, such as keeping the Sunday after the Epiphany as the **Baptism of the Lord** or the last Sunday of the church year as **Christ the King** or **Reign of Christ**. The Lutheran practice of commemorating the Sunday before Ash Wednesday as Sunday of the **Transfiguration of the Lord** has been adopted by many churches. (Roman Catholics have observed this on August 6 since the fifteenth century.)

For the first time in four hundred years, an ecumenical calendar is being followed by Protestants and Roman Catholics around the world. There is basic agreement on most of the greatest feast days, which Roman Catholics now call **solemnities**; less common observance of the subsidiary **feasts**, and still less of **memorials** or saints' days. The newest calendar is the result of a careful attempt to recapture the structure and meaning of the oldest calendar, the one filled out in the fourth century. The new calendar provides a strong witness to the priorities of Christian faith, just as the oldest Christian calendars did.

THEOLOGY FROM THE CHRISTIAN YEAR

How the church kept time in early centuries has been discussed in detail because, as so often happens in Christian worship, if we understand the experiences of the church's first four centuries, we have gained the heart of the matter. It will be worthwhile, though, to reflect a bit on the meaning of this.

The calendar of the early church centered upon what God had done and continued to do through the Holy Spirit. The point of the Christian year is that all is done for us. All we have to do is accept what God has done. Then we really are free to act. The church's liturgical year both underscores the futility of our efforts and exults in God's victories for us. In short, the church year is a constant reminder of gifts that we cannot create but can only accept. Pius Parsch called it "the church's year of grace."[32] Throughout the year, the various seasons and days remind us that salvation is a gift offered to us in all its different aspects. The Christian year can help us sort out for ourselves our real priorities. Keeping time with the rhythms of the early church can be an important means of doing this.

In briefest terms, the church's year of grace functions to proclaim Jesus Christ until he comes again and to testify to the Holy Spirit indwelling the church in the meantime. The church year is both proclamation and thanksgiving. In much the same way as Jewish and Christian prayer recites what we give thanks for, so the Christian year proclaims and thanks God for God's marvelous actions. Christians and Jews praise God, not in abstract terms, but by reciting the marvelous works of God. It is a think/thank process by which we glorify God through recalling what God has done. The liturgical year reflects the very nature of Christian prayer and our relationship to God. Much of its power, as is true of daily prayer, comes through reiteration. Year after year, week after week, hour after hour, the acts of God are commemorated and our apprehension of them deepened. These cycles save us from a shallow spirituality, based on ourselves, by pointing us to God's works instead.

Keeping time, of course, can also become an idolatrous gimmick like anything else that is good. Time can be used simply to dress up our services and to make them look fashionable. Keeping the church year for the wrong reasons is worse than useless for we can end up worshiping our own gimmicks rather than God. But when we do use the structures of time to bring us closer to God, they can serve that purpose exceedingly well by helping us to encounter the wholeness of the gospel.

How does time bring us closer to God? The Christian year is a means by which we relive for ourselves all that matters of salvation history. When we recall the past events of salvation, they come alive in their present power to save. Our acts of remembrance bring the original events back to us with all their meaning. And so we continue to "proclaim the Lord's death until he comes" (1 Cor. 11:26). The various acts of rehearsing salvation history give us anew the benefits of what God has done for us in these past events. Christ's birth, baptism, death, resurrection, and so on are all given to us again for our own appropriation through corporate reenactment of them. These events become no longer simply detached data from the past but part of our own personal history as we relive salvation history by rehearsing it in our worship. Thus Christ dies again in our consciousness every Good Friday. And every Easter and every Lord's Day we are witnesses to the resurrection.

The Christian year becomes a vital and refreshing means through which God is given to us. It is a giving that is never exhausted. Each time, the year, week, and day push us a bit deeper into our encounter with God. We perceive one aspect of Christ's being baptized this year, another next year, but we never touch bottom. So the liturgical year is a constant means of grace through which we receive God's gifts to us.

The year of grace is about what God does for us, not our efforts. The whole structure calls attention to God's work, not ours. And God's work is made known in differing ways through the changing events and needs of every time and place in which Christians worship.

The **Season of Advent** is both a time of thanks for the gift of Christ to us in past time and a time for anticipation of his second coming. It contains both threat and promise. Christmas Day rehearses God's self-giving in the birth of Jesus Christ. The **Season of Christmas** continues this commemoration through the Epiphany.

In the **Season of Epiphany** (or **Ordinary Time**), the appointed Gospels stress the various ways in which Jesus Christ has made God manifest to us by making the Father known through mighty signs and teachings. These begin with the **Baptism of the Lord** (when Jesus' Sonship is declared and his ministry begins). The Sundays after Epiphany continue with readings about the signs and teachings by which Jesus made his glory known through manifesting God. The season ends with the Last Sunday after Epiphany or **Transfiguration Sunday** in which Jesus is once again proclaimed: "My Son, the Beloved."

The **Season of Lent** is the season in which we participate in that final trip to Jerusalem and the self-giving nature of love shown in Christ's passion and death. All is changed as Christ gives himself to us as the resurrected one at **Easter**. The **Season of Easter** begins with **Easter Vigil** and concludes on the **Day of Pentecost**. **Ascension of the Lord** commemorates the ending of Christ's historical visibility and the beginning of his sacramental visibility.

The **Season after Pentecost** (or Ordinary Time or Kingdomtide) signals the long interim of the new covenant church until Christ comes in glory. Both the Old Testament and the New remind us of God's continuing saving works. The Last Sunday after Pentecost, **Reign of Christ** or **Christ the King,** pushes us to anticipate the consummation of all things when Christ comes in glory as King of all, and all human failures and achievements are, at last, made of no account, a most comforting doctrine. Then, the following week, we are once again into the Season of Advent, and the year starts over afresh.

The **minor christological feasts** have evangelical values that we are just beginning to discover. The Name of Jesus, Presentation, Annunciation, and Visitation are christological and call attention to Christ's full humanity and identification with human social patterns. All Saints Day is christological, too. It does not dwell on the virtues of the saints but on the love of Christ who works in people throughout time to accomplish God's purposes. The chief benefit of commemorating the saints is the recognition through them of Christ, who never leaves us without a witness. If commemoration of individual saints could help us realize this, then such piety could once again serve a "valuable end."

In actual parish life, the Christian year is only one of many calendars by which congregations live. There are various national calendars, which add events often deserving commemoration in churches. In the British Isles, such dates as Mothering Sunday, Harvest Festival, or Remembrance Sunday are usually recognized in prayers and hymns. Rarely in the United States do Mother's Day, Independence Day, Labor Day, and Thanksgiving Day go unrecognized. Ethnic groups keep their identity through other festivals (St. Patrick's Day and Dyngus Day). Church life is also affected by the academic year which also governs the vacation plans of parents. And the financial year is a fact of church life that can hardly be ignored.

More directly, local churches usually evolve their own pragmatic calendar, which gives a necessary structure to congregational life. An annual event for many country churches is **Homecoming Sunday** in which former residents return for worship and a meal on the grounds, often in the vicinity of the graveyard where relatives are buried. More common is the annual **revival**, a week of preaching services that often ends with the eucharist. **Rally Day** marks the beginning of the Sunday school year; **Loyalty Sunday** calls for pledges of money to support the congregation's ministry; and the **Christmas pageant** is an annual event involving all generations. Frequently, Sundays are set aside to raise funds for various charities or to promote good causes. Many Protestant churches keep the first Sunday of October as **World Communion Sunday**.

All of these are significant events in the life of local congregations. They do, indeed, call more attention to human activity than to God's actions, but they accent aspects of the congregation's ministry to the world. The pragmatic calendar with its focus on ourselves always needs the balance of the traditional Christian year, which points beyond us to God's work for us. Ultimately that is what makes our work for others possible.

FUNCTIONING OF THE CHRISTIAN YEAR

Every service of Christian worship is composed of two kinds of acts of worship: ordinary and propers. The **ordinary** elements are those that remain the same: the basic structure of the service and the items in it, such as the Lord's Prayer, the offering, the creed, and a doxology. The **propers** are those elements that change daily or weekly. We read different lessons, sing varied hymns, pray a variety of prayers, and (we hope!) hear a somewhat different sermon whenever we gather for worship.

The importance of the propers in Christian worship is that they supply variety and interest. Although the ordinary parts provide a necessary constancy, Christian worship without the proper parts would be deadly dull, a repetition of the same thing week after week. Without the constants that the ordinary parts provide, Christian worship would be chaos.

Variety is an important ingredient. The Good News of the gospel is much too wide and deep to be encompassed by a single service or even a whole season. Each time a congregation gathers for worship is a different event. Never before and never again will exactly the same people be assembled in the same context for worship. But the uniqueness of each gathering goes beyond that. The life of the local community, as well as that of the national and global communities, is never the same from week to week. Christian worship reflects this in its affirmation that every Sunday or special day is a different occasion. Christmas is not Easter nor is the Sunday after Easter the same as the Sunday before Labor Day, though the attendance may be about the same. A wedding is not a funeral though the flowers may be similar. A Sunday evening service is not even the same occasion as that morning's service, for the people are apt to behave in a more relaxed fashion. In a similar way, no two family meals are identical. Each occasion for worship is unique.

Variety, then, is an important characteristic of Christian worship since worship relates both to the eternal gospel and to daily life. A frequent criticism of Christian worship has been that of dullness. Yet this is apt only when Christian worship is unfaithful to its own nature. The surest way to avoid the boredom of constant repetition is to revel in the rich variety inherent in the Christian year. And the best way to ensure dullness is to ignore such a varied array of possibilities.

Nothing is a better source for variety and interest in Christian worship than careful following of the Christian year. The structure of the year provides an orderly pegboard on which to hang all our best ideas and is a stimulus for creativity. The first question to raise when planning any service is, When does it occur in the Christian year? The answer should be our first and best clue to guiding our planning.

The **calendar**, we have said, is the foundation of most Christian worship. The calendar in diagram 6 is that of the *Revised Common Lectionary* of 1992.[33] The reader will probably want to refer to it frequently while reading the following explanations.

The calendar is based on two cycles: one culminating in the resurrection at Easter Day and the other focusing on the incarnation on Christmas Day. The seasons of Advent and Lent serve as times of preparation and expectancy; the seasons of Christmas and Easter rejoice in the events they commemorate. The Season of Epiphany and the Season after Pentecost have less distinct meaning and function as Ordinary Time.

A few details are necessary in keeping time with the church. The number of Sundays in the seasons of Advent, Lent, and Easter are constants. There are either one or two Sundays in the Season of Christmas. The number of Sundays after Epiphany or Pentecost (Ordinary Time) varies and different churches have varying means of choosing the lections for these. For most North American Protestants, the final Sunday of the post–Epiphany season (just before Ash Wednesday) is always the last Sunday after the Epiphany (Transfiguration Sunday). These churches and Roman Catholics keep the Sunday before Advent as Reign of Christ or Christ the King (last Sunday after Pentecost).

It may help to remember that, as far as Sundays and festivals are concerned, each season except Advent begins and ends with a special day. The Season of Christmas extends from Christmas to the Epiphany, the Season of Epiphany from Epiphany through Transfiguration Sunday, the Season of Lent from Ash Wednesday through Holy Saturday, the Season of Easter from Easter Vigil and

SUNDAYS AND SPECIAL DAYS

SEASON OF ADVENT
First Sunday of Advent to Fourth
  Sunday of Advent

SEASON OF CHRISTMAS
Nativity of the Lord (Christmas Day)
First Sunday after Christmas
New Year's Day
Second Sunday after Christmas

SEASON OF EPIPHANY (ORDINARY TIME)
Epiphany of the Lord
First Sunday after the Epiphany (Baptism of the Lord)
Second Sunday after the Epiphany to Ninth Sunday after the Epiphany
Last Sunday after the Epiphany (Transfiguration Sunday)

SEASON OF LENT
Ash Wednesday
First Sunday in Lent to Sixth Sunday in Lent
  (Passion Sunday or Palm Sunday)
Holy Week
    Monday of Holy Week
    Tuesday of Holy Week
    Wednesday of Holy Week
    Holy Thursday
    Good Friday
    Holy Saturday

SEASON OF EASTER
Resurrection of the Lord
  Easter Vigil
  Easter Day
Second Sunday of Easter to
  Sixth Sunday of Easter
Ascension of the Lord
  (Sixth Thursday of Easter)
Seventh Sunday of Easter
Day of Pentecost

SEASON AFTER PENTECOST (ORDINARY TIME)
Trinity Sunday (First Sunday after Pentecost)
Second throughTwenty-Sixth Sunday after Pentecost
Reign of Christ or Christ the King (Last Sunday after Pentecost)

SPECIAL DAYS
Presentation of the Lord (February 2)
Annunciation of the Lord (March 25)
Visitation of Mary to Elizabeth (May 31)
Holy Cross (September 14)
All Saints (November 1)
Thanksgiving Day (Fourth Thursday of November, U.S.;
  Second Monday of October, Canada)

Diagram 6

Day through the Day of Pentecost, and the Season after Pentecost from Trinity Sunday through Reign of Christ or Christ the King. White vestments and hangings are usually used on all these special days except Ash Wednesday, Holy Saturday, and the Day of Pentecost.

A few dates may be unfamiliar or have special problems. In various churches, Epiphany Day may be celebrated on the first Sunday of January, combined with the first Sunday after Christmas, or observed with the Baptism of the Lord. The **Baptism of the Lord** is a new festival for Western Christians though closely associated with Epiphany. Baptism of the Lord comes on the first Sunday after January 6 (the Epiphany).

Passion Sunday or Palm Sunday is now regarded as a single day on which the passion narrative is usually read. The Easter Vigil is usually celebrated on the Eve before Easter Day. Ascension Day is sometimes commemorated on the seventh Sunday of Easter. The Day of Pentecost has recovered its earlier place as the fiftieth day and the last Sunday of the Season of Easter. All Saints Day, in some churches, may be observed on the first Sunday of November when November 1 is not a Sunday. The last Sunday of October, once observed as Reformation Sunday, has now been dropped by many churches. Instead, it now seems more appropriate to commemorate our common inheritance with All Saints Day.

For those who keep the minor christological feasts, there are other possibilities. The color for each is usually white. The **Holy Name of Jesus** (January 1) calls to mind Jesus' humanity and his full identification with human society (cf. Luke 2:15-21). **Presentation of the Lord** (February 2) was traditionally called Purification or Candlemas since the candles to be used each year were blessed on this occasion. It can also call attention to the aged in our society who, Luke tells us, were the first to proclaim the Lord (Anna and Simeon) (cf. Luke 2:22-40). **Annunciation of the Lord**—Lady Day in some countries (March 25)—calls attention to the power of the humblest person to fulfill God's will (cf. Luke 1:25-38). **Visitation of Mary to Elizabeth** (May 31), with its dialogue between two women, calls attention to the incarnation and contains Mary's Song, the radical *Magnificat*—in essence the social creed of Christianity (cf. Luke 1:39-56). **Holy Cross** (September 14) focuses on the sacrifice of Christ.

Roman Catholics also keep other additional **solemnities**: Mary, Mother of God (January 1); Joseph, Husband of Mary (March 19); Corpus Christi, Sacred Heart, Birth of John the Baptist (June 24); Peter and Paul, Apostles (June 29) Assumption of Mary (August 15); and Immaculate Conception (December 8). The course of the normal Sunday readings ought rarely to be broken for special observances without good reason since the lessons are usually constructed to cover scripture in a comprehensive way.

If the calendar is the foundation of Christian worship, the first floor is certainly the **lectionary** or list of **lections** (scripture lessons) based on the Christian year. One of the most significant changes in Protestant worship in recent decades has been the widespread adoption of a lectionary. The use of it in worship as the basis of preaching has affected the worship of thousands of congregations. All too often, earlier, haphazard methods of choosing scripture had, in fact, eliminated extensive portions of God's word and reshaped scripture in the preacher's own image. Social activists might be partial to passages from the prophetic books and conservatives to the more rigid passages in the pastoral epistles. Yet both, in choosing passages they found congenial, were in effect rewriting scripture. Liberals and conservatives were equally guilty of revising God's word in accord with personal preferences.

One of the most useful outcomes of the post–Vatican II era has been an ecumenical lectionary. Begun after Vatican II by the Roman Catholic Church, several years' work by a full-time staff and eight hundred consultants—Protestants, Catholics, and Jews—brought it to its present form. Published as *The Lectionary for Mass*, for Roman Catholics, it is the most carefully prepared lectionary in all Christian history. The *Common Lectionary* was published in 1983 and replaced in 1992 by the *Revised Common Lectionary*. It is now in use in English-speaking Protestant churches around the world. The most distinctive feature is in permitting long Old Testament narratives to unfold, week by week, during the Season after Pentecost.

How do the new lectionaries work? Both are three-year lectionaries, the years are designated A, B, and C. Year C is a year, such as 2001, that is evenly divisible by the number 3. The church year begins between November 27 and December 3 of the preceding civil year, so Advent in civil year December, 2001, is part of the church year 2002 and hence is in year A.

For each Sunday or festival, three lessons are appointed: The first is usually from the Old Testament, the second usually from an Epistle, and the third always from a Gospel. After Easter, lessons from the book of Acts are read as the story of the new creation begins with the resurrection. Chrysostom explained that the book of Acts is "the demonstration of the Resurrection" and, hence, Acts is read during the Easter Season, a custom that Augustine also notes in Africa. Occasionally, readings from Revelation take the place of the Epistle. In the course of three years, when all three lessons are used, most of the New Testament and large portions of the Old Testament are read.

Two principles are in operation here. The Gospels reflect the events of the Christian year with the first lessons more or less dependent on these readings. The second lessons, on the other hand, are usually read in order (**lectio continua**) from each book from beginning to end. First Corinthians, for example, is read chiefly during the Season of Epiphany. For the third lesson, year A is devoted to reading the Gospel of Matthew; year B to Mark; and Year C to Luke. Portions in all three years are filled in from the Fourth Gospel.

The lectionary provides the most comprehensive method available for reading almost the entire Bible in worship within three years. After that, it is time to start over again. There are two exceptional dates: On Passion or Palm Sunday and Good Friday a full passion narrative is read, often in dramatic fashion. For the Easter Vigil, provision is made for nine lessons, seven of them from the Old Testament.

The second question to ask in planning any service is, What does the lectionary provide? More than any other single item, the lectionary guides the choices appropriate for any given Sunday. It is reflected in the opening prayer, the psalm, the hymns, the choral and instrumental music, the sermon, and the visual materials used. The use of a lectionary makes it possible to plan services months or even years in advance. This makes it especially useful for musicians and artists who need a great deal of advance preparation. Since the lectionary shapes other choices, it is important that we examine briefly its effect on each of them in turn.

An **opening prayer** is sometimes an effective way to articulate the general thrust of the lessons for the day and to alert the congregation to the event. The Roman Catholic *Sacramentary* provides opening prayers (and alternatives) for Sundays and special occasions. Episcopalians and Anglicans retain the ancient term "**collect**" for opening prayers, and Episcopalians provide them in "traditional" and "contemporary" language. "Prayer of the Day" is the Lutheran term, "Opening Prayer" the United Methodist, and "Prayer of the Day" or "Opening Prayer" the Presbyterian.

Psalms are used in worship as responses to or commentaries on the lessons. The Roman Catholic and the *Revised Common* lectionaries provide lists of psalms chosen deliberately to relate to the lessons in the lectionary. A psalm serves as a response not as a lesson, but it does relate carefully to the lessons.

Appropriate **hymns** are listed in almost all denominational hymnals for seasons, festivals, and special occasions. Most hymnals have scriptural indexes as well as topical ones.

No one has questioned that J. S. Bach wrote some of the greatest choral and instrumental music while following the careful guidance of the lectionary and calendar. When well planned, choral music can mesh successfully with the ministry of the word by providing a musical commentary on the lessons. Too often, anthems with texts unrelated to the occasion blunder into the otherwise carefully planned flow of a service. This is not necessary. Careful use of the calendar and lectionary can be a tremendous boon to church musicians since it gives them lead time to order and rehearse appropriate music.

Nothing is as thoroughly and obviously affected by the lessons as the **sermon**. There are several direct results from the widespread use of the lectionary. First, it has made financially feasible the publication of a number of top-quality aids to biblical study in the form of commentaries and other resources to improve homiletic use of the Bible.[34] Second, the lectionary has forced many preachers to preach on a much wider selection of scripture than most did previously. That does not mean that one should preach on all three lessons at one time. Sometimes they relate to one another well; more often than not the second lesson goes its own separate way. But to preach on any one of these texts will force the preacher to study and ponder many portions of God's word that are unfamiliar. Third, anyone who really follows the year and the lessons carefully finds himself or herself probing deeper into Christology. One simply cannot preach on the Baptism of the Lord, the Transfiguration, Passion or Palm Sunday, Ascension Day, All Saints Day, Christ the King, and so on, without being forced to make up one's mind about whom one says Jesus Christ is. Without such discipline, it is remarkable how long a person can jump around that vital question. Many preachers have agreed that preaching from the lectionary improves the content of their sermons. And many have been surprised at how relevant assigned passages often are for their congregation's time and place.

Finally, we must say a word on the **visuals** that can be derived from the lectionary and calendar. They, too, provide ordinary and proper components of worship, though of a different type from verbal texts. With the use of textiles, graphics, and other visuals we can have, in effect, a new church setting each Sunday just as the whole appearance of a living room is changed by adding some orange pillows on the sofa. For example, where projections are possible, a wall can be whatever we want to project on it. We are limited only by the horizons of our imagination.

Some of the things we have learned about worship in the last few years seem irrevocable. In 1965 few, if any, churches had ever used a banner. By now, most have. If the Gospel can be proclaimed visually, why should it not be? Each new dimension we add to our perception of the Good News seems to be clear gain.

How do we do it? The simplest concept is just using pure **color**. Colors signify different meanings in various cultures, and we must recognize this. Color helps form general expectations for any occasion. We do not wear flamboyant colors to a funeral. Traditionally, purples, grays, and blues have been used for seasons of a penitential character, such as Advent and Lent, although any dark colors could be used. White has been used for events or seasons with strong christological meaning, such as the Baptism of the Lord or the Season of Easter; yellows and golds are also possibilities at such times. Red has been reserved for occasions relating to the Holy Spirit (such as the Day of Pentecost or ordinations) or to commemorations of martyrs. Green has been used for seasons of less pronounced character or Ordinary Time such as the Season of Epiphany or the Season after Pentecost. These longer seasons need not stagnate in a single color or hue any more than nature retains a monotonous green. After all, nature is not static. The delicate yellow greens of spring progress to the deeper hues of summer and then to the bright yellows and reds of autumn. The absence of any colored textiles from Maundy Thursday to the Easter Vigil is a striking use of contrast. **Contrast** itself is one of the prime forms of communication in visual materials. Different cultures have different concepts of the meaning of colors.[35]

Much may be done with pure color. However, we are coming to realize the need to be equally sensitive to hues and **textures**. A silk purple might be less preferable for Lent than a rough-textured blue or gray. And a splendid, tightly woven gold might be better for Easter than a coarse white material.

Colors and textures can be used most effectively in textiles for hangings on pulpits, on lecterns (if any), for the stoles worn by ordained ministers, or for ministerial vestments. Sometimes bolts of colored cloth may simply be hung as giant abstract banners. It is better not to hide the altar-table under cloth hangings.

Banners can be hung almost anywhere in the church. Increasingly we see a move to large-scale banners, fifteen feet in length or so. They ought to be changed as the year turns. The church building at Easter ought to be quite different from what it is in Lent.

Posters, bulletins, placards, and other **graphics** can express the gospel in forceful ways. Photographs may be blown up cheaply. A few words of press type—"Lord, when was it that we saw you?" (Matt. 25:37) or "Is it nothing to you, all you who pass by?" (Lam. 1:12)—lettered on photos can be a powerful message. Try to discover a few key words for any occasion—"Peace on earth," "My Son," "He is risen"—and use them. Visit a local art supply store to see how many possibilities churches have neglected. Good posters and bulletins will not soon be forgotten, especially when created locally.

Certain **objects**—such as an advent wreath with four candles, a lenten veil, palm branches, and a paschal candle (during the Season of Easter)—communicate to the congregation at different seasons. Symbols pertain to different occasions too: a star, a crown of thorns, tongues of flame, and so on. The lack of objects also is a powerful form of communication. The absence of any flowers and candles during Holy Week can say much.

A word of caution is necessary. None of these colors, textures, images, or objects is a decoration or an ornament. If they are used as such, they are trivialities not worth the time or effort they consume. But if used to add one more dimension to our perception of the Good News, they can be well worth considerable effort and expense. Much work goes into a sermon, meant to be preached only once. Work from a broader segment of the community on visuals to present the gospel is a good plan even though visuals, like the sermon itself, may be used only once.

All in all, Christians are called to proclaim the gospel by every means available. The Christian year and the lectionary based on it are two vital resources for this. If keeping time with the church can make for better Christians, then exploring all the possibilities such a discipline can offer is most worthwhile.

CHAPTER THREE

THE LANGUAGE OF SPACE

t should not surprise us that a religion whose fundamental doctrine is the incarnation should take space seriously in its worship. Not only did Jesus Christ enter human time, but he also came to dwell among us, occupying a specific and definite place on earth in Judea. The New Testament is full of place names; Jesus was at Jerusalem, Bethany, the Sea of Galilee, the River Jordan, and so on.

The same is true for the rest of salvation history. The Jewish and Christian God is made known by events that occur among men and women, not on Mt. Olympus or in Valhalla. It is space on earth that is made holy, not because of the place itself but because of what God does for humans in that place. In the Bible, saving events usually happen at some ordinary field, well, or village street. Today such places would be as ordinary as a shopping mall. The location is indifferent, the event is crucial.

Of course, after the event, the place becomes significant as a bearer of meaning: the place where something happened. Jacob had a dream at a remote place and woke to exclaim that it was a fearsome place, the house of God, the gate of heaven (Gen. 28:17). His dream provoked him to erect a pillar and give the place a new name, "House of God," that all might know about the event. We have already seen how fourth-century Jerusalem shaped all subsequent Christian worship by commemorations at the times and places where climactic events in Christ's life and death occurred. Fourth century pilgrims to Jerusalem were still shown the sycamore tree Zacchaeus had climbed to see Jesus—once an ordinary tree but by then a holy place. Europe eventually became dotted with pilgrimage places where an event had made a spot significant. All these testify to the eloquence of the language of space. A religion of the incarnation has to have its feet planted firmly on the ground. God and humanity meet at a place, whether it is as casual as an ordinary desert bush or as magnificent as the Jerusalem Temple.

Any Christian community needs a place to worship the Incarnate One. It can be anywhere, but it has to be a designated place so the Body of Christ knows where to assemble. Early missionaries in the British Isles simply set a cross on a pole to determine the place for worship. Eventually such places were roofed and walled, and the spaces sheltered thus were organized for the convenience and comfort of the worshipers. We call the art of organizing space "architecture." Today, we are so accustomed to the Christian use of architecture that, in many languages, the word "church" refers to the building just as much as to the body of believers.

The relationships between architecture and what Christians do when they worship are complex. Church architecture not only reflects the ways Christians worship but it also shapes worship or, not uncommonly, misshapes it. Architecture reflects Christian worship by providing the setting and shelter needed by a community to carry out its worship together. This is perhaps obvious—not even a football crowd will sit still in below-zero weather. But, at the same time that architecture is accommodating worship, it is also, in a subtle and inconspicuous way, shaping that same worship. In the first place, the building helps define the meaning of worship for those gathered inside it. Try to preach against triumphalism in a baroque church! Try to teach the priesthood of all believers with a deep Gothic chancel never occupied by any but ordained clergy! Second, the building dictates the possibilities open to us in our forms and styles of worship. We may want good congregational song, but do the acoustics swallow up each sound so that all seem mute? Or do we have to give up any hope of movement by the congregation because everyone is neatly filed away in pews? We soon realize that architecture presents both opportunities and limitations, some possibilities opened and others closed. We could worship with difficulty without buildings; often we worship with difficulty because of them.

The way space is organized reflects and shapes Christian worship, so much that we must examine why and how space speaks a language that is so important for worship. In this case, it is best to interpret theory first, then to survey the history, and to offer practical conclusions from the history of church architecture. Finally, the role of the visual arts will be discussed.

THE FUNCTIONS OF LITURGICAL SPACE

How does the way space is organized reflect what happens in Christian worship? To answer this we may make use of a description of Christian worship involving "public speaking and touching in Christ's name." Another way of saying the same thing is that in worship we speak for God, to God, and to one another as well as reaching out to touch others in God's name. This is unquestionably a severe oversimplification of what happens in Christian worship, but it does make clear that Christian worship is action that requires space. This crucial insight is not apparent in more abstract definitions.

Let us begin, then, by asserting that in worship God acts in self-giving through human words and by human hands and we give ourselves to God through our words and hands. All that happens in worship depends on God, but it occurs through the instruments of human speech and the human body.

How does God act in self-giving through words? God speaks God's word to us through the mouths of humans. That seems a strange way to reach people; it displays a far greater trust in humans than most of us would ever have. But it is God's way as scripture repeatedly testifies: "I have put my words in your mouth" (Jer. 1:9) or, to tongue-tied brothers, "I will be with your mouth and with his mouth" (Exod. 4:15). There can be no doubt that in biblical faith God calls men and women to speak God's word.

Now there are a few, very few, necessities required for one human being to speak to others. One is that in order to communicate best one ought to be able to sustain eye contact with those to whom one is talking. One speaks best to those who can be looked in the eye, not to those to the side or behind one. Eye contact is part of reaching out in love to others and is an important part of speech. Mark tells us "Jesus, looking at him, loved him" (Mark 10:21). Looking is part of loving.

Spatially, this implies a straight line between the speaker and the hearer. The speaker may need to be elevated a few inches so that the heads of others do not interfere with sight lines, but too great an elevation becomes a visual barrier, a moat of height. Pillars, partitions, and other barriers must not intervene. The audience and the speaker must meet face-to-face. The best space for face-to-face encounter is organized along a horizontal axis, as if there were a straight line from the speaker to the person in the middle of the audience. This is the basis of the synagogue where people come together to hear God's word read and expounded or a meeting-house where Christians assemble to hear the gospel.

Self giving occurs in speech to people gathered along a horizontal axis from human speaker to human hearer. If that were all that Christian worship involved, then planning a worship space would indeed be simple. But God not only places God's word in our mouths, but God also uses our hands. And this is where organizing space for Christian worship gets complicated. We must provide not only for receiving the word but also for receiving the sacraments. God's self giving comes in both ways. All good church architecture is a compromise to provide for both types of divine activity. The whole history of church building is the history of compromises between arrangements best for speaking in God's name and those best for touching in God's name.

If the path of the speaking voice is a horizontal axis, the locus of the outstretched hand is on a vertical axis. The reach of the human voice can be artificially extended—not so the human arm. God has created each of us small enough so that we can reach out only about a yard. Others have to come to us, and they come best in a circle gathered about us. The image this projects is one of people gathered in concentric circles around a vertical axis. On that vertical axis may be an altar-table, a font or pool, or simply a person. From there we can reach out—God can reach out through our hands—to the community standing around us.

In other terms, we need both a synagogue and an upper room for Christian worship. We need space in which we can both project our voice and reach out our hands, whether it be hands baptizing a new Christian, hands giving the Lord's body at the eucharist, hands laid on a head, hands uniting the hands of a couple, hands blessing or reconciling, or hands sprinkling a coffin. Not only do we speak for God but we also touch others for God. And we have to be close enough really to touch them. A woman touched the hem of Jesus' garment and power passed to her. We touch others' heads, lips, or hands, and power passes to them. But our reach is limited by arms which, unlike our voice, cannot be stretched by a microphone. We need intimate concentric space to touch in God's name. The scale is that of the human body.

How do we reconcile space organized along a horizontal axis with space situated around a vertical axis? There is a paradigm of worship itself in the problem, the God to human represented by the vertical, the human to human represented by the horizontal. Soon, we shall trace different ways this tension has been resolved historically.

But what of the words people offer to God? There seem to be few spatial requirements for this; prayer and praise can be offered anywhere that people can assemble. Above all else, a church building is a place for people to come together. In Quaker terms, where many candles are brought together there is more light. Christians can speak to God wherever they can assemble for worship. Spatial requirements for this act are not specific. Churches once tended to suggest that God was high and lifted up—maybe in the dim recesses of the rafters or at the end of the chancel. Today we are more inclined to suggest that God is in the midst of the worshipers, not in a remote holy spot. One architect places the cross in the midst of the congregation to state this fact. In addition, there are few requirements for space in which to speak to one another in Christ's name. Access to our neighbor is all that is necessary.

Of course, we cannot touch God, but each of us can touch others in God's name. In recent years, the **passing of the peace** has again become a prominent sign of reconciliation and love as Christians embrace one another or shake hands during worship. Other possibilities include pronouncing God's forgiveness after a prayer of confession, an act that can be done with the hands even better than the voice (a sign of the cross traced on one's neighbor's forehead, for example). Foot washing is a dramatic occasional act. And, in services of reconciliation, touching others for God may be practiced. All that seems necessary for these aspects of worship is accessibility to one another.

We can break down the components of space for speaking and touching in God's name more specifically. Most Christian worship necessitates six different **liturgical spaces** where worship occurs and three or four **liturgical centers**, that is furnishings from which worship is led. It is amazing how few and how simple the physical necessities for Christian worship are. But since we never encounter them in isolation from each other, we may not be aware of them individually. If a church building can be compared to a complete sentence, then, it is time, for a moment, to look at the individual words that compose that sentence.[1]

In recent years, we have become much more aware of the importance of **gathering space** as a key liturgical space. The Christian community needs to assemble in order to worship and this act of coming together may be the most important single activity of the congregation. In the heroic age of the early Church, the very act of assembling produced martyrs. In every age, forming the body of Christ is the first act of worship—one in which all participate. Therefore, space that marks the temporary separation of the community from the world outside, space in which individuals become a community, deserves careful attention in the design of churches.

The second type of space is **movement space**. Christian worship demands considerable movement. Revivalists in the nineteenth century and charismatics today remind us that to move people spiritually we have to move them physically, too. Christians seem to be restless pilgrim people. The people who gather must take their places, but even then processions, weddings, funerals, baptisms, offerings, and receiving communion involve further movements, more rearranging of the community at worship. Movement is an integral part of worship, and aisles and cross aisles demand careful planning.

The largest liturgical space is usually **congregational space**. Basically, a church is a people place. The Greek temple was the reverse; pagans kept the money on the inside and the people on the outside. Christians use the money for the world outside and serve the people inside. Quaker meetinghouses consist almost entirely of congregational space and make it manifest that God's presence is known in the midst of God's people. In an important passage, Vatican II's *Constitution on the Sacred Liturgy* (CSL) lists as one of the ways that Christ is present in the church's liturgical celebrations: "He is present, lastly, when the Church prays and sings, for he promised: 'Where two or three are gathered together in my name, there am I in the midst of them' (Matt. 18:20)" (par. 7). Today, we might also add that Christ is also present in the poor in our midst.

Choir space may be the most difficult liturgical space to deal with, especially when there is uncertainty about the role of a choir in worship. Such space may also need to accommodate instrumentalists or dancers. The chief role or roles assigned to the choir should determine the location and design of this type of space.

We are accustomed to speaking of baptism in terms of a font or baptismal pool; less often do we think of it in terms of **baptismal space**. At worst, baptism has been a private ceremony tucked off in a remote corner of the church. Yet every baptism is an act of the whole community, not just because it adds to the body's number but because it witnesses again and again to the fact that those who have gone through the waters of death and resurrection are united to Christ. Like the wedding service, baptism involves both the whole church community and the more intimate circle of family and sponsors gathered as a special focus of love around the one being baptized. In terms of space, this necessitates access and space for the candidates and baptismal party in a way that does not impede participation by the whole congregation. Baptismal space is people space in concentric circles. Around the font or baptismal pool gather, first of all, the candidates and ministers, then family and sponsors, and finally the whole congregation.

Altar-table space surrounds the altar-table itself. Some traditions call this area the **sanctuary**. Usually it is the most conspicuous space in the building, often blinding us to the fact that its role is to serve, not to dominate. Thus we need to avoid such barriers as excessive height, the glare of too much direct light, overscaled furnishings, enclosure, and other ways of making this space seem a remote and detached holy spot. Strangely enough, in many denominations with little eucharistic piety, this is the one spot in the church never approached by the people. It remains more aloft and aloof than in those denominations where people gather around it weekly.

There are also three or four liturgical centers essential to Christian worship. Again, their use reflects how we perceive the presence of Christ in our worship. A **baptismal font** or **baptismal pool** is a necessity for the sheer physical fact that water demands a container. It can be a recess in the floor (as the earliest surviving baptistery buildings reveal) or a basin mounted on a pillar. The one necessity—that it can contain water—seems more concealed than revealed in many designs. The *Constitution* reminds us: "By his power he [Christ] is present in the sacraments, so that when someone baptizes it is really Christ himself who baptizes" (CSL, par. 7). Without a container for water, we cannot baptize or experience this form of Christ's presence.

Christ is also "present in his word, since it is he himself who speaks when the holy scriptures are read in the Church" (CSL, par. 7). One could argue in a strict sense that a **pulpit** or **ambo** is not a necessity but a convenience. Yet if the reading and preaching of God's word is understood as a fresh theophany each time the people of God gather, then we need physical testimony to that belief in the form of a pulpit. The Bible is displayed when it is not being read, and it is held so that the reader's or preacher's hands are free when reading or preaching. The visual aspects of this form of Christ's presence are not to be minimized. This also means that bookbinding must again become a major art form for the church.[2] A lectern is unnecessary and weakens the focus on the unity of reading and preaching of God's Word.

There is no need to emphasize the importance of the **altar-table** for Christian worship, but we need to be reminded that it is not present as the architectural focus of the building or even as a symbol of Christ. It is there because it is used, in short, just as fonts hold water and pulpits hold Bibles, altar-tables hold the communion vessels. The altar-tables depicted in early Christian art were hardly larger than a card table. They were ministerial altar-tables, quite adequate for holding what was put on them but not monuments to fill space or to create an architectural focus or religious symbol. In Western culture, it would seem most inconvenient to have to put the communion vessels on the floor, so an altar-table is a necessity.

In the early church, the **presider's chair** was the center from which much of the service was conducted and the place for preaching until late in the fourth century. There has been a revival in the importance of the presider's chair since Vatican II in Roman Catholic circles. Many Protestants are still recoiling from the ugliness of the inevitable three pulpit chairs the nineteenth century provided for preacher, song leader, and guest preacher. As a result, many Protestants, are reluctant to make clergy seating very conspicuous. The *Constitution* speaks of Christ's presence "in the person of the minister," but it is questionable how much a living person can be identified with a chair in the way we associate water with a font, the Bible with the pulpit, or communion elements with the altar-table. A chair does not function in quite the same way, since Christ's presence in a person does not need a furnishing to make it visible. Certainly the presider's chair is a convenience, but it ought to be designed and located with reticence and not resemble a throne.

No more is necessary. There is a certain sense of poverty or economy of means about Christian worship, but too often, we gild the lily. Other spaces, other furnishings (lecterns, prayer desks, communion rails) are not necessary and may confuse by concealing those that are. Restraint and understatement are the most powerful forms of statement. The essential spaces and centers—and only these—reveal what is basic in Christian worship.

There is also a quality in church space that rarely takes visible form, and it is one of the most easily and tragically overlooked factors: the way space affects sound. Every church building forms a unique **acoustical environment**, and few things affect worship more profoundly than the way sound behaves in space. Sound, of course, exists in time too, and it could well have been treated in chapter 2. The relation of sound to space, however, needs emphasis, especially since it is so frequently overlooked when liturgical space is planned. Churches are built to be used; they are usually photographed empty of people, but a church functions chiefly when peopled by a congregation. The very act of people assembling is an event with sound, often commencing with bells calling them out of the world.

Sound exists in space, then, as well as in time. Our concern here is with all the sounds that exist within a church building and the way those sounds act in that space to shape and determine the nature of the worship offered therein. A few examples may be helpful. The large dimensions and hard surfaces of medieval stone buildings made necessary the practice of chanting prose recitations in melodic form in order to ensure audibility. The psalms were usually chanted in unison to plainsong melodies; a practice well adapted to such an acoustical environment where sound lingers. On the other hand, it is not accidental that congregational song in England developed in the small meetinghouses of dissenters rather than in stately medieval parish churches. Hymnody was picked up in time by Anglicans, but Congregationalists and Methodists took the lead. Their small intimate meetinghouses encouraged congregational song by making everyone feel that they are "on stage." In similar fashion, it would be hard to imagine the silent waiting for God in Quaker worship in any place where sound is as resonant as in a large stone cathedral. In a small domestic space, Quaker worship seems natural; in a vast area, such speaking from the Spirit would appear difficult.

Worship involves a wide range of sounds. How do people interact as they gather? There is the sound of feet, voices, and moving chairs mixed into worship. Babies cry and children whine. These are not sounds to be suppressed; they are the natural and welcome sounds made when forming the body. But there may be annoying sounds from outside that need to be subdued or internal mechanical hums from lighting, heating, or air-conditioning that ought to be absorbed.

More crucial, though, is the spoken voice. If there is an echo bouncing off hard or curved surfaces, preaching may be difficult. Hearing the word of God ought not to be prevented by echoes. There are also similar problems with an environment that is too absorbent; it can make each person think she or he is singing solo, so each one usually stops singing. Too much absorbency can make organ music lose much of its brilliance. Although requirements are not the same for the speaker and the musician, poor acoustics can frustrate both of them. The speaker wants no echo while the organist relishes a bit of reverberation. Compromises between the two are usually necessary.

HISTORY OF LITURGICAL ARCHITECTURE

A look at how Christians have arranged these liturgical spaces and centers over the course of history can teach us much. The relative prominence or reticence of various spaces or centers, their relation to one another, and the design of the liturgical centers themselves give us a clear indication of shifts in practice and theological perspective. This variety in worship spaces indicates the diversity inherent in Christian worship. Yet the persistence of the same six spaces and the three or four centers is a clear witness to the large degree of constancy in Christian worship. We can only give a rapid survey of diversity and constancy, but this survey will indicate the great variety of liturgical arrangements that have been found useful.[3]

The early church had to worship in makeshift quarters during periods of persecution, yet we know buildings of some magnificence were occasionally built—even while Christianity was an illicit religion. We have very little documentary or architectural evidence of the architectural setting of Christian worship before Constantine. Apparently, early Christians often met in private homes, usually those of the more well-to-do members of the community. During periods of persecution, there was always danger that Christians could be put to death for the crime of assembling for worship or become the victims of mobs who considered such assemblies unpatriotic or irreligious. Thus it was probably wise to use regular family furniture and rooms for such worship then return them to their places immediately.

The domesticity of these spaces in private homes gave a sense of hospitality and intimacy that was lost when Christian worship went public. Yet the advantages of such intimate space recur again and again whenever Christians are persecuted or an impoverished minority, such as the Anabaptists, the Amish, the Quakers, and even Christians in some countries today. We probably deceive ourselves if we think this same domestic feeling of hospitality and intimacy can be easily imitated in public buildings yet we are equally misled if we forget the need to seek these qualities in good church architecture. These characteristics clearly shape the style of worship practiced within these settings.

We do have an astonishingly well-preserved example of a house-church from **Dura-Europos** on the Euphrates River. It is a home that was adapted permanently for Christian worship early in the third century (long before persecution ended in A.D. 313) and destroyed in A.D. 256. The ruins indicate that a wall had been removed and two rooms were joined to provide space for the eucharistic assembly (fig. 1).[4] At one end is located a small platform, possibly for the altar-table and the bishop's throne. A room on the opposite side of the house was probably used as a baptistery. It had a font covered by a canopy and walls ornamented with frescoes. Thus, even at this early date, there appears an explicit allocation of spaces for different liturgical functions, a pattern reflected in most subsequent church buildings.

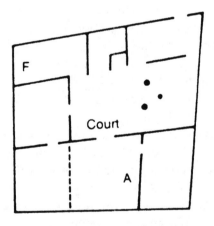

Figure 1

In the fourth century, Christianity not only became legal and respectable but was also espoused by the emperor Constantine who showered magnificent gifts on the church: nine new churches in Rome and others in Jerusalem, Bethlehem, and Constantinople.

The worship in these magnificent new buildings matched all the sumptuousness of the imperial court—a far cry from that of the persecuted Christians huddled together in secret meetings. The emperor's architects simply adapted a well-developed building type, the **basilica** or Roman law court. The civil basilica served much the same functions as the county court house and high school auditorium do in American towns. Most were rectangular buildings with a semicircular space, the **apse,** at one end, opposite a long people's part, the **nave.** In the apse, there was a platform with a throne for the judge, who might be flanked by scribes. The basilica was basically a **longitudinal** building organized along a horizontal axis. The church made this building type its own in the fourth century (fig. 2).

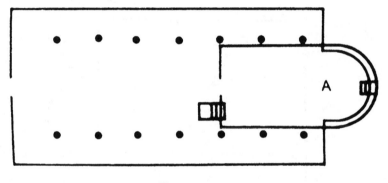

Figure 2

The bishop's throne replaced that of the judge, and presbyters sat on either side of him. A platform for the singers extended out into the nave (indicated here by solid lines). The altar-table usually appeared near the junction of the apse and the nave, and an ambo (pulpit) stood on the end or side of the platform. Preaching, at first, was done from the bishop's throne, and the eucharistic prayer was offered facing the people across the altar-table. The rest of the building was unencumbered by seating, the mobile congregation moving wherever they could best hear and see.

From an early time, the tradition of a **centralized** building organized around a vertical axis in the center of the building has also existed. A separate type of building for baptism, the **baptistery**, was often designed on this basis—as was the **martyrium,** or chapel over the grave or relics of a martyr. Both of them were based on the mausoleum. New technology for building domes over square naves led to the gradual adoption of centralized buildings among Eastern Orthodox churches instead of the elongated basilicas favored in the West. Frequently, three apses are walled off by an **iconostasis** (screen covered with images of the saints) from the central congregational space, which is frequently covered by a dome (fig. 3). The iconostasis shielded the people from the awe and mystery of the service surrounding the altar-table. **Icons** (images) of the saints surround the congregation, reminding them that they worship amidst the whole company of heaven.

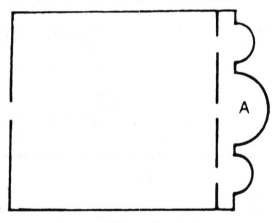

Figure 3

In the West, churches tended to develop longitudinally, partly, because of technology. (The maximum width of Gothic vaulting was about eighty feet, but by repeating bays a church could be extended lengthwise.) This tendency, however, was also the result of a growing complexity in the forms of worship and the specialization of priests and lesser clergy, as well as those in religious orders. The complexity and specialization can be seen most dramatically in the retreat of the altar-table from proximity to the congregational space until the sanctuary space became located at the farthest extremity of the building, away from congregational space.

The Middle Ages saw the development of highly specialized types of churches: pilgrimage churches or shrines, churches for monastic communities, collegiate churches, cathedrals, preaching churches, and ordinary parish churches. The pacesetters, though, were the **monastic churches**. Since a large part of the time in these communities revolved around saying and singing the seven daily offices and the night office and since large communities could include as many as a thousand monks, it is not surprising that a magnificently functional type of building evolved, specifically designed to accommodate such worship. The most important space was the choir stalls (since the whole community was a choir), arranged in two parallel sections so that psalms could be sung **antiphonally** (alternative verses sung back and forth). In effect, these elongated choirs provided a church within a church, often sectioned off from the nave by screens (fig. 4).

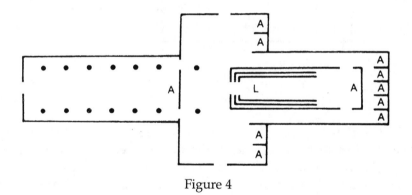

Figure 4

For a monastic community, it was a functional arrangement. A high altar-table in the sanctuary served for mass, and other altar-tables were scattered throughout the building for private masses. Various other arrangements were tried for monastic communities: a choir in a western apse in Germany and a walled-in space in the middle of the nave in Spain. Cathedral churches followed the monastic pattern, often subdividing the interior space into more specialized compartments for chantry chapels where mass was said for the repose of the dead.

It should not surprise us that these highly specialized churches had a disproportionate effect on **parish churches,** where most people worshiped in their village (fig. 5). These buildings, too, sprouted large screened chancels, spaces used only by the local clergy and the family of the lord of the manor. But the congregation was not monks or clergy, it was lay people relegated to the nave, where they could glimpse mass being said at the altar-table at the other end of the chancel. The nave often contained a pulpit around which they could stand.

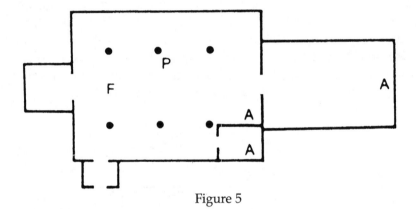

Figure 5

Unlike the monastic church, each parish church contained a font. The services of baptism and marriage, by the late–Middle Ages, began in a porch, just outside the nave, which was decorated with a vast array of sculpture, painting, and stained glass meant to instruct and to stimulate devotions. Until the fourteenth century, the nave was clear of chairs and pews; a mobile congregation moved where they could see and hear best. The late and gradual introduction of pews meant sitting down on the job and a congregation that was no longer mobile. Their time had come to be spent in private devotions.

Clergy and people had become so divorced that a sixteenth-century Catholic bishop wrote: "The people in the church [nave] took small heed what the priest and clerks did in the chancel. . . . It was never meant that the people should indeed hear the

Matins or hear the Mass, but be present there and pray themselves in silence."[5] The division between nave and chancel, so functional in a monastic church, was inappropriate in parish churches but, nevertheless, imitated with zeal. The medieval parish church had become an excellent place for personal devotions (which was indeed primarily how the people used it) but a very poor place for genuinely liturgical worship with that "full, conscious and active participation in liturgical celebrations which is demanded by the very nature of the liturgy" (CSL, par. 4).

Another medieval development was attributing symbolic meanings to every bit of space, furnishings, and actions of worship. This fanciful development often betrayed the lost comprehension of how items were once functional and obvious in purpose.

The Protestant and Catholic Reformations saw great changes in the arrangements. The Jesuits, who had no need for choir space to say the daily office together, led the way among Roman Catholics in building sumptuous churches where the mass could be a dazzling spectacle. The altar-table once again became conspicuous without the intervening space of a choir or screens. Ornate pulpits were common.

It is hard to generalize about the Protestant experiments in liturgical architecture, so richly varied were they in trying to leapfrog over medieval developments to achieve what they, rightly or wrongly, considered to be primitive (early church) patterns in building. It was difficult, if not impossible, to teach the priesthood of all believers in a building rigidly divided into clerical chancel and lay nave. Medieval buildings were adapted by bringing all the communicants into the chancel for communion or by moving the whole service out into the nave. Sometimes the chancel was simply walled off and used for schools.

When Protestants began building numerous new buildings in the seventeenth and eighteenth centuries, the variety of shapes they experimented with was extraordinary, though many were of a centralized type. Figure 6 shows (left to right) several patterns that were drawn from German, Dutch, and Scottish examples.

The same variety of experimentation continued in eighteenth-century America. Figure 7 shows (at top) a typical Congregational

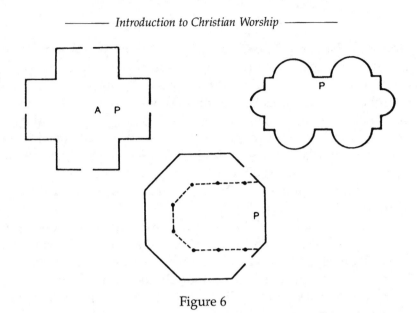

Figure 6

meetinghouse, one of the many arrangements tried by Anglicans, and (at bottom) a Quaker meetinghouse with the movable partition between men's and women's meetings (indicated by a zigzag line).

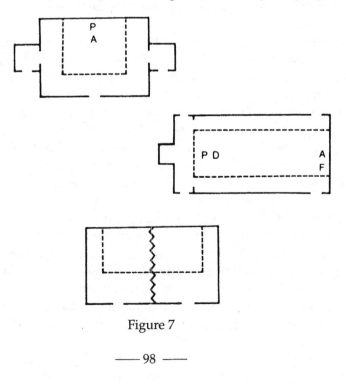

Figure 7

What do these have in common, if anything? None has a chancel; it virtually disappeared from buildings constructed for Protestant worship for nearly three centuries. Instead, congregational space was magnified, and choir and sanctuary space have shrunk or disappeared. The Quaker building is entirely congregational and movement space. A characteristic Protestant addition was balconies to enable speakers to be heard by a large number of people. Balconies also helped bring the total community together about the pulpit and Lord's table, although movement was difficult.

The nineteenth century saw a strange reversal. The romanticism of the **Cambridge Movement** led many churches in the English-speaking world to see the Middle Ages by moonlight and to clamor for a return to a neo-medieval type of building (fig. 8—compare with fig. 5). Revivalism, on the other hand, emphasizing pulpit personalities and massed choirs, developed the concert stage arrangement (fig. 9). Roman Catholic churches of this period tended to be variations of figure 9, with the altar-table at C, a font near the door, and a diminutive pulpit off to the side of the chancel.

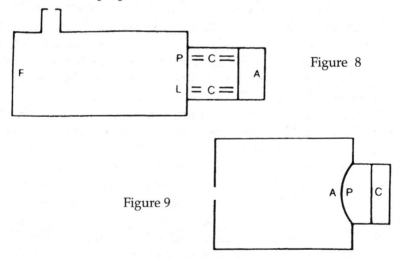

Figure 8

Figure 9

Recent years have seen drastic changes, especially since Vatican II. Many of these modifications represent a move to a centralized plan, but with compromises necessary to make the spoken word function well and still allow concentric arrangements of people.

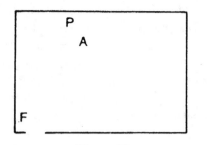

Figure 10

Figure 10 shows an arrangement that might appear in either a Protestant or a Roman Catholic church built today. Protestants would be more inclined to place the font before the congregation, but this is not unknown in new Roman Catholic churches. Roman Catholics would be more likely to feature a presider's chair; Protestants are currently reacting to overly dominant clergy seating. Both groups are inclined to seek centralized shapes with the congregation gathered around the altar-table. The fan shape has a wide popularity among Roman Catholics.

Some of the most pronounced characteristics of current church buildings are the result of economic necessity and new construction methods. But others, such as low profile buildings, nondirectional interior space, and flexible seating, show deliberate attempts to recover some of the hospitality and intimacy of the house churches in which early Christians worshiped.

What practical conclusions for our times can we draw from this rapid survey of the Christian experience with liturgical space? Obviously there is enough diversity mentioned here to make generalizations of any type difficult, yet when we look at these experiences with a critical eye, there is much to admire and much to deplore in each. Obviously, our point in time has different standards of judgment than these of other ages, but if we accept the qualification that we are speaking from the beginning of the third millennium, we can propose some criteria of practical relevance for those who build or remodel space for Christian worship today.

Our first criterion is that of **utility**. How well does a building function in being used, not admired but used, by worshipers? The question can be resolved only by seeing how adequately the building serves for speaking and touching in God's name. If speaking cannot be heard because of atrocious acoustics, even though the space functions well for music, it can hardly be considered adequate. Or if the speaking is fine but the congregation is fractured into inaccessible balconies so that giving communion is difficult the building again flunks. Clearly, there must be compromises between an ideal preaching church and a perfect sacrament church. The criterion of utility covers all uses. Churches are built to be used, not to be monuments for tourists to admire or art historians to chronicle.

Much of the success of the space organized most usefully for Christian worship is the result of a devotion to **simplicity**. Only when we understand clearly what is basic and essential *in* worship can we build well *for* worship. Restraint and discipline are crucial. Too many church buildings have been ruined by too much money and effort expended on nonessentials and too little concern directed to basics. The six essential liturgical spaces and the three or four liturgical centers provide the core of our discipline of simplicity. Knowing when to stop is all important. One must talk worship before one talks architecture. Church building committees are notoriously poor clients because they do not do their homework to make up their mind about what the church is and what it does in its worship. Without this information, even the best architects cannot design buildings adequate for use in worship. The most they can do is design very attractive facades.

Our survey has shown that the circumstances of Christian worship and the needs perceived are subject to change. The events of the last few years, especially, have also taught us the importance of **flexibility**. Despite the constancy in Christian worship, there are strong forces shaping and changing the outward forms through which these constants are expressed. The most difficult churches to deal with today are those built, not so long ago, when we had not yet come to accept the reality of change in worship. A most important new element in our thinking about church architecture is the frank acceptance of change. John Ruskin's romantic "when we build, let us think that we build for ever" belongs to another age.[6] Instead, we should say, "When we build, let us not tie knots in the future." For we know it will be different, maybe even in a very short time. Immovable pews, massive pulpits, and fixed choir stalls, belong to an age that could not even imagine the possibility of change. Both history and recent experience have taught us that what seems so true and obvious in one period of time may not be so in the next. Let us not try to impose our will irrevocably in concrete on those who come after us. They deserve a voice, too.

An elusive strand throughout our historical survey has been the need for buildings that foster a sense of **intimacy**. This was certainly true in the early church, recovered again in many Reformation traditions, and now ardently sought in building today. The sense of intimacy is important as we emphasize participation by the entire worshiping community. Current revulsion against monumental type buildings is a healthy sign that a servant people has learned that architecture is meant to serve the community, not dominate it. This means smaller scale and less expensive buildings that allow each worshiper to feel he or she is on stage and playing an important role in worship instead of being a lonely spectator lost in the audience. Intimacy implies a sense of hospitality, of welcoming the stranger.

The human spirit associates **beauty** with worship. Beauty is an elusive quality, and consensus about what things and places are beautiful is not always easy to obtain. Excess height seems to be almost the only constant factor associated with making worship space beautiful. Other design features will continue to change as architects seek to build the best possible space of which their era is capable.

Utility, simplicity, flexibility, intimacy, and beauty seem to be the criteria by which we can best judge how adequately liturgical architecture serves the church today. These are obviously not the standards by which the great cathedrals of the thirteenth century were built or even the churches of the 1950s, although we can learn much from both. But the directness and honesty sought in our time can indicate new directions to add to the varied legacy of the past.

Those who have the responsibility of building or renovating space for a worshiping congregation have a wonderful opportunity to renew the life of their community. A building project can be the catalyst that makes church renewal possible. It can also be sheer hell. The *process* (planning to build) can be more important than the final *product* (the building). After all, the church is people, not a building. But planning for a building can often help the people discover, or rediscover, what it means to be the community of God's favor. Much depends on the leadership given in guiding the planning process and the willingness to take the time needed to prepare adequately.

Nevertheless, the building is not unimportant, either. After it is built, it will continue to shape worship in its image for generations. Although it is not completely true that the building will always win, we must at least recognize in it a powerful ally and a formidable foe. Its witness will outlast its builders. The more carefully we study and reflect on Christian worship, the better equipped we will be to help plan a building that will provide the best space for speaking, acting, and touching in God's name.

LITURGICAL ART

Space provides the setting for an important component of Christian worship: the **visual arts**. Ralph Adams Cram, the famous architect, was fond of referring to architecture as the "nexus of the arts." To a large degree this is true; architecture provides shelter not only for music and dance but also for sculpture, painting, and a variety of visual arts and crafts. But architecture does far more than just shelter the other arts; it adds to or subtracts from their effectiveness in helping Christians express their relationship to God.

What function do the various visual arts play in Christian worship? Some traditions have avoided them altogether. At times, in the early church and the Reformation, there were violent outbursts against them, though these various outbreaks of **iconoclasm** (image smashing) were in themselves strong testimony to the power of visual images. In the opposite extreme, the arts are sometimes used simply to ornament space. Thus tamed and innocuous, they have little potency for contributing to worship and merely provide superfluous decoration.

We must distinguish between religious art in general and **liturgical art** (sometimes called cultic art, especially when non-Christian examples are being considered). Most briefly stated, liturgical art is art used in worship. "Religious art" is a much broader category and, by some definitions, includes illustrations in Sunday school literature, Van Gogh's landscapes, or abstract art. Paul Tillich was willing to apply the term "religious" to any art that had a dimension of depth, penetrating beneath superficial observation.[7] Liturgical art, by contrast, is defined more by its use, although its subject matter is usually the divine or those through whom God has worked.

The prime function of liturgical art is to bring us to an awareness of the **presence of the holy**, to make visible that which cannot be seen by ordinary eyes. Liturgical art does not make God present, but it does bring God's presence to our consciousness. As a photograph brings to mind loved ones who may be absent from us, so liturgical art opens our eyes to the unseen presence of God. There is a difference, of course; liturgical art makes us aware of a presence, not an absence.

Adequate liturgical art has a tremendous potency because of its **religious power**.[8] This is the power to penetrate beneath the obvious and to convey the divine. Much of the art placed in churches in recent centuries was profoundly deficient in this respect. Liturgical art has to use the objects of this world to represent the immaterial. But when painting and sculpture simply reflect naturalistic reproductions of the appearance of persons or objects, they fail to penetrate beneath the surface, no matter how skillful the artist. Many popular paintings of the head of Christ represent only the human nature of Jesus and never lead us beyond the obvious. A mid–twentieth-century painter, Georges Rouault, on the other hand, could treat this type of subject with such sensitivity that we know we stand before a suffering God. The far less skilled makers of *santos* of the nineteenth- and early twentieth-century Hispanic culture of New Mexico and Colorado created a liturgical art of extraordinary religious power. Their images are primitive and crude, but no one can contemplate them without being called to worship. They let loose numinous power in a piece of wood or canvas by relying on conviction and insight far more than academic artistic skills. Our inner eye is addressed by such art and we discover how close seeing is to believing.

Those who destroyed liturgical art in the past recognized clearly its religious power, but they feared that ignorant people might confuse the mirror with what it reflected. This is probably the least dangerous form of idolatry we face today. Indeed, when liturgical art calls us from indulging in the egocentric satisfying of our emotions and self-centered lives, it can break down a far worse form of idolatry.

Another characteristic of good liturgical art is its **communal nature**. What is projected is not the individual experience of the artist but the insights of the total community. Good liturgical art is not noted for originality in subject matter but for capturing the experience of a community. This does not mean that the artist must even be Christian. From the ancient catacombs to modern France, successful liturgical art has been created by non-Christian artists working under the careful guidance of the Christian community, and many Christian artists have failed to produce satisfactory liturgical art because their muse called them to a personal vision rather than a communal one. An architect can no more design a good church without understanding the life of the community that will use it than an artist can produce good liturgical art without comprehending the same life.

The community whose life together is meant to be served by such art is not just one generation old. It is a community of traditions. Those traditions reflect the way other generations have experienced and rejoiced in God's actions. These communities have found that some ways adequately reflect these realities in visual form. Past experience is always our point of departure in creating liturgical art for today. That is not to say liturgical art is unchanging; historical research can easily chronicle the introduction of new styles and contents. But beneath all its diversity, there is a strong underlying current of constancy in returning again and again to the same visual contents, just as we still prefer many of the same words and acts that link us to other Christians in different ages.

Part of the inherited vocabulary takes the form of **visual symbols**. Every mass movement creates its own visual symbols. Think of bumper sticker art on gun control, the environment, or feminism. Each is an instantaneous way of recalling shared beliefs. The church has long used the same kind of visual shorthand. A crown of thorns, a manger, or tongues of flame—all these, and many more, convey shared beliefs and have done so for centuries. But symbols are mortal. Where now is the World War II "V" for victory? To how many Christians now does a pomegranate or a peacock speak of resurrection? It is not easy to create fresh new symbols intentionally. They sneak up on us spontaneously. Probably thousands of people simultaneously thought of the aptness of the mathematical equal sign for expressing the justice of equality for women and men. We can await the appearance of new symbols and bury those that have died, for symbols have died when they become an esoteric code. Symbols are meant to be used because they reflect realities of compelling importance for the lives of those experiencing them. They can be visual (images), audible (words), and kinetic (movements), but in all cases they must refer us to realities we experience.

We shall speak briefly of several media used as liturgical arts. The visual arts function in worship in two ways. Some are fixed and permanent; others are seasonal or only used occasionally. Both the commonness and the uniqueness of each event can be underscored by different liturgical arts, which can portray both continuity and change.

One of the most important of the fixed and permanent art media used in worship is **sculpture**. It has been greatly mistrusted in the Eastern Orthodox churches, which generally forbid sculpture in favor of two-dimensional representations. Until recently, most Reformation traditions also avoided three-dimensional forms as too tangible. It is hard, though, to doubt the religious power sculpture can have after seeing Henry Moore's madonnas or Sir Jacob Epstein's figures of Christ.

Painting seemed dangerous to some of the Reformers, but it must be remembered that each medieval church was itself a whole catechism, painted from floor to roof with sacred history, past and future. Some of the images (God the Father with a long beard) proved offensive to Roman Catholics as well and much of such art was obliterated. It was easier to print new catechisms, far less imaginative, no doubt, but far more explicit in teaching correct doctrine in an age of religious controversy. Georges Rouault, Graham Sutherland, Stanley Spencer, and a host of others have shown us how much painting can contribute to knowing the object of our worship in ways that transcend most verbal categories.

Much that was said about painting applies equally well to colored light, that is, **stained glass**. Few human creations are more beautiful or more changing than the warm splash of colored light on cold stone or plaster. We have misunderstood the medium too often by trying to make it explicitly pictorial. Its nature is closer to instrumental music, an abstraction that says something words and pictures cannot. There is no denying the emotive factors present in all worship, and stained glass seems to make an almost universal appeal to these.

Every church makes use of **basketry, glassblowing, ceramics,** or **metalsmithing** for communion vessels. These art forms provide opportunities for expressing the community's joy in its Creator. Good quality baskets, glassware, ceramics, and silverware are available commercially in most areas. They are often superior to those stocked by church-goods suppliers. Almost any community college has a studio art department that would welcome a chance to produce or help a congregation acquire these vessels.

Bookbinding, too, is a neglected but necessary art that deserves much more cultivation by the church today. If we regard the contents of Bibles and service books as vital, then there ought to be outward and visible testimony to the importance of these volumes in worship.

Liturgical arts for seasonal or occasional use include many possibilities, especially textiles, graphic arts, and the new electronic media. There has been an explosion of interest in **textile arts** in recent years, though their use is ancient. Undeniably part of the attraction of textiles is their impermanence. They can be removed, even discarded, after a single occasion or season. The variety of uses that textiles serve is impressive. **Antependia** or **paraments** are hangings or falls on the pulpit and lectern, and **frontals** serve in the same way to cover altar-tables (though the preference today is not to conceal the form of the altar-table). Seasonal colors and symbols are often used. Liturgical **banners** may be carried in processions or suspended where air currents give them movement.

More controversial are **vestments** or sacramental garb for the clergy. They are really testimony to the conservatism of the clergy.[9] When barbarians swarmed down from northern Europe in the fifth century and introduced men's trousers to Rome, the clergy kept sartorial faith by continuing to wear the everyday garb of imperial Rome: the **chasuble**, a poncho-like outer covering; the **alb** or white dress-like tunic worn by men and women alike; the **stole** draped around the neck, a symbol of public office (comparable to a police badge); and the **cope**, a cloak. Derived from the tunic are the **dalmatic** with wide sleeves and slit sides, and the **surplice** with full sleeves, often worn over a long black outdoor garment, the **cassock**. Special garments are worn by bishops in some churches. Protestant clergy, academics, and judges continued to wear the black medieval scholar's gown. The eighteenth century saw the survival of a secular collar in two small white neck **bands** or **tabs** which some Protestant clergy wear over a black **preaching robe**. The alb is now often used as an outer garment and is favored by many as appropriate to women and men alike. Stoles add variety in colors, textures, and designs to whatever other garments are worn under (or over) them. Clothing is a means of communication, and what clergy wear says something about the event.

The **graphic arts** take as many forms as textiles. The first impression of worship is often a printed bulletin thrust into one's hand upon entering the building, then a hymnal or other service book. Gradually, we are coming to see that the way a page looks is almost as important as what is printed on it. Liturgical graphics have moved in recent years from depressingly drab to halfway exciting, although good examples are still rare.

Posters may be present in churches. Enlarged photos can make poignant statements, especially when lettered with key words in the lessons for the day. Every worship committee should make regular visits to the local art supply store. Obviously some spaces are more adaptable to the display of banners and posters than others but suitable lighting and places to hang seasonal art forms ought to be considered.

The most recent varieties of visual art forms utilize **electronic media**. Motion picture films are too disruptive to employ in worship, but still images may be projected with sensitivity, provided the building allows this method of presentation. Where adequate control of lighting, flat reflective surfaces, and electrical outlets exist, projections can add a new dimension to worship that no other generation has known. Today a wall can be anything we want to project on it. The ability to use projections must be used with care, however, so that it supplements and underscores the rest of the service rather than overwhelming it. Like good liturgical music, visual art must be carefully coordinated with the entire service.

In all of these art forms, we depend upon what the space will allow. The building can greatly enhance the effectiveness of the various liturgical arts, or it can hamper them. For better or for worse, the influence of the space in which we worship is crucial. How could it be otherwise in a religion grounded in the incarnation?

CHAPTER FOUR

THE SOUNDS OF CHURCH MUSIC

oth time and space come together when we begin to think about church music. Music exists in time because it has duration. But time is intrinsic to music itself since time dictates rhythm. Even the most elementary tune uses rhythm, melody, and sometimes, harmony to play out its message. Church music is very much determined by the specific occasion in the church year or the event (wedding, funerals, and so forth).

What is heard is also determined by the space in which music is produced. Each church building is actually a musical instrument that determines the quality of the music heard. Sometimes this sound is enhanced (or degraded) by electronic amplification; even opera houses have felt the need for amplification in recent years.

It is appropriate, then, to keep in mind that music must exist in both time and space and that these have major significance for the use of music in worship. But Christian worship can and does exist without music. Frequently, we grasp the importance of music best when we are deprived of it, as at a Good Friday service in some traditions. Some traditions, such as the Quaker, generally avoid the use of music altogether.

We must begin by asking ourselves why music is considered so vital to Christian worship. Why do many congregations gladly spend a major portion of their worship budget on music? Then we must discuss what the major components of **church music** (or **sacred music** or **liturgical music**) are. We shall discuss the various forms music takes in Christian worship. Finally, we shall quickly review how music has functioned in Christian worship both in the past and in the present.

WHY DO CHRISTIANS SING?

The chief function of church music is to add a deeper dimension of participation to worship. By now, almost every choir room has a sign quoting Augustine to the effect that whoever sings prays twice, but Augustine's fears about the overattractiveness of music never seems to be displayed. There is much truth to the statement about praying twice; one must be more fully aware and conscious of what one is doing in order to sing. Dancing would add yet another layer of consciousness. To sing a text requires more concentration than just reciting something aloud, although overfamiliarity can make singing threadbare at times. When there is music, a deeper level of performing or listening is involved, usually, than when there is no music. Music, then, gives an added dimension to an event.

One of the reasons music aids worship is that music is a more expressive medium than ordinary speech. Music enables us to express an intensity of feeling through variety in tempo, pitch, volume, melody, harmony, and rhythm. Thus one has a greater range for expressiveness when singing than when speaking. Music can, and often does, convey a greater intensity of feeling than would be expressed in its absence.

Another factor is the beauty of music. We must be cautious here because the creation of beauty is not the purpose of worship (or of some music either), though beauty may be of considerable value in worship. Music with minimal aesthetic qualities, nevertheless, seems to function well as a satisfactory vehicle for some individuals to express their worship. One cannot criticize a church service using the same standards applied to a concert. Many who have been taught to know what is "good" church music for "sophisticated" people fail to recognize that they should also have been taught what is "good" for various people and the circumstances in which this music is actually used. At every level of cultural sophistication, there are a number of different possibilities—some more appropriate than others for each situation. Thus, if we do not select music in accord with the culture and situation of our congregation, we are apt, instead, to be elitist in choosing.

One function of music, then, is to offer something we consider to be beautiful, no matter how meager our own musical accomplishments may be. This is why actually singing oneself involves more active participation than listening to someone else singing, no matter how superior the other's musical attainments may be. Fortunately, we do not often have to choose between the two; we can have both choral music and congregational song in the same service. But congregational song does have the distinct advantage of giving everyone the opportunity to offer to God the best sounds he or she can create. This cannot be replaced by someone else's effort.

Church music is essential in adding further dimensions of feeling and beauty to our worship. If music is so important to worship, then the effects of the building on music are crucial. Sound vibrates in a church building or is absorbed into it just as in any other musical instrument. Some new concert halls are actually built to be "tunable" with adjustable louvers so that the walls can absorb or reflect more sound. To a certain extent, this adjustment happens in church buildings too. The acoustics change as more people assemble and more sound is absorbed. The building functions in a variety of ways to affect different types of church music. It can enhance or deaden every kind of church music.

The needs of **instrumental music** vary somewhat according to the instrument or the combination of instruments used. Usually, a bright, lively sound is desired and some reverberation preferred, but not enough to create an echo that would interfere with speaking. The increasing use of instruments other than the piano or organ demands provision of space. Usually this is part of choir space. It is best to have singers and instrumentalists adjacent to each other since it is difficult to sing to accompaniment from a distance. This flexibility is especially important for choir space. It is difficult to wedge a cello between choir stalls or to lug a piano up stairs. The whole interior of the building must be carefully planned so that sound is not expected to turn a right angle to emerge from a chancel or so a hundred-thousand-dollar pipe organ is not buried in a transept. The effects of surfaces and materials throughout the building will have a great impact on the quality of instrumental music heard, no matter how talented the performance.

Space has other effects on **choral music**. Indeed, the sound of this type of music will be largely conditioned by the space provided for it. Before we build, we must ask, What is the function of choral music? Unfortunately we usually get a chorus of confused voices for an answer. Most congregations devote far more time and energy to building bigger and better choirs than to examining how they conceive choirs to function in their worship. But what we consider to be a choir's chief functions will certainly determine the organization of choir space and its location with regard to the other five liturgical spaces.

If the chief function of the choir is conceived to be a sharing in the ministry of the word—singing *to* the congregation—a location facing the congregation may be necessary. But the choir is meant to be heard rather than seen and this location can cause problems. Other ministers should not have to vie with the choir for the congregation's attention, especially during preaching. If a choir is considered necessary chiefly for the offering of beauty—singing *for* the congregation—a less conspicuous location could serve just as well. Increasingly, it is realized that one of the prime functions of a choir is leading congregational song—singing *with* the congregation. This is particularly true when introducing new hymns or leading difficult music. This support function is often best accomplished from behind the congregation. In any case, the choir ought to be as close to the congregation as possible, maybe even mingled with it. The old basilican arrangement (with the choir in the front of the nave and surrounded by the congregation on three sides) has much to offer for all three of these functions.

Wherever the choir is located, its placement will determine the sense and meaning with which the choir and the congregation hear what is sung. Thus the location of the choir is probably the single most vexing problem in organizing space for worship today. Ideally, since the role of a choir can change from week to week, choir space is treated as mobile space. On some occasions, such as Good Friday, it might be omitted entirely. Some congregations, after much thought, use a choir only on special occasions and for sacred concerts. Choir space ought always to be related closely to congregational space so that choir and congregation readily identify with each other instead of the one appearing to be performers and the others listeners. In worship, all are performers.

Most important of all is **congregational song**. This type of music provides an opportunity for all those present to express themselves. The prime criterion here is not beauty but adequacy of expressiveness. Congregational song must pass the test of expressing the inmost feelings and beliefs of the worshipers. When it succeeds in doing this, it is frequently (but secondarily) of great beauty.

Congregational song is divided into **psalmody** (singing the psalms), **hymnody** (hymn singing) and **service music** (music to a fixed set of words in the liturgy, such as the *Sanctus*—"Holy, holy, holy"). Augustine called a hymn "the praise of God in song," but in a narrower sense, most hymns are metrical poetry set to melodies. Hymns can vary tremendously in form and content.

The importance of congregational song does not always prevent it from neglect. Carlton R. Young has said that we often tend to treat the choir as if it were the congregation whereas we ought, instead, to treat the congregation as if it were the choir. The choir is only a supplement to the congregation, except at sacred concerts. The choir exists only to do what the congregation cannot accomplish or to help the congregation do its singing better. Choral music is not a substitute for congregational song.

Much of the effectiveness of congregational song depends upon acoustics. A building that absorbs sound too well embarrasses every member out of singing by reinforcing the fear that he or she is singing solo. Hard surfaces in flooring and walls can help singing greatly. In addition, the congregation should not be divided into separate transepts or balconies unless necessary. Such arrangements may be good for responsorial singing, but this form of singing is used less frequently than singing together.

Music is a body art. Our inhibitions may keep us from acknowledging it, but music calls our whole body into motion. Children, unfortunately, learn *not* to dance. Younger children frequently break into dancing at the sound of music, but age stills them. At times, Christians have used **liturgical dance** as a major part of worship: Clement of Alexandria, in the second century, spoke of prayer as involving hands and feet. Throughout most of the nineteenth century the Shakers made dance an important part of their worship. They gave it up only when advancing age made it difficult for all members of their community to participate. Some Christians in Africa find drumming and dancing natural ways to worship with hands and feet. Most American Protestants are only a few generations removed from ancestors who understood hand clapping and foot tapping as a natural part of church music. In many Eastern Orthodox churches, the whole congregation is still as mobile today as Western Christians were before the introduction of pews in the late–Middle Ages.

The whole body participates in worship through various **postures** (kneeling, standing, sitting), **gestures** (embracing, breaking of bread, making the sign of the cross), and **movements** (communing, assembling, offering). In recent years, the ancient **procession** of the whole congregation on special occasions has been rediscovered as a stirring form of witness, especially when accompanied by appropriate hymnody. Even **clothing** is an important part of worship. It testifies to our understanding of the occasion and our role in it, as well as facilitating or constraining meaningful movement.

Liturgical dance has become more common in recent years. In many respects, it is comparable to choral music with the trained and skilled performers providing leadership. When possible, the congregation also ought to participate actively, just as with congregational song. Where congregational space is packed full of immovable pews, the possibilities of congregational dance are greatly limited. Once again, the building is hard to fight.

Silence, too, is an important part of worship. The absence of sound can often communicate much. The Quakers can teach all Christians much about silence. The best use of silence depends upon discipline; silence comes to be fully corporate by being directed in such a way that all worshipers focus together in confessing sin, reflecting on a lesson just read, or offering intercession. Directed silence can be intensely communal while undisciplined wool-gathering can be anything but. To remain uninterrupted, silence may require shielding space from outside noise or subduing mechanical sounds within the building. Even in silence, space is all important.

FORMS AND FUNCTIONS OF CHURCH MUSIC

It is impossible to recreate the music from nearly half of the Christian era simply because musical notation had not been invented. Early church musicians depended entirely on memory. Eventually, ascending or descending lines were sometimes placed above the words of a text. By the eleventh century, an Italian monk, Guido D'Arezzo, had begun to develop a means of placing signs, which we now recognize as notes, on parallel lines, thus indicating pitch by location.[1] Only later was a means found to indicate the duration of each note. During the twentieth century, Thomas Edison invented a means of actually preserving sound: the phonograph. Thus what the first millenium could preserve only by memory, we can recreate through musical notation or reproduce through electronic means.

Technology has always influenced the development of church music as new musical instruments made their advent. The most dramatic of these was the pipe organ which, coming from secular origins in classical antiquity, did not make its advent in churches in the West until the tenth century. Organs first became present in large abbeys and cathedrals, but they did not become common in small parish churches until much later. Organs originally functioned to support choral singing at mass and in the daily office. During the Reformation era, organs came to support congregational song. Other musical instruments were often used for solo or group performances, and each century expanded the possibilities available. The late–twentieth century brought new electronic instruments with new sounds.

Here lies a perennial problem for church music: its relationship to music in the secular world. Early Christians were aware of the religious music of paganism, such as that at weddings and funerals, and took deliberate steps to avoid the associations these brought. The music of Judaism also posed a problem. The Hebrew Scriptures, especially the psalms, made abundant reference to the use of musical instruments in worship, but Christians were nervous about too close a resemblance in their worship. In modern times, the advent of gospel blues posed a similar challenge: how much could church music resemble ballroom music?[2] The challenge has reappeared with every new musical form and will, no doubt, continue to do so. Usually, Christians have managed to baptize each new style and, eventually, appropriate it for church use.

At the other extreme has been sacred music that has somehow escaped the church and been turned into concert music. Many of the so-called masses written in the eighteenth to twentieth centuries were never meant to be sung during the eucharist. They turned the texts of traditional service music into performance pieces for the concert stage. Johannes Brahms' *German Requiem* would make for an unbearably long funeral but a gorgeous musical tribute. Leonard Bernstein's *Mass* might be considered blasphemous in church. Such music often finds performance in concert halls rather than churches. The relation between the church and the world in the area of music has been, and continues to be, ambiguous.

One factor, however, remains constant. Church music is meant to have a high element of participation even when it is performed by others. It is the offering of ourselves even when we are not the actual players or singers. We share in the offering of sound by the intentionality of our being present in order to worship. The concert hall may be purely detached performance; the church is participation. And this is most obvious when we "lift every voice and sing," whether in service music, hymnody, or psalmody.

As far as we know, some forms of music were present in Christian worship at its origins. Even at the Last Supper, a hymn was sung (Matt. 26:30), probably Psalms 115-118. Christians were exhorted to sing "psalms, hymns, and spiritual songs" (Eph. 5:18-20 and Col. 3:16-17). It is quite possible that in the New Testament we have actual examples of **canticles** (songs), such as the *Magnificat* or Song of Mary and the *Benedictus* or Song of Zechariah in Luke 1 and the *Nunc Dimittis* or Song of Simeon in Luke 2.

Much had been inherited from synagogue worship: "This non-clerical, lay-led, word centered worship—where a spiritualized sacrifice of praise occupied the heart of the worship—provided an important model to the followers of Jesus."[3] Yet Christian worship tended to have more elements of spontaneity, even the ecstatic, than Jewish. There is early evidence of the development of **metrical hymns**, that is, divided into stanzas, each with repetitive meters and number of lines. Of the first three centuries, Edward Foley concludes "[t]he whole of worship is musical and to the extent that the worship belonged to the whole assembly, so did the music belong to them"[4] rather than to special singers or cantors.

When Christianity became legal and respectable under Constantine, worship in general and music especially became much more complicated and sophisticated. Musical instruments could be tolerated if free from pagan associations. **Cantors** appeared in the fourth century to lead the worshipers in singing texts or as solo performers. In time, choirs emerged so the worshiping assembly now had a variety of musical specialists. A debate arose over whether women could sing in public worship. Opponents argued from Jewish precedent and Paul's words in 1 Corinthians 14:34 that "women should be silent in the churches." Eventually this was resolved with the acceptance of choirs of women singers or women participating in congregational song.

Music came to play a large role in theological battles. Ambrose of Milan composed many hymns; some, such as "O Splendor of God's Glory Bright," are still sung.[5] The sixth-century Venantius Fortunatus is represented in modern hymnals by "Hail Thee, Festival Day" or "Sing, My Tongue, the Glorious Battle." Augustine, sensitive to the power music had to distract worshipers with its beauty, insisted on the need for the text to dominate. Since the fourth century, metrical hymns have continued to be added to the treasury of church music. Hymn singing was part of the people's daily public prayer as Eusebius of Caesarea noted about 337 A.D.: "the delights of God are the hymns poured forth everywhere on earth in his Church, both morning and evening" (*Commentary on Psalm 64:10,* author's translation, *PG* 23, 640).

In the Middle Ages, many of the advances in church music, such as musical notation, came from the monastics. Monastic life revolved around singing daily public prayer eight times each day and night in the section of the church known as the choir (or quire). Hence a very distinctive type of church music developed that reflected monastic life itself. This life was heavily communal, but it also focused on individual contemplation and edification. The music that evolved focused on the singing of liturgical texts, especially the entire psalter—to be sung weekly—as well as many hymns written for the liturgical year and cycle of saints. The choir space was usually divided into two parallel sections of stalls where the psalms could be sung responsorially. Sometimes, single verses were repeated as an **antiphon**. Dialogues were sung as responsories or invitatories ("O Lord, open thou our lips / And our mouth shall show forth thy praise").

The musical style that developed is known as **Gregorian chant** or **plainsong**. Like monastic life, it is austere and ascetic. Gregorian chant is sung in unison rather than in harmony, so all voices are united in a single pitch. Embellishments were avoided, and the words shaped the rhythm. It is communal and contemplative. **Office hymns** were written to add to the scriptural components, for various times of day, and to commemorate special occasions; most end in a **doxological stanza** of praise addressed to the Trinity and show a wide array of non-sexist possible terms. A late example of an office hymn is Bishop Thomas Ken's "All Praise to Thee, My God, This Night" which ends with the familiar doxology: "Praise God, from Whom All Blessings Flow."

In the Middle Ages monastic forms of worship were most influential in molding daily public prayer for parochial use, developing church music, and shaping church architecture. In the mass itself, service music evolved in parish and cathedral settings as well as abbeys. The ordinary parts (fixed musical texts of the mass) include the *Kyrie* (Lord, Have Mercy), the *Gloria in excelsis* (Glory Be to God on High), the *Credo* (I Believe), the *Sanctus* and *Benedictus* (Holy, Holy, Holy . . . Blessed is He), and the *Agnus Dei* (Lamb of God).

The propers (varying texts) changed to fit the lessons: introit (psalm verse at the entrance rite), gradual (after the epistle), alleluia (before the Gospel), offertory, and communion (usually a psalm verse during communion). Thousands of sequences or original poetic texts elaborating the occasion developed out of the alleluias. Virtually all of these were eliminated in 1570. Many were salvaged as hymns for congregational use by the nineteenth-century translator, John Mason Neale: "All Glory, Laud, and Honor" for Palm Sunday or "O Sons and Daughters, Let Us Sing" for Easter.

Most singing at mass was done by choirs and in Latin. But there were areas, such as Poland, that developed a vernacular hymnody to be sung by laypeople. The late–Middle Ages saw the gradual introduction of pipe organs in larger churches.

A development of the late–Middle Ages was **polyphony,** or the use of many voices simultaneously, sometimes to different texts and melodies. This demanded professional choirs and a high degree of musical skill. Secular tunes made their way into service music and one military tune, "The Armed Man," became the basis for many settings of the mass. Some questioned the appropriateness of polyphony in worship.

The Protestant Reformation of the sixteenth century saw an explosion of new functions for church music, ranging from a total abolition of music in worship to a service that was almost completely musical. Within Roman Catholicism, a debate arose over whether music had become too secular to be tolerated. The Council of Trent even debated the "total suppression" of church music rather than its reform. Fortunately, reform won out, although with the provision that the clergy "shall also banish from the churches all such music which, whether by the organ or in the singing, contains things which are lascivious or impure."[6] Still, it was a narrow escape.

St. Ignatius Loyola took a dim view of much music and forbade it for his novices. Yet brilliant composers of service music abounded: Giovanni Gabrieli in Venice, Orlando di Lassus in Rome, and Tomas Luis de Victoria in Madrid. Above all others, Pierluigi da Palestrina excelled in writing music with such restraint that the counterpoint did not interfere with the audibility of the text. His *Missa Papae Marcelli* of 1555 became the ideal of sophisticated music that did not submerge the text. Palestrina reached a compromise between liturgical austerity and musical elaborateness written for six parts.

Martin Luther was the first to glimpse radical new possibilities for church music. Theologically, music could enable that full participation which belongs to the priesthood of the laity. Luther loved music and placed it second only to theology as a gift from God. He envisioned a form of worship in which virtually everything but the sermon would be sung. His *German Mass*, published in 1526, consists of detailed instructions for singing the liturgy. In addition to the traditional instrumental and choral music, Luther urged the laity also to sing the ordinary parts of the mass (*Kyrie*, and so forth). He made significant contributions to hymnody, publishing a

Priorities in Church Music: 1500–1800

	Roman Catholic	Lutheran	Zwingli	Calvin, Scots, and Puritans	Anabaptists	Church of England	Quakers	Methodists
Instrumental	X	X						
Choral	X	X				X		
Service Music	X	X				X		
Hymnody		X			X			X
Psalmody		X		X	X	X		X

Diagram 7

vernacular hymnal as early as 1524 and encouraging musicians and poets to compose and write for congregational song. Luther himself wrote and composed at least thirty-seven hymns and tunes—many of them based on the psalms.

Thus there is a strong theological basis for church music in Luther. All the baptized help fulfill their priestly rights and duties by singing in worship. Music provides a spiritual sacrifice that is acceptable to God. Luther envisioned what we would call musical liturgy rather than liturgical music. His successors also found that hymnody provided an ideal means for teaching the demands of the Christian life. Eventually, a "hymn of the day" was designated for Lutheran churches to complement the Gospel lesson for each Sunday and feast day.

Lutheranism's greatest single contribution came in Johann Sebastian Bach (1685–1750) who, working most of his career in the parish church of St. Thomas in Leipzig, wrote a multitude of instrumental and choral music for the weekly eucharist. At his hands, many **chorales**, usually based on a nonbiblical text, were written for both choir and congregation. He also wrote choral **cantatas** (that is meditations on the lessons), **oratorios** as sacred dramas, such as the *Christmas Oratorio*, and **passions** to tell the passion narrative, as in St. Matthew or St. John.

A quite contrary direction was taken by Luther's contemporary reformer, Ulrich Zwingli, the reformer in Zurich. Zwingli was a fine musician and had composed music, but he felt guided by unconditional obedience to scripture which, for him, meant no music.[7] As a result singing ceased in the Zurich churches in 1523 and in 1527 the city council gave orders for the destruction of the pipe organs. Obedience to scripture was Zwingli's motif, and it led to drastic results, the total elimination of music.

Although they agreed with Zwingli on the basic austerity of worship, the Anabaptists—known today as Mennonites, Amish, or Hutterites—took a different view. Their furtive gatherings for worship certainly did not allow for pipe organs, but they did develop a very rich hymnody. Their singing was devoid of instrumental accompaniment but rich in fervor. These are not ordinary hymns; they are filled with the anguish of suffering and martyrdom, the fate of so many early Anabaptists. Not only do they keep alive the memories of those who have already given their lives for the faith, but they also anticipate that many of the people now singing will join their predecessors in suffering. The identification of the present with apostolic times is constant. Recent Mennonite hymnals have moved more toward the mainstream in hymnody, but hymns are still sung unaccompanied. Old Order Amish still use the *Ausbund*. First published in 1560, it is the oldest Protestant hymnal in use. Hymns function to fortify the Christian against a hostile world.

John Calvin was more reticent than either Luther or Zwingli. Instrumental, choral, and service music as well as hymns disappeared. Still, Calvin relished the possibility of the congregation singing from such "inspired" texts as the psalms. Since the psalms were from scripture, they obviously took priority over hymns which were "uninspired," or of human composure. Calvin's stratagem was to have the psalms translated into French in the form of **metrical paraphrases**, not exact translations but in stanza form. Calvin may have been influenced by hearing hymn singing in the German-speaking church of Martin Bucer in Strasbourg. At any rate, he found excellent composers, such as Louis Bourgeois (known for "Old 100th"—often used for "All People That on Earth Do Dwell" and the doxology, "Praise God") and Claude Goudimel. Calvin sought poets, such as Clément Marot, and published French versions of all the psalms. Despite a liturgy that can be excessively pentitential, visitors to Geneva noted the solemnity and joy that psalmody gave to services and were impressed by the high degree of active participation achieved. All singing was congregational, biblical, and (with the singing of the Decalogue) essentially from the Hebrew Bible.

Geneva became an international pilgrimage spot for visitors from all over Europe, and many returned home with the same musical ideals as Calvin. The Presbyterian Church of Scotland adopted the exclusive use of psalmody for church music. There are still some Presbyterian churches that allow nothing else. They argue that only the words of scripture are worthy to praise God. The English Puritans were of a similar mind. It is not by accident that the first book published in English in the new world was their *Bay Psalm Book* (1640). Usually the method of singing was the introduction of each line by a leader then its repetition by the congregation.

A subsequent development was led by **Isaac Watts,** an English Congregationalist, who, trying to make David "speak like a Christian," produced such hymns as "O God, Our Help in Ages Past" (Psalm 90) but moved on to topics David never contemplated, such as "When I Survey the Wondrous Cross." Watts' innovation of hymn singing for the English people met stubborn resistance and did not prevail among many Puritans (Congregationalists) and Presbyterians until well into the nineteenth century.

Until mid–nineteenth century a large section of the Church of England embraced more musical variety but very little hymnody. There was no theological objection to singing hymns, as there was among the Scots and Puritans, but neither was there the impetus the Lutherans and Anabaptists found for hymnody. Psalm singing fared much better, and there was a strong tradition of congregational singing of the psalms in the metrical paraphrases of Thomas Sternhold and John Hopkins, published in 1562, and later the *New Version* of Nahum Tate and Nicholas Brady, introduced in 1696.

Service music flourished especially in the cathedrals and collegiate churches. John Merbecke composed music for the Anglican eucharist as early as 1550; he was followed by William Byrd, Thomas Tallis, and Orlando Gibbons. In 1662, the prayer book provided anthems after the third collect at morning and evening prayer. Based on scripture or other texts, the anthem provided a magnificent repertoire for those in "Quires and Places where they sing" (Rubric, 1662, *BCP*). Until the nineteenth century, these places were not likely to be parish churches, but the cathedrals and colleges developed a magnificent tradition of choral music.

Several major musical changes came about in the nineteenth-century Church of England. Increasing affluence made possible the introduction of pipe organs in most parish churches, architectural changes increased the desire for parish choirs vested in surplices, and eventually, the singing of hymns by the congregation became popular despite aspersions that it was "Methodistical." The work of John Mason Neale in recovering medieval hymns and the collaboration of a host of Victorian hymn writers and composers (such as Arthur Sullivan, John Dykes) made hymn singing a major part of worship in the Anglican communion.

The most drastic position was taken by the Quakers in the

seventeenth century. They felt that prepared texts were out of place in worship and were based on human will rather than God's. Thus they dispensed with all forms of music including congregational song. It was possible, but rare, that an individual might share his or her concern with the meeting in a sung version. Silence could often suffice for a gathered meeting in the Spirit.

Methodism emerged in the eighteenth century. Since most Methodists were poor, pipe organs were not available. John Wesley opposed anthems because they were not "joint worship," that is, common, and no provision was made for service music. But John and Charles Wesley, drawing on ancient history, the work of Isaac Watts, and their contacts with the Moravians, saw a clear need for hymns. Since the framework for Methodist worship was missional within the national church, the Wesleys saw hymns as an ideal way of reaching out to the unchurched. Hymns were not only to give praise to God but to teach doctrine.

Wesleyan hymns became highly educational. It was the genius of Charles Wesley, who wrote over six thousand hymns, to incorporate doctrine in his hymns. One focus was the church year, with a set of hymns on the Lord's nativity and another collection on the resurrection. In 1745, the Wesleys published *Hymns on the Lord's Supper*, which still remains the greatest treasury of eucharistic hymns in English. When one studies it, one soon recognizes that much of it comes from a theological treatise on the eucharist by Daniel Brevint. The Wesleys turned the treatise into poetry. The Wesleys' converts both sang and learned their new faith.

The nineteenth century discovered other functions for church music. In the crusade to convert a largely pagan America, the Frontier tradition discovered that music was particularly useful. In campmeetings and revivals all over America it was realized that music was an important factor in preparing people to be receptive to preaching intended for conversion. Churches that had not tolerated choirs were soon adding soloists, trios, quartets, and full choirs to their worship. Choirs were still controversial as late as the 1830s, but they soon became omnipresent, along with pipe organs, as wealth increased.

Hymnody underwent a transformation. The campmeeting blended the spirituals of both African Americans and whites, often with simple texts for illiterate converts. Increasingly the hymns moved away from the objectivity of Watts and Wesley to a much more subjective, individualistic approach, singing in first person of one's experience of Jesus or of one's fervent anticipation of heaven. In effect, Charles Wesley's "Jesus, Lover of My Soul" became "My Soul, Lover of Jesus." The most influential writer of gospel hymns, was Fanny J. Crosby (1820–1915), whose texts, such as "Blessed assurance, Jesus is mine," or "Rescue the perishing," are still popular.

Roman Catholic service music during this period had adopted an operatic style, a type of music that was highly dramatic and emotionally manipulative. It demanded highly trained choirs and professional musicians. But change was imminent in reaction to this music, which focused heavily on individual emotional reactions. Study of medieval chant by the monks of Solesmes Abbey in France brought about a rediscovery of the austere objectivity of the Gregorian chant. With the strong support of Pius X (Pope 1903–1914) a major effort was made to reintroduce Gregorian chant so that it could be sung by congregations, albeit in Latin. For fifty years, millions of school children were taught the Ward method (named after Justine Ward) of singing Gregorian chant. From today's perspective it seems like a good run down the wrong road: the musical style was as foreign as the Latin texts, but the object was to increase lay participation in the mass.

Many mainline Protestant churches in the first half of the twentieth century moved to a more or less frankly acknowledged aesthetic approach to worship. This involved founding schools of sacred music (Westminster, 1926; Union, 1928) to produce competent church musicians. Thousands of churches worked to build better choirs and to install pipe organs. Hymnals were revised, each generation becoming more musically sophisticated. Professor Archibald T. Davison of Harvard personified this quest for "good" church music. Musicians, such as Ralph Vaughan Williams (known for tunes such as "Sine Nomine," "King's Weston," "Forest Green"), wrote or arranged an abundance of quality tunes.

Meanwhile, various folk traditions persisted. Many folk melodies had found their ways into collections such as *Southern Harmony* (1835) and *Sacred Harp* (1844), and shaped note music was developed for the musically illiterate. The Shakers developed their own hymnody with much of it addressing God in feminine language. Dance became an important form of expression for their members.

Eventually the gospel blues, promoted by Thomas Dorsey ("Precious Lord, Take My Hand"), became accepted in many African American churches despite considerable opposition, since many African American church leaders preferred to emulate the music of white churches. In recent decades, much of the music of the African American churches has been cherished by African Americans and whites alike. African American church choirs have produced more than their share of opera singers, and gospel sings now have a following well beyond the churches.

Vatican II brought a revolution in church music for Roman Catholics. At first, the result was constant borrowing from the Protestants, but in recent years new Catholic hymns have found their way into Protestant hymnals ("You Satisfy the Hungry Heart," "One Bread, One Body," and so forth). Nothing is more ecumenical than church music. The music of the Taizé Community in France, with its repetition of simple texts, has been popular throughout Western Christianity. Currently, one of the most popular writers of service music for Roman Catholic masses happens to be a Lutheran who is now resident in a United Church of Christ congregation.

Much of the revolution in Catholic church music has shown that Catholics can sing with enough encouragement and experience. Pride of place has clearly slipped away from Gregorian chant to metrical hymnody. Psalmody has been recovered, often with a cantor singing the verses and the congregation repeating a refrain. Paradoxically, American Catholic congregations have greater freedom in choosing hymnals than most other American denominations. Most recent hymnals have a wide variety of texts from Ambrose to modern composers reaching the present through the poetry of Brian A. Wren, Fred Pratt Green, and Frederik H. Kaan.

The variety of uses for church music continues to expand. In the praise and worship style, music dominates at least the first half of the service with simple and repetitive texts often projected on a screen and sung to syncopated music. The texts are often based on single verses from scripture, and the musical instruments may include almost anything but a pipe organ. Brass, woodwind, and percussion instrumentalists are often well-paid professionals. "Praise and Worship services introduced the church to new visual and aural technologies. . . . Everything in the worship service can be heard and seen"[8] due to technological advances.

Seeker services have found another function for church music. Usually very little is sung by the congregation, but professional musicians provide "entertainment evangelism" with music that resonates in nostalgic style to whatever age group is targeted. Drama in the form of monologues or skits usually precedes the sermon. The emphasis on participation by singing found in the praise and worship model is often replaced in the seeker service by a stress on performance by highly competent musicians.

Present-day hymnals represent another significant development: the advent of a new global consciousness in the churches. As Christian churches grow in various parts of the world, they are in the process of developing their own musical styles. While earlier missionaries usually imported the music they were familiar at home, today's maturing churches increasingly compose and sing in musical idioms of their own culture. Furthermore, as many of these people immigrate to the United States, they bring their new musical styles with them. This means that we all are enriched by unfamiliar musical traditions. Many mainline churches now have hymnals with some texts in languages other than English and with tunes unfamiliar to the English-speaking majority.

At the same time, modern technology has enabled us to hear sounds never heard before. New electronic musical instruments bring possibilities that seem almost infinite in variety. Just as the pipe organ moved from the tavern to the church in the tenth century, so the electronic keyboard has moved from the laboratory to the church in the twentieth century. The only limits in producing sounds of praise seem to be in our imaginations. God has given us not only tongues but hands to use in praise.

CHAPTER FIVE

DAILY PUBLIC PRAYER

We have seen, in previous chapters, how important both time and space are as vehicles of communication in Christian worship. Indeed, it is quite possible that non-Christians gain most of their impressions of Christian worship by noticing the holy days their Christian neighbors keep and the buildings Christians frequent on such days. The impressions many Christians have of Jewish and Muslim worship are largely founded on similar observations. If time and space communicate to those who never enter a church for worship, they work even better as communication vehicles for those who do congregate there.

But the community gathered for Christian worship relies even more heavily on two other forms of communication: the spoken word and the acted sign. The importance for worship with words and acts should not surprise us; they are the primary ways people relate to one another. Saying and doing are as vital in our relating to God through worship as these activities are for our communicating with other humans. The Creator knows us best, and God communicates with us through words and actions, using human speech and acts. Our concern in this chapter, and the following one, is the spoken word as the primary form of communication for much of Christian worship. In the chapters following these two, we shall explore how words combined with actions form the basis of sacraments and other related forms of worship.

The term "word" is so important as a symbol of presenting oneself that the Fourth Gospel uses it *(Lógos)* for Christ himself (John

1:1, 14). Though frequent, references to "the hand of God" are only half as numerous in the Scriptures as "the Word of God." The Word of God became a prominent term referring to Jesus Christ, the Bible, and the event of communication of God through human speech in the Protestant Reformation and subsequent theology. It is with the last of these, the spoken word, that we are concerned at present. The ambiguity that arises from use of "the Word" to imply God, book, and speech simply underscores the complexity and importance of this image for Christian life.

Two structures of worship are built primarily on the spoken or sung word. Actions are present but only in subsidiary ways. Those structures are services of daily public prayer (which we shall consider in this chapter) and the service of the word (to be discussed in chapter 6). The latter is the primary form of worship in most Protestant churches and in an increasing number of Roman Catholic congregations because of the shortage of priests.

We begin by looking at the ways Christians have prayed together on a daily basis. After surveying these various histories, we shall describe the theological priorities present. Then, we shall suggest the bases for pastoral decisions in planning, preparing for, and conducting daily public prayers. Our concerns are with public prayer, not private—as important as it is.

HISTORY OF DAILY PUBLIC PRAYER

Our knowledge of the daily worship of the earliest Christians is meager. Apparently, a variety of Jewish customs with set prayers at set times had a strong appeal. We see early evidences of the gradual development of private devotions for individual Christians. Late in the first century or early in the second, the *Didache* advised Christians to pray the Lord's Prayer three times a day.[1] Others sought disciplines in the Bible itself as ways to make the scriptural injunction to "pray without ceasing" (1 Thess. 5:17) practical. Psalm 55:17 suggested "evening and morning and at noon," and Daniel prayed three times a day (Dan. 6:10). Sacrifices had been offered in the temple daily, a lamb in the morning and another at evening (Exod. 29:38-39) and devout Jews prayed daily at these hours. Psalm 119:164 mentioned "Seven times a day I praise you for your righteous ordinances," and verse 62 added "At midnight I rise to praise you."

The proper number of times for prayer during each day concerned many early Christian writers although Clement of Alexandria felt that the true Christian "prays throughout his whole life."[2] Tertullian and Cyprian called for prayer thrice during the day, referring to Daniel's example and to various acts of the apostles at the third, sixth, and ninth hours mentioned in the Bible.[3] This threefold discipline is a "sacrament of the Trinity," according to Cyprian. Both North Africans also insisted on prayer at dawn and evening (see diagram 8.).

The Apostolic Tradition, written around A.D. 217, tells of Christian practice in Rome at that time.[4] It describes seven daily hours of private prayer, presumably followed by the more devout. The day began with prayer, after which all were encouraged to participate in public instruction "in the word" when it was offered. At nine, prayer was enjoined "for in this hour Christ was seen nailed upon the tree," at noon when "it became darkness," at three when Christ died, before going to sleep, and at midnight for "in this hour every creature hushes for a brief moment to praise the Lord; stars and plants and waters stand still in that instant," and again at cockcrow when Peter denied Christ.[5] It was a rigorous pattern which structured much of the day around the passion and death of Christ.

Perhaps even more important than the hours of private prayer is the note of a daily gathering for instruction and prayer. Particular emphasis is placed on the attendance of the deacons. "When all have assembled, they shall instruct those who are in the assembly and having also prayed, let each one go."[6] This may indicate the beginnings of an almost lost tradition in the West, the so-called **cathedral office** or **people's office**.[7] These were daily services of prayer and praise in the chief church of a city, attended by all Christians. Evidence about these services mounts as we look to the fourth century A.D. and the growing respectability of Christianity after persecution ceased. The people's office points to what may be the biggest gap in Roman Catholic liturgical life today: an alternative to the eucharist that could be celebrated daily by the laity. In the West, the people's office became submerged in a few centuries,

Patterns of Daily Prayer

	Private Prayer		People's Office			Monastic	Reformation		Modern	
	Tertullian	Apostolic Tradition	Apostolic Constitutions	Egeria	Basil	Benedict	Lutheran	Anglican	Various Protestant	Roman Catholic
12M						Nocturns				(Office of Reading variable times)
3		Cockcrow	(Sunday Vigil)	(Sunday Vigil)	Before Dawn					
6	Morning	Morning	Morning	Dawn	Morning	Lauds Prime	Matins	Matins (Morning Prayer)	Morning Prayer	Lauds
9	Third	Third			Third	Terce				
12N	Sixth	Sixth		Midday	Sixth	Sext			Midday or Noonday	Middle Hour
3	Ninth	Ninth		Afternoon	Ninth	None				
6	Evening	Evening	Evening	Lychnicon	After Work	Vespers	Vespers	Evensong (Evening Prayer)	Evening Prayer	Vespers
9		Bedtime			Nightfall	Compline				Compline
12M		Midnight			Midnight				Compline, Close of day, or Night	

Diagram 8

much to the loss of Christianity. Daily public worship, other than observing the eucharist, became an almost exclusively clerical and monastic tradition for many centuries.

We get some fleeting views of the people's office during the fourth century. Eusebius of Caesarea mentions that "throughout the whole world, in the churches of God, hymns, praises, and true divine delights are arranged for God at morning sunrise and in the evening. . . . These 'delights' are the hymns which are sent forth in his church everywhere in the world in the morning and evening hours."[8] Late in the fourth century, the *Apostolic Constitutions* instructed Christians: "Assemble yourselves together every day, morning and evening, singing psalms and praying in the Lord's house."[9] In a later book, the same document tells us: "When it is evening, thou, O bishop, shall assemble the church; and after the repetition of the psalm at the lighting up [of] the lights, the deacon shall bid prayers for the catechumens. . . . But after the dismission of these, the deacon shall say: 'So many as are of the faithful, let us pray to the Lord.'" A bidding prayer, other prayers, a blessing, and dismissal follow. The morning pattern is similar but without the lighting of the lights. Chrysostom told newly baptized Christians they ought to gather "in the church at dawn to make your prayers and confessions to the God of all things, and to thank him for the gifts He has already given," and then each one "at evening . . . should return here to the church, render an account to the Master of his whole day, and beg forgiveness for his falls."[10]

Egeria took careful notes of the daily round of worship in fourth-century Jerusalem. She noted that three groups participated in daily worship at the Church of the Holy Sepulchre: monks and virgins, laypeople, and clergy and bishop. Worship by the monks and virgins is the most extended with hymns, psalms, antiphons, and prayers occupying much of the day and night. Some laity join them, but the laity and clergy mostly share in the "Morning Hymns," at daybreak, again at lesser or **apostolic hours**—at 9:00 A.M. (in Lent only), at noon, and at 3:00 P.M.—and in the evening at the lighting of the lamp (which she calls **lucernare**). There are psalms, antiphons, hymns, prayer for all and commemoration of individuals by name, blessing of both catechumens and faithful, and dismissal.[11] On "the Lord's Day," the whole multitude assembles before cockcrow for an early morning vigil with psalmody, prayer, a reading of the resurrection narrative, a procession to Golgotha with singing, a psalm, a prayer, a blessing, and dismissal. At daybreak on Sunday, the eucharist follows with many sermons and "a thanksgiving" afterward.

To be sure, Jerusalem as a pilgrimage center was not typical, but daily gatherings of the devout for praise and prayer before and after the day's work seems to have been common in the chief church of most cities by the late–fourth century. As Robert Taft describes it, "The morning hour of prayer was a service of thanks and praise for the new day and for salvation in Christ Jesus. . . . And vespers was the Christian way of closing it, thanking God for the day's graces, asking his pardon for the day's faults, and beseeching his grace and protection for a safe and sinless night."[12]

The daily people's service survived relatively intact among East Syrians and Armenians. Its demise in the West was a slow process. Eventually it was supplanted there by the **monastic office**. This is known variously as the divine office, daily office, choir offices, or liturgy of the hours, all a series of several daily services or individual **offices** or **hours**. We have just seen this type of monastic prayer anticipated in Jerusalem where the monks and virgins pursued a course, the **cursus**, of reciting the psalms. Egeria was impressed by how "suitable, appropriate, and relevant" these were, but it is clear most of the laity and clergy did not attend for much of the psalmody. Increasingly, the monastic office came to dominate non-sacramental worship until the people's office disappeared in the West, leaving only remnants—such as tenebrae in Holy Week or certain services in Milan and Toledo. Both the people's office and the monastic office were attempts to obey the biblical injunction to "pray without ceasing." However, each "interpreted this differently, the former understanding it to mean that one's whole life should become an act of worship offered to God, the latter that one should try to spend as much time as possible in actual prayer."[13]

Monasticism originated as a revolt against what seemed to be an overly lax form of Christianity after the alliance of church and empire and the end of persecution. It was basically a lay movement in its origins. In the fifth century, Cassian reported that the early Egyptian monks observed "a prescribed system of prayers . . . in their evening assemblies and nocturnal vigils,"[14] that is, at the end of the day and during the night. He tells of an angelic visitant who departed after the twelfth psalm thus establishing that a dozen psalms at matins was enough for angel or monk. In addition to psalmody and prayer, the Egyptian monks read an Old Testament and New Testament lesson on weekdays and an Epistle and Gospel on Sundays and in the Easter season.

In Eastern regions, the development of monasticism brought the refinement of a daily cycle of worship. Basil, in his fourth-century *Long Rules* cites various precedents of the apostles for prayer also at the minor hours and at midnight, along with prayer "early in the morning, so that the first movements of the soul and mind may be consecrated to God," and "when the day's work is ended, thanksgiving should be offered for what has been granted us . . . and confession made." "At nightfall, we must ask that our rest be sinless and untroubled by dreams" and early in the morning "we must anticipate the dawn by prayer." He summarizes: "None of these [eight] hours for prayer should be unobserved by those who have chosen a life devoted to the glory of God and His Christ," meaning all Christians, not just monastics.[15]

Chrysostom tells us of another scheme in religious communities where, "having divided the day into four parts, . . . at the conclusion of each they honor God with psalms and hymns,"[16] and the day begins and ends with worship. In the *Institutes*, Cassian tells of the addition of another morning service in Jerusalem monasteries so that the series of seven services "clearly makes up according to the letter that number which the blessed David indicates . . . 'Seven times a day' [Ps. 119:164]."[17]

The cycle was completed in the West by adoption of the existing seven along with an office of compline on going to bed. In the early sixth century, Benedict set up the definitive Western pattern (slightly different from that of the Eastern churches), which operated until shortly after Vatican II. The scheme of daily and nocturnal prayer was:

Vespers (at the end of the working day)
Compline (before bedtime)
Nocturns or **Vigils** or **Matins** (middle of the night)

Lauds (at daybreak)
Prime (shortly thereafter)
Terce (middle of the morning)
Sext (at noon)
None (middle of the afternoon)

To these were frequently added the Little Office of the Blessed Virgin, the Office of the Dead, a litany, seven penitential psalms, and fifteen gradual psalms. Praying these services each day meant a strenuous, but not exhausting, daily and nightly cycle of work, prayer, and rest. Benedict equated both work and worship as service to God: "In all things let God be glorified."[18]

Monasticism and the daily office evolved together, being virtually identified with each other. Increasingly, the eight daily and night offices (the canonical hours) moved away from identification with life in the world of the laity. Monasticism set the tone for this type of worship. Parochial clergy copied the monks by holding eight services daily in the chancels of their largely empty churches. Even these chancels, as we have seen, were copies of monastic choirs, and the music sung reflected monastic chant. Secular and religious lifestyles produced only one kind of daily worship, the monastic office. Clergy were obliged to follow it; laity were free to ignore it. And ignore it they did so that "the Offices ceased to be in practice, if not in theory, the common prayer of the Christian people."[19] A few may have listened in on weekdays and more at Sunday vespers but the medieval office was made effectively clerical. In the late–Middle Ages, well-to-do people might possess simplified service books, the lay **primers** which they read (aloud) in public or private. These usually contained such items as the offices of the Blessed Virgin and of the dead. Such vernacular books helped prepare for later Reformation services.

If the daily office served ordinary people poorly, these services did succeed magnificently in digging a deep channel for the liturgical life of religious communities. In contrast to the people's office with its selective use of psalms, Benedict had provided for systematic weekly recital of the entire psalter. Psalmody, sung responsorially back and forth across the monastic choir with appropriate **antiphons** (a key verse as the refrain) was the heart of the monastic office.

Weekly recitation of the psalms throughout a lifetime of stable community life shaped the lives of thousands of men and women for centuries. The monastic office also used a continuous reading of scripture—almost an athletic discipline—instead of reading only edifying portions of it as the people's office had. A wide assortment of office hymns grew up from the fourth century onward. Fragments of patristic sermons and expositions, legends of the saints and martyrs, a rich collection of prayers, and **responsories** (dialogical prayers) and **invitatories** (calls to prayer) filled out the monastic hours. All focused on contemplation and edification.

Change continued during the Middle Ages. Increased mobility of the clergy, the development of universities, and less time for saying the office led to widespread adoption during the twelfth century of the shortened *modernum officium* used in the papal chapel in Rome. It featured an abbreviated lectionary, more hymns, and a modified calendar. The advent of the Franciscans in the following century brought further pressures for brevity and an office that could be said while traveling. Structurally, the office underwent a change: further curtailment in the amount of scripture read and more festivals of saints. The office became more and more a succession of festival days and less and less the orderly recitation of the psalter and scripture week in and week out. Even more important than change in structure was change in practice. The office had developed up to the thirteenth century as a **choral office**, said and sung together in choir by religious communities and (in parish churches) by priests and minor clergy, making use of memory and several books. New conditions of travel and study brought about private and individual recitation from a single volume, a portable **breviary**, which was certainly a convenience but also a subversion of the principle of worship together in choir. But so firmly did this revolutionary development assert itself that, in the sixteenth century, a newly founded order, the Jesuits was freed from the obligation of choral recitation altogether, a fact underscored by their choirless church buildings.

The wild tangle of festivals and complicated rules led to attempts at reform, the most successful being those of the Spanish Cardinal, **Francisco de Quiñones** in 1535, revised in 1536.[20] After sudden popularity, it was suppressed in 1558 and supplanted by the **Roman Breviary** of 1568. All other breviaries that were less than two hundred years old were superseded, leaving a few, such as the **Monastic Breviary,** in operation. But, for the overwhelming majority of clergy and religious, strict uniformity was imposed, and, except for some reforms under Pope Pius X in 1911, the 1568 breviary endured until the 1970s.

The *Constitution on the Sacred Liturgy* (1963) of the Second Vatican Council mandated a thorough reform of what is now called the **liturgy of the hours**. Morning and evening prayer were declared the "two hinges on which the daily office turns; hence they are to be considered as the chief hours. . . . Matins . . . may be recited at any hour. . . . Prime is to be suppressed . . . outside of choir it will be lawful to select any one of these three [terce, sext, none]" (CSL, par. 89). Not only was the daily schedule rearranged but also the psalms were distributed over a period of four weeks instead of one. "Readings from sacred scripture" were to be provided for "in more abundant measure," readings from the fathers "better selected" and saints' legends chosen "to accord with the facts of history" (CSL, par. 92). The *Constitution* did not anticipate the subsequent abandonment of saying the office in Latin, but it did encourage the laity "to recite the divine office" (CSL, par. 100).

The result was the publication in 1971 of *The Liturgy of the Hours* in which the day hinges on the old offices of lauds and vespers, familiar to both people's and monastic offices. An office of readings, centering in scriptures and the fathers or readings about the saints, can take place at any time during the day. A person may select one of the midday hours "so as to preserve the tradition of praying in the middle of the day's work."[21] And compline is provided at the end of the day. The new *Liturgy of the Hours* has been heavily criticized as bearing "a monastic stamp . . . more a contemplative prayer than a popular devotional service, . . . suitable for the private prayer of clergy and religious."[22] The need for a recovery of a true people's service remains unmet in official Roman Catholic sources.

The Protestant Reformers took more drastic steps to reform the practice of daily public prayer. As we have seen, by the sixteenth century, daily public prayer had become almost entirely a clerical and monastic monopoly. The religious needs of this small segment of society had prevailed over those of the majority of people. Whereas the early people's service was composed of familiar and popular psalms, hymns, and prayers, the monastic life provided the leisure to treat the entire psalter as a weekly challenge and make a gesture toward reading all of scripture. Since this monastic model was the only one widely known in the West, it was widely assumed that the early people's service had been similar. This was a dangerous bit of liturgical misinformation for it gave a quasimonastic structure to Protestant efforts to reform daily worship, leading them to make edification more important than prayer and praise.

Various Reformers found different solutions to the problem of recovery for popular use of daily public prayers. The solutions can be categorized as those for regular parish worship, for groups within the parish, for special communities, and for family worship. There was also the possibility of terminating such worship altogether as monastic communities were abolished.

There were many attempts to adapt daily prayers for use in parish churches. In Zurich, the Reformer **Ulrich Zwingli**, inaugurated daily services which consisted largely of readings from and exegesis of scripture. The emphasis was largely on edification; the people of Zurich could attend fourteen sermons a week if they were so minded. This provided a model for a later surreptitious practice among English Puritans in which clergy gathered for weekly "prophesyings" in which all were free to question the preacher's exposition of a text. In a sense, the monastic need for edification reached its logical conclusion in Zwingli's daily services, devoted almost exclusively to edification.

Under **Martin Bucer**, the chief Reformer of Strasbourg, the city saw the abolition of monastic life and the development of daily offices in parish churches for everyone. This involved the translation of services, composition of music, and simplification into two daily services, morning and evening.[23] The *Strasbourg Psalter of 1526* anticipated the reforms by Quiñones a decade later by disposing of the antiphons but keeping the essential structure of the Latin offices. More scripture reading and exposition were added.

Martin Luther was conservative. In 1523 and 1526, he proposed a return to two daily services: matins and vespers on **ferial** days (weekdays, not feast days) comprised of lessons, psalms, canticles, hymns, the Lord's Prayer, collects, the Creed, and preaching.[24] Although they were intended for laypeople, Luther seems to have had a special interest in the use of matins and vespers by schools and universities.

Daily public prayer survived longer in Lutheran circles than may be apparent today. During J. S. Bach's years in the Saxon city of Leipzig (1723–1750), there were several prayer services each day of the week, as well as additional penitential services or sermons. A contemporary of Bach could exclaim: "Happy is he who can live in a city where worship is conducted publicly every day. . . . Dresden and Leipzig are fortunate, because in these two cities preaching and prayer services are held every day."[25] Not until the end of the century did such services disappear, and in parts of Romania they survived among Lutherans up to the twentieth century.

The 1978 *Lutheran Book of Worship* adds to Luther's pattern with "Morning Prayer: Matins," "Evening Prayer: Vespers," and "Prayer at the Close of the Day: Compline." A musical setting is printed for each. Morning Prayer includes psalmody, canticles, lessons, hymnody, prayers, and provision for an optional sermon and offering and a paschal blessing recalling the resurrection for use on Sundays. Evening Prayer may begin with a service of light (procession with a large, lighted candle) and contains psalmody, hymnody, canticles, lessons, a litany, and an optional sermon and offering. Prayer at the Close of the Day includes confession, psalmody, a brief lesson, a responsory, hymnody, prayers, a canticle, and benediction. Provisions are also made for two services of "Responsive Prayer," the "Litany," "Propers for Daily Prayers," "Psalms for Daily Prayer," and a "Daily Lectionary."

The success story in daily public prayer of the Reformation was in the Church of England. Archbishop **Thomas Cranmer**, chief architect of the *Book of Common Prayer* of 1549 and 1552, was familiar with the work of the continental Reformers and Cardinal Quiñones. He combined matins, lauds, and prime from the medieval English Sarum Breviary into "Matins" while vespers and compline were condensed into "Evensong." In the 1552 edition, the names became "Morning Prayer" and "Evening Prayer." The midday hours disappeared altogether. Cranmer made his purpose clear in "The Preface," where he occasionally even followed

Quiñones' words. He hoped: "that the people (by daily hearing of holy scripture read in the churches) should continually profit more and more in the knowledge of God, and be the more inflamed with the love of his true religion."[26] Believing (wrongly) that the "ancient fathers" had provided systematic daily reading to cover the "whole Bible (or the greatest part thereof)" each year for the people, Cranmer eliminated all "anthems, responsories, invitatories, and such like things as did break the continual course of the reading of the scripture."[27] "The rules," he claimed, were "few and easy" and only the prayer book and Bible were necessary for conducting services. National uniformity would be secured since "all the whole realm shall have but one use."

The scheme is simple enough; the psalms are "read through once every month"—several each day at morning and evening prayer, starting afresh at the beginning of the month. The Bible is read through in course *(lectio continua)* starting with Genesis, Matthew, and Romans (Old Testament and Gospel at matins, Old Testament and Epistle at Evensong). The rest of the service consists of a masterful blend of the elements of the Sarum breviary offices. These include the Lord's Prayer, versicles, psalms with *Gloria Patri*, two lessons, canticles, *kyrie*, creed, Lord's Prayer, versicles, and three closing collects. A change came in 1552 with the addition of a penitential prelude consisting of penitential sentences from scripture, a call to confession, a general confession, and absolution. Precedent for this manner of beginning is found in both Quiñones (at matins) and in the continental Reformers. In 1662, additional prayers and provision for an anthem were added at the end of the services. A great tradition of sung daily offices distinguishes worship in English cathedrals and collegiate churches.

There can be no question of Cranmer's success. Indeed, his morning and evening prayer, besides providing the daily service, became the normal Anglican Sunday service for three hundred years. The Litany, the service of the word from the Lord's Supper, and a sermon were usually joined to morning prayer on Sundays until well into the nineteenth century, causing a bit of redundancy. Popular eucharistic piety and frequent communion in England had to await until the Methodists in the eighteenth century and the Tractarians in the nineteenth.

The widespread popularity of morning and evening prayer is quite understandable. Both services have a large amount of scripture and considerable congregational participation, especially when psalms and canticles are sung. The services are deficient in their lack of hymns. Cranmer bemoaned the lack of suitable poets to translate the medieval office hymns. As daily services, intended to be supplemented on Sunday by the eucharist, they were not provided with a sermon or an offering. Cranmer's morning and evening prayer became the well-beloved worship of the English people for centuries and nurtured a rich biblical piety instead of a sacramental one. No doubt, part of the offices' enduring popularity was due to the state of the English language in 1549 and Cranmer's skill in using the spoken language of his time with its carefully balanced cadences: "erred and strayed," "wrath and indignation."

Much of the quality of Cranmer's work is reflected by the fact that only minor changes occurred in the two offices in more than four centuries. The 1979 American *Book of Common Prayer* shows, at long last, considerable development in the daily office, including 110 pages of materials. The most important change is frank recognition that this is an age of pluralism in worship as in society. Diversity within the Episcopal Church is recognized by printing both "traditional" and "contemporary" wording of the same services. Many options appear for the first time in an American *BCP*: a short noonday service, "An Order of Worship for the Evening" including symbolic bringing in of light, and a service of compline. A two-year lectionary, based on the church year, provides the lessons. But aside from supplying more options for opening sentences, antiphons, canticles, and collects, the basic pattern has changed remarkably little since Cranmer put down his pen in 1552. A basically conservative revision appears in the English *Alternative Service Book 1980* with increased alternatives for the canticles and shorter forms of morning and evening prayer.

Other churches have recently produced a variety of forms of prayer. The most ambitious is the 1987 Presbyterian Church (U.S.A.) volume *Daily Prayer* with a wealth of resources for the entire cycle of the Christian year. Much of this was included in the 1993 *Book of Common Worship*. In addition to morning and evening prayer, forms appear for "Midday Prayer," "Prayer at the Close of the Day," and a "Vigil of the Resurrection" for use on Saturday night. The 1989 *United Methodist Hymnal* introduces, for the first time, orders for morning and evening "Praise and Prayer." In addition, the 1992 *United Methodist Book of Worship* provides orders for midday and night plus a "Midweek Service of Prayer and Testimony." These are a deliberate attempt to recover the pattern of the ancient people's service. Unlike the new Presbyterian services and others of the Reformation era, the reading of scripture is made optional, prayer and praise being given priority in this newest and yet most ancient form of daily public prayer.

A variety of patterns of weekday worship for groups within parishes eventually developed in various Protestant bodies. Much impetus to these was given by the movement known as Pietism in the late–seventeenth and eighteenth centuries. Pietism encouraged disciplined groups within the parish that were meeting on weekdays for Bible study and prayer. These were imitated in early Methodism in class meetings that met for spiritual direction, hymn singing, and prayer, much of it spontaneous. In the nineteenth century, this became the midweek prayer meeting, an important component of worship in American Protestantism. Not only were these lay dominated but they were also the first to give women the opportunity to speak in public worship (other than among Quakers). These informal services were social dynamite because they gave voices to those often voiceless on Sunday. The prayer meetings contributed much to the empowerment of women and led them to engage in major reform crusades and political activity, such as women's rights, temperance, and the abolition of slavery.

Various Reformation churches also produced a variety of intentional communities, which frequently found daily public prayers natural. The Little Gidding community in England, revived in recent years, carried on a daily cycle of prayer services for two decades in the seventeenth century. Their day began with prayer services and concluded with similar services including considerable congregational song. In the eighteenth century, the Moravians evolved a system of "choirs" of single brethren or single sisters living and worshiping together with daily prayer and hymnody. Notable, too, were hourly intercessions carried on unceasingly by delegated individuals. Daily public prayer was common among many utopian communities, such as the American Shakers. The Taizé Community in France has developed its own daily office.

An important Reformation tendency was relocation of daily public worship to the family. Family worship became an important part of the worship of English Puritans, Scottish Presbyterians, Victorian Anglicans, and their American relatives. The Scottish *Directory for Family-Worship* of 1647 laid out a daily pattern of prayer and praise, reading of scripture, and conference on the application of it. Numerous manuals and collections of prayers were published over the next two and a half centuries to guide this form of daily prayer. It is hard to document the prevalence of family prayers, although Victorian novels, such as George Eliot's *Adam Bede*, give examples of a daily round of prayer, psalmody, and scripture reading within the family circle. These patterns are far from extinct today and sourcebooks still abound such as *The Upper Room Discipline*.

THEOLOGICAL REFLECTIONS

One has to see daily public prayer in the light of the totality of the Christian life to see what is significant and distinctive about it. Obviously, the great majority of Christians neither practice nor miss such a form of worship. Are we to conclude then that it is just a pious option, available for those who like that kind of thing? Or does it fulfill an important need of which many Christians have been deprived?

When one reviews the dynamics of other forms of Christian worship one is struck by the degree to which they predominantly express God's gracious self giving to people. The normal Sunday service of the word is oriented around the proclamation of God's word through readings, a sermon, music, and other arts. The eucharist, too, largely focuses on God's self giving through actions with bread and wine. It is true that such services do include elements of hymnody, psalmody, and prayer, but their emphasis is elsewhere.

Daily public prayer has a different and more personal focus: our response in praise to God in the midst of daily life. It is a response not just to word and sacraments but to the totality of daily experience—the sun coming up, the squabbles in the family, the tedium of work. Thus it is a sharing of our words to God in a corporate fashion. Even though common forms must be used to make it fully communal, each of us supplies the gifts for which we give thanks, the complaints that we express, the joys for which we give praise. This ability to express ourselves in the setting of daily life makes daily public prayer distinctive.

Much of the importance of this kind of worship is in giving balance. This operates on several levels. There is a need to balance daily public prayer with the weekly rhythm of Sunday (or Sabbath) worship. We have previously mentioned the differing dynamics of the Sunday service of the word and the eucharist. It is, of course, possible to have daily sermons as Zwingli did in Zurich or a daily eucharist as some Roman Catholics and Anglicans do. But these have dynamics that services focusing on prayer and praise do not, and the more intimate quality of prayers provides a desirable balance to services better seen as weekly than as daily.

There is also the matter of balance between public prayer and private prayer. We have not mentioned the latter, but it is assumed that public prayer is usually accompanied by prayer in private at other occasions during the day. Neither replaces the other; each strengthens its companion. We must, then, see private prayer as the other end of the same pole, not as a distinct object. Private prayer brings energy and focus to public prayer. But public prayer provides a good balance for private prayer in relating it to the whole of praying Christianity. Essentially, the company of many voices makes Christian prayer Christian. We do not pray against people but for them and with them. And we need the discipline of public prayer to make our own private prayers fully Christian. Otherwise they may stray from the mark and voice private fantasies and aberrations.

In this sense, daily public prayer is a school of prayer. It teaches us how to pray, something in which we all need help whether we live in the first century (Luke 11:1) or the present century. It may not teach us how to pray for John or Alice, but it does teach us the need to reach out to them when they need help. The 1662 prayer for "all sorts and conditions of men" now seems somewhat exclusive but the instinct was to teach Christians to be beside all other humans in prayer. In this way, public prayer teaches us how to pray since it transcends the limitations of our own lives.

The third type of balance we need to reflect on, is the balance between prayer and praise and the reading of scripture. As indicated by the remarks above, the circumstances of monastic life encouraged the discipline of constant prayer which encouraged covering the psalter weekly and the scriptures yearly. This may have been appropriate in such communities, but it provided the only model the Protestant Reformers had for ordinary people so the Reformers tended to make edification the chief function of daily worship.

The ancient people's service relegated edification to other occasions: catechesis and the Sunday service. This left the daily public prayer free to concentrate on prayer and praise in terms that were familiar. In some communities since that time, such as the Moravian, not needing to use the hymnal when singing was a real sign of belonging to the group. A wide variety of hymns might be more edifying; familiarity allowed one to voice with gusto one's own personal feelings. So careful decisions must be made about whether daily public prayer is really meant to focus on scripture and be edifying or whether it serves a fundamentally different purpose. Certainly, scripture reading can and ought to continue in private, but it may be better that the daily public assembly is chiefly concerned with prayer and praise.

PRACTICAL CONCERNS

Much of the value of daily public prayer is that it is adaptable to the people and circumstances present. All recent revisions seem to stress flexibility, adapting things to the people and their situation. This has meant the addition of many options and alternatives. If one can judge from these new forms, *adaptability* is at a premium. Each community has its own distinctive lifestyles and these ought to be reflected in how it prays together. A group of high school students on a retreat should not expect to pray together the same way seminary students would.

Basically, *simplicity* seems to be an important factor in modern reforms. That ties in closely with another desirable quality, *familiarity*. The point of daily prayer is frequently to be able to reflect on words that are familiar and meaningful. In this sense, the use of a *mantra* or repeated phrase in some oriental religions is not irrelevant. One never plunges to the bottom of the Lord's Prayer. The twenty-third and other well-known psalms prove inexhaustible. Certain prayers and hymns continue to lead us to greater depths. Structures of daily prayer that are simple and familiar seem to be favored increasingly in our day. Much of popular religion focuses on repetition.

Familiarity also makes relative *brevity* desirable. If ten minutes are good, that does not mean twenty are twice as good. The quality of daily prayer is our concern, not the quantity of it. Short services can also induce more people to stop in the middle of a busy day or evening.

In recent years, there has been a growing sense that more *actions* should be coupled with daily prayers. Such things as the kiss of peace given through a handshake or embrace, the ceremony of lighting a large candle in the evening, or the use of incense appeal to the body and senses and make it clear that our whole being worships God, not our lips alone.

No other form of worship is affected so much by the *time of day* as daily prayer. The term "Liturgy of the Hours" recovers this sense. People are different at different times of the day; they behave differently, feel different, and have different needs. Physical metabolism is not unrelated to how people pray at different hours. Anyone planning or preparing for public prayer will need to be sensitive to the fact that humans change throughout the day. This is both part of the appeal and the challenge of daily public prayer.

CHAPTER SIX

THE SERVICE OF THE WORD

We have looked at one form of worship, shaped largely by the spoken word, in the preceding chapter on daily public prayer. Now we turn to another form of worship which also stems primarily from the spoken word, the service of the word. Although in both forms of worship, far more happens than just what is done by speech, the spoken word is the primary mode of communication. It is orally that the corporate memories of the community are recalled and reinforced.

The subject of this chapter includes the first half of the Lord's Supper or mass, but the service of the word is also the normal Sunday service of most Protestant groups when the eucharist is not celebrated. The term "service of the word" is thus the most comprehensive designation. Other terms used for the first half of the mass also include foremass, ante-communion, synaxis, or proanaphora. For the usual Protestant service, other terms abound: Sunday service, morning order, preaching service, or divine worship.

Our method will be to trace the various histories of this type of worship as they manifest themselves in the Lord's Supper and in noneucharistic services. Then we will survey some of the theological principles at stake before moving on to see how both historical and theological concerns are reflected pastorally today.

HISTORY OF THE SERVICE OF THE WORD

We begin our discussion of the service of the word with a glimpse at the worship of the Jewish **synagogue**. We have already

seen that the church adopted much of the Jewish rhythm of time
and the mentality that made such a rhythm a means of remembering. And we shall see again and again that both Jewish structures
of worship and underlying mentalities made Christian worship
possible.

The Jewish synagogue service and its mentality underlie the
Christian service of the word. So we must ask, What functions did
the synagogue service fulfill? Strangely enough, it seems to have
originated to fulfill a nationalistic function: the survival of Israel
while in exile in Babylonia. Although we lack clear information on
the origins of the synagogue service, it appears to have originated
sometime in the sixth century B.C. while the Jews were in captivity
in Babylonia. The Jerusalem Temple lay in ruins and the nationalized worship centered there had come to an abrupt halt. There was
no way to pick up elsewhere the temple cult of sacrifice, which by
that time had become identified exclusively with Jerusalem. A new
beginning had to be made to enable Israel to survive.

The synagogue apparently originated as a survival agency, in the
same way many immigrant groups in North America have established nationalistic clubs. Israel kept its identity by remembering.
It remembered what God had done for God's chosen people whose
history made them unique. In answer to the pitiful question, "How
could we sing the Lord's song in a foreign land?" (Ps. 137:4), Israel
invented the synagogue service. Survival, for Israel, meant the ability to remember God's actions that had made them a distinctive
people. And for them, the best ways to remember were through
instruction and prayer together. It is difficult to tell whether synagogue worship began primarily for worship or for educational
purposes, just as it is difficult to tell if some television is meant to
educate or to entertain. Recalling what God had done and rejoicing
in those memories—is that worship or education? It does not much
matter, the result is the same. Israel could survive through worship
when countless other kingdoms were obliterated by the sword.
And the power to remember, reinforced generation after generation by worship, was too powerful even for the tyranny of
Babylonia.

It was soon realized that putting the corporate memories of
God's actions into writing was highly useful for recalling what

God had done to make the Jews a unique people. Teaching these writings through synagogue classes was useful, but the memories really came alive when they were read aloud, reflected upon, and rejoiced in by the gathered community. Maybe this was not intended as worship at first but worship it became and remains: the synagogue service. Homesick Jewish exiles gathered to read, reflect on, and rejoice in what God had done for their people. And every time they told the familiar stories their self-identity was renewed.

No temple was needed for this kind of instruction or worship nor were priests needed. It was a type of worship that laypeople could lead; anywhere ten Jewish men could gather, a synagogue could be formed. All that was needed was a book and people. The lay character of such worship, unlike worship in the Temple, cannot be overemphasized.

The synagogue service focused on what God had done. Jews celebrated God's actions not only by reading their history (scripture) but also in songs rejoicing in this history (psalms), in prayer blessing God for that history, and in reflection on that history (sermons). Eventually, the prayers that recalled what God had done also began to anticipate what God promised to do. This took the form of supplication to God to act, a natural development in prayer. Stylized in time, the prayers eventually began to function as creeds as well as praise and supplication. Reading of the law and prophets became standard practice as Jews recalled God's gift of the law and God's use of the prophets to speak to them.

Thus worship became a way of teaching and transmitting the corporate memories of a people with whom God had covenanted. Survival came through remembering. It was not just a dead detached past that was recalled but a living God, who was made known through past events encountered in present worship. As past events were recited, they became present reality through which God's power to save could be experienced again and again. Through worship, people could relive for themselves the whole history of salvation. Individual lives were changed by sharing in the recital of common memories, just as an adolescent gains individual identity by looking through the family photograph album with the rest of the family. The core of synagogue worship is identification with the community's corporate memories of what God has done for God's people. And the spoken word is the medium through which this occurs.

This was the worship familiar to the earliest Christians, most of whom were Jews. We glimpse fragments of this worship in the Nazareth synagogue in Luke 4:16-28. Jesus read the lesson from the prophet Isaiah and sat down to preach. At the synagogue in Pisidian Antioch, "after the reading of the law and the prophets, the officials of the synagogue" invited Paul and companions to speak (Acts 13:15). It was a style of worship thoroughly familiar to the earliest Christians; their Lord had sanctioned it by regular attendance (Luke 4:16) and the apostles had utilized it to the fullest.

Christian converts from Judaism would all be familiar with such a pattern of public worship and probably many continued to worship in the synagogue while also celebrating the eucharist "at home" (Acts 2:46). But soon Christians were expelled from the synagogue, and by the middle of the second century A.D., we find that a fusion of these two types of worship had taken place, tentative at first but soon becoming permanent. The synagogue pattern was grafted onto the upper room pattern or two media fused, the spoken word and the acted sign. From the sixth to the sixteenth century, the service of the word and the eucharist became inseparable except on rare occasions such as Good Friday.

Though the union of word and sacrament may have occurred earlier, our first evidence of it appears in **Justin Martyr's** *First Apology* written in Rome around the middle of the second century. Justin has given us two examples of a eucharistic gathering. The first follows a baptism. The newly baptized (probably at Easter) are led to the eucharistic assembly, which offers prayer for the one just baptized, gives the kiss of peace, and immediately starts the eucharist. It would appear that initiation, when celebrated, replaced the service of the word but not the eucharist. The other service Justin describes seems to be the normal Sunday service:

> And on the day called Sunday there is a meeting in one place of those who live in cities or the country, and the memoirs of the apostles or writings of the prophets are read as long as time permits. When the reader has finished, the president in a discourse urges and invites [us] to the imitation of these noble things. Then we all stand

up together and offer prayers. And, as said before, when we have finished the prayer, bread is brought, and wine and water.[1]

In modern terms, there were readings from the Old and New Testaments, a sermon, and **general intercessions** or **prayer of the faithful**, that is, prayer for others. Apparently, the amount of reading was flexible but included several lections.

The Apostolic Tradition indirectly corroborates these details two or three generations later. The two eucharists described are both on special occasions: baptism and ordination. Neither eucharist mentions the service of the word which, apparently, is still separable when another celebration precedes the eucharist. Even today, on Good Friday, the service of the word is detachable and stands in its original simplicity apart from the eucharist. This illustrates Anton Baumstark's discovery: In feasts of the greatest solemnity the earliest elements are likely to endure the longest.[2] Even today, the first part of the Good Friday service shows the same conspicuous simplicity as we see in Justin: lessons, psalmody, sermon, and intercessions. The form of the Good Friday intercessions—bidding to prayer, silent prayer by all kneeling, and a summing up prayer where all stand—is primitive (early). No nonessentials appear in the early service of the word. Augustine tells us: "I came into the church, greeted the people with the customary greeting, and the lector started the lesson"[3]—about as sparse and abrupt a beginning as one could imagine.

But it was not long to remain that simple. If we think of a river laying down sediment, we can imagine successive layers of liturgical strata being deposited. This is a useful way to picture developments except that liturgical items were also moved around or dropped entirely, something even an earthquake cannot quite duplicate! First to disappear were the **Old Testament lections** from the law and the prophets which started to vanish in the fourth century. The **dismissal of the catechumens** (those who had not yet been baptized) disappeared in the West by the end of the sixth century, although it still remains in the East. Catechumens had been allowed to be hearers of the word but not to participate in the prayers of the faithful, the kiss of peace, or any of the eucharistic action. The intercessions or prayers of the faithful also disappeared from the service of the word in the Roman rite by the seventh century.

The rest of the earliest stratum survived: the greeting, the epistle, responsorial psalm, Gospel, and sermon. The passage of time brought further accumulations, especially at the beginning of this stratum.

The second stratum represents basically introductory materials, including both song and prayer. Apparently these accretions began in the fifth century after Christian worship had become public and more elaborate. Functionally, many of them tended to embellish such vital actions as getting the clergy to the altar-table and everyone in place to begin worship. Acts performed in silence, no matter how essential, always seem to invite verbal or choral accompaniment as if we never quite trust simple action.

Clearly, these developments occurred at different times in different parts of the Christian world. We can suggest only the outlines of development in the Roman rite of the West. We have seen how terse the beginning of Augustine's service was, but within a few decades after his death an **introductory rite** had appeared that still persists: introit, *Kyrie, Gloria in excelsis*, and collect. This second stratum of liturgical development seems to have been the result of unrelated accretions. The introit, the first in order of the variable parts of the mass, was originally basically travel music to accompany the procession of clergy to the altar-table in the manner of a psalm verse set to music. Late in the fifth century, the older prayer of the faithful was replaced in Rome by prayer in the form of a **litany** (a series of petitions each followed by a recurring response) located before the lessons and sermon. The response was *Kyrie eleison* ("Lord Have Mercy"). By the beginning of the seventh century, the petitions themselves had disappeared in Rome though complete litanies still remain in the Byzantine rite. Only the *Kyrie* remained in Rome, a tiny Greek island in a sea of Latin words. The successive disappearance of the prayer of the faithful and the litany left the Roman service of the word devoid of intercessions. A third item added was the *Gloria in excelsis* ("Glory to God in the Highest") or greater doxology, usually sung. Although of Eastern origin, its use as part of the service of the word is confined to the West, and the *Trisagion* ("thrice Holy") fills an equivalent role in Eastern rites. The **collect, oration,** or **opening prayer** brings the entrance rite to a close. A Western form, the collect follows a formal literary pattern usually consisting of (1) an address to God, (2) a relative clause referring to some characteristic of God, (3) a petition, (4) a result clause, and (5) a concluding doxology. At this point, the collect functions to conclude the introductory rite and to introduce the lessons for the day. Collects are another variable part of the eucharist. Compilations of collects form an important part of the great **sacramentaries,** or prayer texts for masses.

Let us recapitulate. The fifth and sixth centuries had seen a great elaboration of the introductory rite. Gone was the terse greeting and direct move into the lessons and in its place was a stately and musical progression of introit, *Kyrie, Gloria in excelsis*, and a collect.

But there is yet a third stratum, deposited through gradual accumulation during the early Middle Ages. It is common today for those leading public worship to spend a few moments of preparation in personal devotions in the sacristy before entering the church to begin the public service. Gradually such personal devotions crept out of the sacristy and into the chancel. They tended to have a specific character; they were basically **apologies** for the presider's unworthiness and petitions to be made more worthy to serve God in presiding at worship. Such devotions, then as now, tend to be individualistic, subjective, and introspective. These are not bad qualities in themselves but when the function of these personal devotions was changed by incorporating them into public worship itself, an important shift occurred. It was a slow and subtle change, not something debated and decided in public synods. It signaled a shift in emphasis away from an assembly gathered to rejoice in what God had done to an assembly of individuals met to bemoan their sin before the Almighty. Eastern churches escaped much of this transformation; Western churches unconsciously majored in it.

The result was a **preparatory rite** of opening devotions appended to the very beginning of the service of the word. These began with Psalm 43 (42), of which verse 4 of the Latin version provided an apt text: "I will go to the altar of God." The fourteenth century prefaced the psalm with a Trinitarian blessing. The next of these prayers at the foot of the altar-table is the *confiteor* or prayer of **confession** and an **absolution** or declaration of **pardon**, operating as a cleansing station before the priest is really prepared to begin. The penitential language of the confession shaped much of medieval, Reformation, and modern eucharistic piety. Short prayers next accompanied the priest's approaching and kissing the altar-table before beginning the introit.

A further medieval accretion was musical elaboration of the responsorial psalm, the **gradual**, which originally followed the Old Testament lessons. When these disappeared, the gradual was transferred after the epistle and shortened to a single verse. There it joined other sung items, the **Alleluia** or **Tract** (for penitential occasions). Nonbiblical elaborations of the Alleluia known as **sequences** flourished in the Middle Ages but were virtually abolished in 1570.

The Middle Ages (in the West) also added the **Nicene Creed** immediately after the sermon. This appears to have occurred as a rearguard action against Arianism (which denied the divinity of Christ) and in forgetfulness of the proclamatory nature of the eucharistic prayer. This practice of saying the creed probably originated in Spain, was promoted by Charlemagne, but was not adopted in Rome until the early eleventh century. In the East, it was adopted in the sixth century as a part of the eucharist itself.

The result of all these developments is the service of the word which the sixteenth century inherited, the Reformers changed slightly, and the Counter-Reformation altered even less. Diagram 9 charts the various strata using parentheses to mark those items that disappeared, at least temporarily.

For better or for worse, the Protestant Reformers themselves had been shaped by the late medieval version of this service with its heavy dose of penitential elements and losses of the Old Testament lection and intercessory prayer. If they had known more of the history of the rite, they would have had more freedom to reform it, but without that knowledge, history could not set them free. The Reformers did contribute greatly in advancing preaching, congregational song, and vernacular rites. In his *Formula Missae* of 1523, Luther saw little to change in the service of the word.[4] He delighted in the musical elements, the introits, *Kyrie*, *Gloria in excelsis*, graduals, and alleluia and sung creed. He eliminated the opening devotions and nonbiblical sequences but encouraged congregational song in German especially after the gradual. He once suggested

The Service of the Word

First three centuries	Fourth to sixth centuries	Medieval
greeting		Psalm 43
	introit	confiteor
	(litany), *Kyrie* response	
	Gloria in excelsis	
	collect	
(Old Testament lections)		
(psalm)		
Epistle		
(psalm)		
Gospel		
Sermon		
	gradual, alleluia, tract	(sequence)
		Nicene Creed
(dismissal of catechumens)		
(prayer of the faithful)		

Diagram 9

that the sermon might precede the entire service. In 1525, Luther produced his *Deutsche Messe* (German Mass) and introduced more vernacular hymns and a paraphrase of the Lord's Prayer after the sermon.[5]

Though Luther did not intend it, by a long slow process the service of the word or "ante-communion" by itself came to be the normal Sunday service among Lutherans, thus dividing the two so long wed, word and sacrament. The Enlightenment of the eighteenth century brought an end to weekly eucharists in most Lutheran countries. The (1978) *Lutheran Book of Worship* returns to the sixth-century pattern. There is a "Brief Order for Confession and Forgiveness" which may precede the service. Three musical settings are provided. The sequence when the eucharist is not celebrated is: entrance hymn, greeting, *Kyrie, Gloria in excelsis,* collect, first lesson, psalm, second lesson, alleluia or tract, Gospel, sermon, hymn, creed, offering, prayers (which may be intercessions), Lord's Prayer, and blessing. The pattern would have seemed familiar to a sixth-century Christian.

In the Reformed tradition, greater change occurred on the assumption that the early church was being followed. We shall look at **John Calvin** primarily since his *Form of Church Prayers . . . According to the Custom of the Ancient Church*[6] of **1542** (Geneva, Strasbourg 1545) was the fountainhead from which this tradition spread, although much of its originality is due to the reformer of Strasbourg, **Martin Bucer**. The service is heavily penitential and didactic. This tradition seemed to relish the medieval apologies. The rite begins with a vigorous prayer of confession noting that we are "incapable of any good, and that in our depravity we transgress thy holy commandments without end or ceasing." Absolution follows, then an item introduced by Bucer, the singing of the Decalogue. Extempore prayer is offered, a metrical psalm is sung, a collect for illumination—an item which it was believed was common in early Christian worship but which, instead, has become a distinctive Reformed contribution is said, and the lesson and sermon follow.[7] A long pastoral prayer of intercession, a petition, and a paraphrase of the Lord's Prayer precede the concluding blessing.

Calvin preferred the eucharist to follow weekly but was thwarted

Plate 1: The Church of St. Sabina, Rome, Italy; view toward the apse (Alinari/Art Resource, NY)

Plate 2: Abbey Church, St. Denis, France; view of the choir (Scala/Art Resource, NY)

Plate 3: Il Gesu, Rome, Italy; interior view of the Gesu toward the main altar (Scala / Art Resource, NY)

Plate 4: Castle Church, Torgau, Germany; first church built for Protestant worship; dedicated by Martin Luther in 1544 (photograph by James F. White)

Plate 5: The Interior of St. Odulphus in Assendelf, Pieter Jansz Saenredam; Rijksmuseum, Amsterdam, The Netherlands (Rijksmuseum Amsterdam, Object number: SK-C-217)

Plate 6: Fort Herkimer Reformed Church, New York, 1767, 1812 (photograph by James F. White)

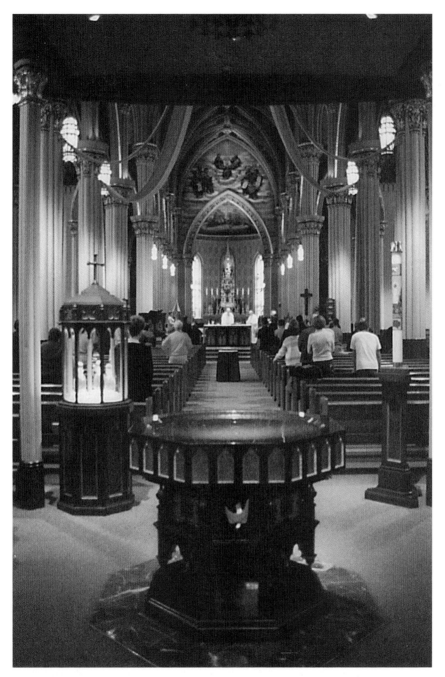

Plate 7: Basilica of the Sacred Heart, Notre Dame, Indiana, 1870–87, with new baptismal font and ambry (for oils) (photograph by James F. White)

Plate 8: Unity Temple, Oak Park, Illinois; Frank Lloyd Wright, architect (photograph by Unity Temple)

Plate 9: Greek Orthodox Church of St. Andrew, South Bend, Indiana, showing icon screen and baptismal font (photograph by James F. White)

Plate 10: Iconostasis of the Russian Orthodox Cathedral of St. John the Baptist, Washington, D.C. (Sisterhood Kiosk and Bookstore, Russian Orthodox Cathedral of St. John the Baptist)

Plate 11: The Church of St. Elizabeth Seton, Carmel, Indiana; Frank Kacmarcik, interior designer (photograph by James F. White)

Plate 12: Eucharistic vessels: chalice, paten, and straw; German ca. 1235 (photograph © The Metropolitan Museum of Art, The Cloisters Collection, 1947. [47.101.26–29])

Plate 13: Eucharistic vestments: left, representation of an archbishop, wearing mitre, gloves, crozier, pallium, chasuble, amice, maniple, stole, 2 dalmatics, and alb; right, representation of a priest, wearing chasuble, amice, maniple, stole, and alb.

Plate 14: *The Last Supper,* Eucharist, agape, or refrigerium; Catacomb of St. Callisto, Rome, Italy (Scala/Art Resource, NY)

Plate 15: *The Mass of St. Giles in the Cathedral of St. Denis*, the Master of St. Giles; National Gallery, London, Great Britain (Erich Lessing/Art Resource, NY)

Plate 16: The Wittenberg Altar: painting of the Last Supper and scenes from the life of Martin Luther, by Lucas Cranach the Elder, Marienkirche, Wittenberg, Germany (photograph by James F. White)

by the conservatism of the Genevan magistrates who were not accustomed to receiving communion frequently. But it is important that the model for Sunday worship in the Reformed tradition was the service of the word, not the daily office. Singing of psalms came to be a hallmark of Reformed worship. They give joyful contrast to the stern penitential and disciplinary character of the service.

The **Westminster Directory**[8] imposed the Puritan approach to worship on the national churches of England, Scotland, and Ireland in **1645**, superseding the *BCP* for fifteen years and terminating the authority of the Scottish *Book of Common Order* (1564). The *Directory* is more than a book of rubrics, less than a prayer book. The order for the "Publique Worship of God" is as follows: The minister calls the congregation to worship and begins prayer by reminding the people of "their own vileness and unworthiness to approach so near him [God]; with their utter inability of themselves, to so great a work." Reading of the Word follows ("ordinarily one chapter of each testament" on a *lectio continua* basis), singing of a psalm, intercession (a very long pastoral prayer of confession and intercession), preaching of the word, a prayer of thanksgiving, the Lord's Prayer, a sung psalm, and a blessing. This service of the word has, for several centuries, provided the basic structure of worship for much of the English-speaking Reformed tradition. Preaching is obviously the dominant act of worship. The medieval, apologetic, and penitential approach looms large but there are clear gains in the recovery of Old Testament lections, the high regard for congregational psalmody, and the importance of preaching.

The 1993 Presbyterian *The Service for the Lord's Day* represents greater historical consciousness of early patterns and yet reflects Reformation tendencies. Its structure is four part. First comes "Gathering": call to worship, opening prayer, hymn of praise, psalm or spiritual, confession and pardon, the peace, and canticle or psalm, or hymn, or spiritual. Second comes "The Word": prayer for illumination, first reading, psalm, second reading, anthem, hymn, psalm, canticle or spiritual, Gospel reading, sermon, hymn, canticle, psalm or spiritual, affirmation of faith, and prayers of the people. The third part, "The Eucharist," contains, on noncommunion occasions: offering, prayer of thanksgiving, and Lord's Prayer.

The final part is "Sending": hymn, spiritual, canticle or psalm, charge and blessing, and going forth. The *Service for the Lord's Day* encourages the use of the eucharist each Lord's Day but this has not yet become common.

Different decisions were made by the **Anglican Reformers** who benefited from the gratuitous advice, based on two decades of experience with vernacular liturgies, of the continental Reformers. Basically a conservative revision of the Sarum service of the word, Cranmer's 1549 rite began with an introit psalm, Lord's Prayer, the collect for purity, *Kyrie*, *Gloria in excelsis*, greeting, collect of the day, and collect for the king.[9] The epistle and Gospel follow immediately, then come the Nicene Creed and sermon. The service then moves into exhortation and the eucharist. Two items have been transplanted into the eucharist itself: Intercessions appear right after the *Sanctus* and confession comes before communion. In the 1552 version, there was a lurch in the Reformed direction: the introit psalms disappeared and the Decalogue was added immediately after the collect for purity.[10] The intercessions have been returned to just after the sermon and offering, and the confession now follows the exhortations, just prior to the *sursum corda*. The *Kyrie* disappeared, and the *Gloria in excelsis* was banished to just before the final blessing in the eucharist. A rubric was provided for ending the service after the general prayer of intercession when communion was not celebrated. This allowed detaching the service of the word from the eucharist after a thousand years of unity. For three centuries, this "ante-communion" or "second service" with sermon followed morning prayer and the litany on most Sundays. The eucharist was not celebrated frequently in most parish churches.

The years since have seen a gradual unscrambling of this pattern. The 1979 American *BCP* represents significant gains in the restoration of the Old Testament reading and psalmody and the downplay of confession. The service of the word is entitled "The Word of God" and includes a greeting, collect for purity, *Kyrie* (or *Trisagion*), *Gloria in excelsis*, collect of the day, two or three lessons (interspersed with psalms, hymns, or anthems), sermon, Nicene or Apostles' Creed, prayers of the people, optional confession of sin, and the peace. In short, this is the sixth century pattern again.

Similar changes have been made in the *BCP*s of other nations and the *Alternative Service Book 1980*.

Quaker worship does not necessarily involve the spoken word. It takes its center in a silent waiting upon God. After a period of centering down, people may rise to speak as the Spirit prompts them. There is a high sense of discipline, a strong reluctance to rush into words or to speak from oneself. Such worship does not fit into any of our patterns traced for other traditions although some American Friends have moved to structured worship.

Methodism inherited the Anglican Sunday pattern of morning prayer, litany, and ante-communion with sermon. The *Sunday Service of the Methodists in North America* **(1784)** made minor changes in the service of the word aside from omission of the creed.[11] The principal change was the expectation of hymn singing, which brought a distinctive warmth to Methodist worship. Some British Methodists tended to cling to Anglican morning prayer. John Wesley proved to be a poor judge of his followers in America. In 1792, the year after Wesley's death, the printed text of the service of the word was set aside.

What happened in the nineteenth century? The official book of Methodist church law, the *Discipline*, carries only a scant outline during this century: "Let the morning service consist of singing, prayer, the reading of a chapter out of the Old Testament, and another out of the New, and preaching." On balance, that sounds slightly more like morning prayer than the service of the word, though a monthly eucharist was also appended to it. Nineteenth-century Methodism moved close to the revivalism of the Frontier tradition.

Revivalism having paled, Methodism turned increasingly toward aestheticism in the early twentieth century and to historicism by the middle of the century. This has been superseded by an era of ecumenism with a common concern to recover the early roots of Christian worship. For United Methodists, this has taken the form of *A Service of Word and Table*. "The Basic Pattern of Worship" without Holy Communion includes: gathering, greeting, hymn, opening prayer and praise, prayer for illumination, lesson, psalm, lesson, hymn or song, Gospel lesson, sermon, response to the word (for example, invitation to Christian discipleship, baptism, or creed), concerns and prayers, confession, pardon, peace, offering, prayer of thanksgiving, Lord's Prayer, hymn or song, dismissal with blessing, and going forth.

In the early nineteenth century, the **Frontier Tradition** sprang up in the American West, bringing with it a whole new function for the service of the word. Basically, Christians on the frontier were ministering to unchurched people whom they hoped to convert to Christianity. A form of worship for the unchurched was necessary. This developed out of **campmeetings,** held to bring the populace from a large area together for preaching, spiritual direction, baptism for those converted, and a concluding eucharist. Such new measures proved effective on the frontier and were gradually incorporated into the worship life of more sedate, settled regions on the East Coast.

The result was a tripartite form of the service of the word, one that is the most common today in American Protestantism. It can be experienced on national television each Sunday. The first part begins with a service of song and praise, which places great emphasis on music. A special type of hymn developed, the gospel song, which was deeply introspective and highly individualistic, expressing the feelings of the devout. The first portion of the service also included prayer and reading of a scripture lesson. The second portion was the sermon, which was and remains highly evangelistic, calling souls to conversion and the converted to renew their commitment. All of it climaxes in the final harvest, a call to those who have been converted to acknowledge this change in their lives by coming forward, being baptized, or making some other indication of their new being. Although the sermon is the longest portion of the service, all the parts are carefully integrated.

The Pentecostal Tradition, beginning at the onset of the twentieth century, has preferred spontaneity to clear structures. Its most dramatic form involves the use of the gift of speaking in tongues and interpretation. But more important is the insistence on freedom from set forms and on the unexpected possibilities in spontaneous singing, testimonies, and biblical readings.

If one thing can be clear in recent developments in all of these traditions—Protestant and Roman Catholic (except the Quaker, Frontier, and Pentecostal)—it is the return to the priorities of the first six centuries. We now see how captive the Reformers were to medieval assumptions by making the service of the word so heavily penitential, didactic, and disciplinary. Even recent elimination of more penitential portions of services does not remove lingering feelings among many people that they still go to worship primarily to be scolded, to feel sorry, and to make amends.

Much of the impetus for the newer (and older) reforms came from Vatican II. It mandated simplicity and clarity in the mass and stressed that "the treasures of the Bible are to be opened up more lavishly" (CSL, par. 51), that preaching should be normative on Sundays (CSL, par. 52), and that "there is to be restored, after the Gospel and the homily, 'the common prayer' or 'the prayer of the faithful'" (CSL, par. 53). The results can be seen clearly in the **Roman Missal of 1970**. The "Order of Mass" is: entrance song, greeting, blessing rite or penitential rite or neither, *Kyrie, Gloria in excelsis*, opening prayer, first reading, responsorial psalm, second reading, alleluia or gospel acclamation, Gospel, homily, profession of faith, and general intercessions. Not only could it be used almost interchangeably with the newest rites of the Protestant traditions mentioned here but also it could almost pass for what Roman Christians did each Sunday fifteen hundred years before. Muted is much of the penitential preparatory material and recovered are emphases on Old Testament lections, responsorial psalmody, preaching, and prayer of the faithful.

Two modern variants of the service of the word emerged in the 1980s. The first, praise and worship, devotes the first half of the service to songs of praise generally sung by the whole congregation, often from words projected on a screen. The second half is given over to preaching or what is frequently referred to as teaching. This has its focus on a biblical text or some topic relevant to living the Christian life.

The second, frequently known as the seeker service, may not be considered worship at all but a form of evangelism. It begins with a musical preformance in a familiar style which often alternates with a skit or monologue to present and resolve an issue with which seekers may be wrestling. The talk that follows pursues this issue further, sometimes using a scriptural basis, sometimes not. Frequently, these congregations also provide a weeknight service for committed members that is somewhat more traditional.

THEOLOGY OF THE SERVICE OF THE WORD

Fundamental to the traditional service of the word is hearing and responding to God's word, mediated and expressed through human speech. First of all, God speaks to us through the lessons and sermon, read and preached by humans. What God does here is done primarily through the spoken word. We must recognize the medium and its powers and limits. Speech acts in worship as a means of giving oneself. Through words we are present to others, and God is present to us. Words express our thoughts, our emotions, and our very being so that others may share in them. In worship, God gives God's selfhood to us through human speech, and we, through God's power, give ourselves to God through our speech.

Structurally, this means that these types of worship revolve around God's word as read in the lessons and expounded in the sermon (if any). This was certainly the intent of the Reformers and has become much more obvious in the post–Vatican II Roman Catholic Mass. A Reformation collect declared that God "has caused all holy Scriptures to be written for our learning" (cf. Rom. 15:4). That "all," it is recognized today, means that both covenants, old as well as new, must form a part of worship. To communicate the corporate memories of the community of faith, its written records—the scriptures—need to be read again and again. The corporate memories contained in scripture give the Church its self-identity. Without the continual reiteration of these memories, the Church would simply be an amorphous conglomeration of people of goodwill but without any real identity. Through the reading and exposition of scripture, the Christian recovers and appropriates for his or her life the experiences of Israel and the early church: escape from slavery, conquest, captivity, hope for a messiah, incarnation, crucifixion, resurrection, and mission. The Church's survival depends on reinforcing these memories and hopes just as Israel's did. Worship is indeed the recapitulation of salvation history.

Of course it is not just the recollection of past events that occurs in the readings and their interpretation. In the events narrated in scriptures, the Christian community discerns meanings that illumine all history. The black and white of all history is transformed into a color presentation as the scriptural events give history meaning. Historical events which are bearers of meaning are chronicled in the Bible and give the Christian community clues for interpreting the present and future as well as past events. It is as if the playwright steps into the play to tell us what it is all about.

An excellent description of the service of the word would be "Bible service." The reading of scripture—whether done selectively or consecutively—is basic. The spoken word doubtlessly will continue to be central just as it is and will be the primary mode of communication for the rest of human life. Transmitting the corporate memories narrated in scripture is crucial to this service.

The importance of preaching is closely linked to the centrality of scripture. Many guides to a theology of proclamation are available.[12] Preaching is a form of communication based on the conviction that God is central in the process. The preacher speaks *for* God, *from* the scriptures, *by* the authority of the Church, *to* the people. Four items are vital in conceiving of preaching: the power of God, source in scripture, authority from the Church, and relationship to people.

It would be presumptuous to believe that we preach on our own power. God uses our voices to speak God's word; what we have to say has little power by itself. But through the power of God our voices have the power to heal and reconcile. The substance of preaching is grounded in scripture. Otherwise we get solemn lectures, not preaching. It is simply not true that the only difference between a sermon and a lecture is thirty minutes! Preaching is grounded in God's word, although all other forms of learning may help interpret the scriptures. The value of preaching from a lectionary is that it gives us a catholic canon (even though imperfect) rather than a private canon of favorite passages. We do not preach an individual faith but rather the faith of the church, which examines and licenses us, thereby authorizing us to speak for it in preaching the faith of the universal community of believers. Preaching cannot occur without hearing. A congregation of faithful people who can hear and respond to preaching is a necessary part of preaching. Through the presence of hearers of the word, God acts in self giving through preaching.

Not only does God speak to us through lessons and sermon, but we also speak to God. This takes place through prayer, psalms, canticles, and hymns. Understanding worship as revelation and response is useful at this point. God takes the initiative and we respond with our words to God's word. God's word does not return empty; it evokes ours. But we can respond only on the basis of what God has done.

Prayer takes many forms: invocation, praise, thanksgiving, confession, supplication, intercession, oblation, and others. Each of these operates in a somewhat different way, yet all have in common that they are the creature's voice to the Creator. We may beg forgiveness, offer praise, or plead for someone else, but whatever the function the method is similar: the articulating of deeply felt human needs as we confess, rejoice, or beg. Prayer gives us the opportunity to speak the right words, to say to God whatever concerns us most deeply. It is an essential part of all worship. Recovery of the importance of the intercessions in the service of the word is an important advance for both Protestants and Roman Catholics.

A rediscovery of psalmody is underway among Western Christians. The psalms are not substitutes for lessons; they are responses to or commentaries on lessons. In many services, psalms, or canticles are interwoven between the lessons. They provide a jubilant form of congregational or choral response to what has been read. The psalms articulate our wonder and our marvel (and occasionally our despair) at what God has done. Sometimes they are deeply and intimately personal; at other times they are a recapitulation of salvation history. Psalms may also be used as an invitatory to worship or as an opening act of praise. **Canticles**, poetic fragments from other books of scripture along with a few early Christian hymns, function in the same way as psalms.

In the fourth century, Christians began to supplement biblical poetry with hymns. Hymns, like prayer, function in a rich variety of ways. There are hymns of praise, thanksgiving, proclamation, contrition, invocation, oblation, and a long list of other purposes. Like prayer and psalms, hymns are usually addressed to God and frequently recite God's acts. But hymns add another dimension: the ability to shade our meaning by adding melody, harmony, and rhythm. Hymns provide a more intense form of address to God than ordinary speech by adding another layer of participation:

music that involves our whole body. Frequently, hymns provide a rather subtle bridge between different portions of a service, sometimes eliminating the need for a spoken rubric.

Finally, there are times in worship in which we speak to one another, especially the greeting, announcements, various spoken rubrics ("Let us . . ."), dialogues, the creed, the peace, and the blessing and dismissal. These are not just necessary stage business; these reflect the communal nature of our approach to God. We come to meet our God and we meet our neighbor first. It is as a community that Christians worship and members of any community talk to one another. Greetings and dialogues encourage us and provide us with cues while the creed helps us to build one another up as, together, we profess allegiance to the church's faith as symbolized in spoken words.

God speaks to us, we address God, and we speak to one another. All these are vital parts of worship in the service of the word.

PASTORAL CONCERNS OF THE SERVICE OF THE WORD

Only on the basis of historical and theological priorities can we best make the necessary practical and pastoral decisions that worship leadership entails. The practical decisions will vary from tradition to tradition. For Roman Catholics, Lutherans, and Episcopalians, the decisions will chiefly involve choosing the most apt materials provided in service books and, of course, preaching the most suitable sermon possible. Even these traditions have become increasingly open to prayer composed for the occasion *(ex tempore)*. Considerable time must go into planning and preparing for worship in these traditions. Decisions of a pastoral nature must take place in terms of where we are in the liturgical year, where worship will be located, and, above all, the actual people who will be worshiping.

For people in the Reformed, Frontier, and Methodist traditions even more decisions are necessary. Although denominational publications are available in most instances, many pastors prefer to devise their own **order of worship**. Many, though not all, of the decisions to be made revolve around the order of worship.

Frequently local orders ignore important historical and theological issues and, consequently, fail pastorally as well. Sometimes the order is a legacy from the last pastor. (The tradition hardest to overcome is usually the most recent one.) And sometimes the order of worship seems to be designed after a system that passes all understanding.

Quite clearly there is no one "right" order of worship. Nevertheless it may be of help to suggest some criteria to keep in mind while planning an order of worship in those traditions where this is determined locally. First of all, we must realize the **centrality of scripture**—all of scripture—in this type of worship. All churches are rediscovering the importance of a richer diet of God's word in worship. Gone are the days when we could be content with a few verses read as a sermon text. God's word speaks for itself and should be read whether there is a sermon or not.

Second, there ought to be an obvious **sense of progression** in worship as one goes from greeting to benediction. This can be overdone. There is no clear indication where, for instance, the Lord's Prayer belongs. But one can trace development from introductory types of acts to proclamation and on to commitment with a sense of "flow" or movement.

Third, is the need for **clarity of function**. Generally acts of worship that have the same function ought to come together. It is astonishing to see how far the location of preaching strays from the reading of scriptures. Yet the reading and the preaching of God's word are about as similar in function as any two acts can be. Money, service, and prayers offered for others also have a similar purpose. Questions need to be asked about the function of each act. What does it do? What is its purpose? Usually this will help clarify the link. To be pastorally responsible, orders of worship must be designed so that clarity of function enables the congregation to follow the order with ease.

In addition to the basic problem of ordering the service, there are several areas where problems are common. The first of these is that we have usually not been sensitive to the process of gathering and scattering and to how people interact during these preliminary and final acts of worship. But these are important parts of worship and need to be pondered and planned more carefully rather than simply masked by music. Areas outside the worship area must be inviting and stimulate a desire to linger and socialize rather than to hurry inside or outside.

The problem of penitential portions of the service has been mentioned. They may make sense as personal devotions for minister or priest in the sacristy before leading public worship, but that does not mean that penitential acts are the best way to begin public worship. They need not appear at all in most services. Contemporary thought seems inclined to suggest that penitential rites be occasional acts, particularly appropriate in Advent and Lent. But when they do occur, they often make more sense after God's word is read and interpreted and the congregation knows for what omissions and commissions confession is needed.

Until recently, psalmody had to vie with the pastoral prayer for the distinction of being the most dull part of Protestant worship, but neither need be in this unenviable position. At best, the psalms ought to be sung. There are a variety of ways of doing this ranging from metrical paraphrases (hymns) to the various settings where a cantor or choir sings the verses of varying lengths and the congregation joins in the refrains. The *United Methodist Hymnal* prints responses and music for one hundred psalms. Most of these methods can easily be taught to congregations, especially with choir help. When the psalms cannot be sung (if there ever are such circumstances) they ought to be shouted back and forth across the central aisle between halves of the congregation at a fairly rapid pace. The psalms make more sense when tied closely to the lections read and most easily done by following the psalms listed in some versions of the ecumenical lectionary.

The chief problem with the **pastoral prayer** is that it often tries to do everything and often ends by doing nothing. At its best, it can be a magnificent articulation of the congregation's deepest feelings and needs. Some pastors have this gift; others of us do not. Too often the pastoral prayer is simply overloaded and tries to cover confession, thanksgiving, intercession, and all points in between as if one try were better than several. If we think through the differing functions of these (and other) types of prayer, it may make better sense to have separate prayers for each main purpose. Some lend themselves well to various forms of congregational participation, such as confession (unison), supplication (litany or bidding), or intercession (spontaneity). Then the pastoral prayer can fill a single function and do it well. The Reformed tradition, which gave us this type of prayer, too often yielded to the temptation to use it for instruction. We would now consider this a dubious function for prayer, no matter how badly Christians in the sixteenth or twenty-first century need instruction. But the pastoral prayer can enlarge our vision while leading us in intercession or in thanksgiving, for example. One thing done well may be better than many done poorly.

The function of choral music, especially anthems, is problematic (cf. chapter 4). Frequently the anthem can be used as a part of the proclamation of the word, provided it is carefully selected to join with the lections read. When simply dropped in as a musical interlude to cover some action or, worse still, as a bit of entertainment, it is highly questionable. The lectionary is as useful for good choral work as it is for comprehensive preaching. When the anthem functions as a musical commentary on God's word, it can be a strong asset to worship. Even then, it ought not deprive the congregation of opportunity for singing hymns and songs.

The creed is a rather late addition to worship in the West, and far from necessary. But it can function as an appropriate response to the word, especially after a doctrinal sermon, by giving an opportunity to affirm together the faith that makes the church one. It is hard to see how a recently composed affirmation of faith can function in this way. The ancient Apostles' and Nicene Creeds can be joined in by all Christians, and maybe even the Athanasian Creed on rare occasions such as Trinity Sunday. All other affirmations of faith are denominational or local and fail to function as symbols of the faith of the universal church.

Acts of offering seem to come best as a result of what has been said and heard, whether they be the offering of money, service for others, or prayer for them. "Concerns of the Church" may be statements asking for help for those in need. Prayer of intercession reaches out to all of humanity: the church, those in positions of power, those in need or distress, the local community, the world community, and (in some traditions) the dead. Clearly, this is the most worldly part of worship. It is far too easy to thank God that we are not like other people. Intercessory prayer opens us to the needs of all peoples and is an important act of growth and love on our part.

The service of the word will continue to evolve in form and yet retain much the same function as it enables the church to remember and to hope. The survival of the church depends upon it just as the survival of Israel depended on the synagogue service.

CHAPTER SEVEN

GOD'S LOVE MADE VISIBLE

n the last two chapters, we have discussed God's love made *audible*, primarily through the use of the spoken word in worship. But there is another medium of equal importance in Christian worship, the use of certain meaningful actions known as sacraments which also make God's love *visible*. For the majority of Christians worldwide, the sacraments are the most common experience of worship. In the worship life of almost all Christians, the sacraments certainly play a significant, if not dominant, role. Accordingly, the second half of this book will examine the sacraments. This chapter treats what is traditionally called **sacraments in general**; the last three chapters will study them individually.

Sacramental worship is distinguished by its use of **sign-acts**, that is acts that convey meaning. **Sacraments** are a type of sign that involves acts, words, and (usually) objects. Calvin repeats Augustine's dictum: "Add the word to the element, and there results a sacrament, as if itself also a kind of visible word."[1] More specifically, we might say that in sacraments words become part of an action using an object such as bread, wine, oil, and water.

In Christian worship, both the spoken word (as found in daily public prayer or the service of the word) and the acted sign (as found in the sacraments) reinforce each other. A handshake does not compete with a spoken greeting, each strengthens the warmth and meaning of the other. The washing of baptism underscores words spoken about God's action in forgiving. Like eating and drinking, speaking and acting belong together in Christian worship. The same God who gave us ears to hear also gave us eyes to see.

Worship is true to the ways humans communicate with one another. The kiss does what words cannot; words impart meaning to the kiss. Much of the beauty and color of life would be lost if we had to choose between one medium or another. Instead, we say much through a nod of the head, a wave of the hand, or an embrace. Each of these sign-acts, though small in itself, is nevertheless part of the whole galaxy of actions that add to what we express in words. These revelatory actions are a means of giving ourselves to others as we convey to them what we mean or even who we are. Words do so, as well, but neither more nor less, only differently.

Ever since New Testament times, the church has found certain sign-acts essential for expressing the encounter between God and humans. These sign-acts have signified sacred things and have become ways of expressing through the senses what no physical sense could perceive, God's self-giving. The sacraments call us to "O taste and see" (Ps. 34:8), to touch, to hear, even to smell "that the Lord is good." In them, the physical becomes a vehicle of the spiritual as the sign-act causes us to experience what it represents. Obviously, only a very few sign-acts out of the myriads we use in daily life function as sacraments. The process of reaching consensus about just which sign-acts to designate as sacraments has been complex, as we shall shortly see.

The number of sign-acts that can be used universally in worship is limited, and there seems to be a built-in bias to conservatism in retaining those that communicate well. Those in common use today would have been familiar at any time in Christian history. Sign-acts do not change as rapidly as spoken words do. Perhaps this is one reason they seem so faithful at the solemn crises of life: birth, marriage, sickness, and death.

There is a tendency in Christianity when the original function of something becomes obscure to overlay it with symbolic meaning and then at a later date to lay it aside as irrelevant. Puritans and Catholics alike have tended to trivialize actions and to bury them under a haystack of words. A meal became a snack, or the act of washing got underplayed while we interpreted in words what was happening instead of actually doing it. Only in recent years have we become fully aware of the sign value that actions have in and of themselves and have at last become willing to let them "speak" for themselves.

In this chapter, we shall trace the gradual development of Christian reflection on what the church experiences in sacraments. Part of this discussion will involve familiarizing ourselves with terms Christians have selected over the centuries as the least inadequate ways to explain what they were experiencing in the sacraments. Then we shall attempt to interpret the meaning that sacraments have today. And we shall trace the consequences of this interpretation for practice.

THE DEVELOPMENT OF REFLECTION ON THE SACRAMENTS

The practice of the sacraments has seen few dramatic changes over the centuries. Development in practice, for the most part, has been like the slow unfolding of a bud. Nor have new ways of understanding what was experienced in the sacraments been articulated rapidly except in a few times of controversy. Many terms we now regard as essential were unknown in the first thousand years of church history. Even the number of sacraments remained indeterminate throughout most of the Christian centuries.

Once again, we must begin with the Jewish mentality and practices that made sacraments a possibility for Christians. It is hard to imagine a sacramental life evolving from any religion other than Judaism. The Jews held in tension the transcendence of God with God's concrete involvement in the actual events of human history. God was made known through events and objects that disclosed the divine will but were never confused with the Deity. Humans, in turn, could respond to God by appropriate actions.

Christianity's deepest debt to Judaism in this area, then, is the mentality that conceived the use of certain actions and physical objects as a means God and humans could use to communicate with each other. Yet God remained transcendent, never to be confused with the created. In this way, even inanimate objects could gain a power to speak yet never become identified with God themselves. A pillar of fire, a cloud, a volcano, daily bread, all could become ways through which God was revealed though God is none of these. Thus a false split between the material and the spiritual was avoided. Even ordinary objects such as water could be used to convey God's love to us. From time to time, Christians need to remember that they are not called to be more spiritual than God; the path to the spiritual leads through many material realities.

Throughout the Old Testament, we encounter a variety of forms of **prophetic symbolism** in which dramatic actions signify God's will and purpose. Frequently the actions not only reveal but also help initiate events. Jeremiah makes a yoke of iron or smashes a pot of clay. Such actions give impetus to the ensuing denouement of what God intends. They are part of the very events they anticipate and thus have potency to fulfill God's will.

From Judaism also comes a profound understanding of each meal as a sacred event. This most common of human social activities became, for Judaism, an opportunity for praising and thanking God as well as for forming a bond of unity between partakers. Far from being simply physical necessity, the meal became a means of encountering God as provider, host, and companion.

Judaism discovered that humans could also use actions to reach God. Practices of sacrifice of food and drink became ways of establishing and maintaining relationships with God. Although the forms and interpretations of sacrifice are complex, the central concept seems to be the use of objects of value to convey one's meaning, one's very being, in surrender of self for communion with God.

Without this Jewish mentality and these practices, the sacramental life of Christianity would never have been born. But, since many of the earliest Christians were also Jews, these ways of thinking and doing things came naturally to them. Though surrounded by a wide variety of idolatrous religions, early Christians were nevertheless able to use, but not confuse, the material as a channel of the spiritual. Their sense of the transcendent set them free to use the material in spiritual ways without risk of idolatry. It was a freedom tempered by responsibility to the weaker brethren (1 Cor. 8) who had not yet shaken off the shackles of idolatry.

The Gospels show Jesus and his disciples using the sacramental patterns of Judaism. The disciples, following a custom of baptizing converts to Judaism, began baptizing early in Jesus' ministry (John 4:2). Jesus himself had submitted to baptism at the hands of John the Baptist, a fact the evangelists explain (with some difficulty) as "to fulfill all righteousness" (Matt. 3:15). It was obvious to Jesus, as to any other Jew, that the annual passover commemoration brought to life the crucial moment in their history. The passover meal itself was a series of sign-acts that recalled what God had done to make the Jews a distinctive people. These customs were part of the very air that Jesus and his disciples breathed. Nothing could be more natural than to transform these familiar practices in establishing a new covenant, or rather, a new means of commemorating such an event.

It is not nearly so clear just what Jesus intended for his followers to do. It can be debated whether we have in scripture express commands in the actual words of Jesus to baptize (Matt. 28:19), to remit sins (John 20:23), or to eat and drink as a memorial of him (1 Cor. 11:24-25). On the other hand, there can be little doubt that the early church considered itself to be fulfilling the Master's will in continuing these practices in his name. There is no room for doubt that Jesus received baptism, that he forgave sin, or that he kept the feast. In this sense, Jesus' own actions are a firmer basis for the sacraments than reports of his words. At an even deeper level, Jesus himself, as the visible manifestation of God, is the **primordial sacrament**. The church, in doing what he did, simply continues his sacramental mission to reveal God.[2]

The church continued to repeat Jesus' actions from the time of his death on, that is, long before the scriptures were put into written form. What we find recorded in the scriptures, then, represents sacramental practices the church had already long observed. The various **institution narratives** of the Lord's Supper (Matt. 26:26-29; Mark 14:22-25; Luke 22:15-20; 1 Cor. 11:23-26) may tell us as much about the fulfillment of the Lord's will by churches in various locations as they do of the Lord's directives themselves.[3] In short, the sacraments are older than the written scriptures, which refer to contemporary liturgical practice as well as to a remembered past.

The church's acts of obedience to Christ, then, are our chief evidence of the foundation of the sacraments rather than words of institution. There is no reason to believe that the church's practice did not faithfully obey what it understood to be Jesus' own intentions. The apostolic practices of Jesus' followers who baptized (Acts 2:41), laid on hands (Acts 6:6), prayed (Acts 2:42), healed (James 5:14), and broke bread together (Acts 2:46) are acts of obedience. These actions of the apostles reveal Jesus' intentions as much as any red-letter formulas. This also means that we are not limited to a handful of passages in interpreting Jesus' intentions with regard to acted signs but can draw on Acts and the epistles, which supply far more detail.

The New Testament is full of references to what later generations would call sacraments. Most numerous of all, as might be expected in a church afire with missionary zeal, are references to baptism. Second are mentions of the Lord's Supper. Widely scattered allusions appear to other sacral actions such as laying on of hands, healing, sealing, and forgiving. In none of these instances do we get much more than a glimpse of apostolic practice. Even less do we find an exposition of what these practices meant to the participants. But, taken as a whole, we discover innumerable rich and varied insights into the sacramental faith and practice of the apostolic church. The manifold views of apostolic practice are like the different facets of a jewel. To do them justice, we must turn the jewel around so that all its facets sparkle. Unfortunately, throughout its history the Church has tended to look at only a single facet or two and to ignore the rest. We shall try in subsequent chapters to examine the rich variety of these biblical facets so as to get a balanced view.

Thus we can be thankful there is not a New Testament chapter devoted exclusively to portraying sacramental life and doctrine. In the diverse and scattered fragments, a broader and deeper reality is depicted. In our urge to systematize, we must beware of the temptation to settle for a narrowly coherent view instead of accepting the richly varied assortment scripture presents. The Bible does not give us liturgies or sacramental theologies, but it lays solid foundations on which these can be built. The church uses the New Testament, then, not as a book of laws and statutes but as the fundamental constitution for its ministry of sacraments.

We must beware of asking the early church our questions about the sacraments. The very terms and categories in which we think are products of later ages. Our terms would seem hopelessly legalistic and mechanically precise to an age more inclined to experience the sacraments than to consider them objects of theological study. Yet we, in turn, may learn much from the church's use of the sacraments in the first centuries of the Christian era.

A basic insight is revealed in the Greek word normally used for a sacrament, *mystérion*. The usual translation, "mystery," is misleading. As the New Testament uses the term, it refers to the secret thoughts of God, which transcend human reason and therefore must be revealed to those whom God wishes these secrets to reach. In Mark 4:11, Jesus tells the disciples that "to you has been given the [*mystérion*] of the kingdom of God" while others must depend on parables. Paul uses the term to refer to Christ himself, to the apostolic preaching, to that which is spoken in the spirit, and to the hidden wisdom of God. The basic insight in the use of this same term for those sign-acts that we call sacraments is that *mystérion* implies acts in which God is disclosed to us. These heavenly mysteries are completely dependent upon God's acting in self giving.

Unfortunately, the Latin word chosen by Tertullian to replace *mystérion* has none of that rich depth. **Sacramentum** is a term that referred to an oath of allegiance taken by a soldier or a vow to keep a promise. It is much more legalistic and lacks the cosmic dimension of divine personal self giving that *mystérion* implies. It is, though, the word the Western church chose from the third century onward.

Whatever the term used, the sacraments were more experienced by the early church than debated. Heresies abounded in other areas but relative tranquillity reigned in this aspect of the church's life, aside from occasional defenses of sacraments against those who decried any use of physical objects in worship. The precise definitions with which we are familiar were unknown because no one pushed the church to define what it meant. Concepts such as an exact number of sacraments or the moment the Holy Spirit was given in initiation or the moment the eucharistic elements were consecrated would have been puzzling in the church's heroic age. For well over a thousand years there was no consensus about just how many sacraments there were. For Augustine, the list included such things as the baptismal font, the giving of salt at baptism, the ashes of penance, the Creed, the Lord's Prayer, and Easter Day. One thing mattered: that in these acted signs God was given to humans.

Consequently, what we know about early practice and reflection on the sacraments comes indirectly. Tertullian wrote the short treatise *On Baptism* early in the third century, but it tells us more of baptismal discipline than theology. In *On Penance* he gives us a bit more theology but mostly practical advice. We get glimpses of actual rites in *The Apostolic Tradition* but practically no interpretation. Ambrose, John Chrysostom, Theodore of Mopsuestia, and Cyril of Jerusalem are more detailed in the lectures given to newly baptized Christians, in which they try to interpret what the new Christians have just experienced for the first time. These date from the fourth century but are as dangerous as they are tantalizing. For us, it is tempting to read back subsequent developments in West and East into these terse statements about what occurs in the eucharist. But these are our concerns, not theirs. Augustine baffles us with apparent contradictions in presenting, side by side, realistic and symbolic interpretations of Christ's presence in the eucharist. What to us is inconsistency never troubles this great thinker. Clearly, our categories are not his, and our exclusivistic language seems a bit trite by comparison.

Augustine did nudge the church forward in several irreversible directions in understanding what it experienced in the sacraments. He began the attempt to define a sacrament, finding it a sacred sign which represents what it signifies, just as bread and wine represent body and blood. Most important are his phrases "visible form" and "invisible grace" which shaped the standard late medieval definition (in Gratian and Lombard) that "a sacrament is the visible form of an invisible grace." Furthermore, Augustine distinguished between the visible sacrament itself *(sacramentum)* and the power *(res)* of a sacrament. Apart from the invisible grace, the sacrament has no power of itself; only this invisible power or force can give it effect.

Through his involvement in the Donatist controversy, Augustine had to clarify who had actually been baptized. In refuting a group of North African schismatics known as **Donatists**, who believed only good people could perform good sacraments, Augustine imparted some concepts that have lodged themselves permanently in the church's thinking about the sacraments. First of all, Augustine had to argue that the schismatic Donatists nevertheless possessed genuine baptism, though they had it unrightfully. This is true because the sacraments depend not on the human who administers them but on God. Their power is not a human one, contingent upon the moral character or doctrine of the celebrant, but it depends instead on God, who uses sacraments to bring about God's own purposes. This is at once the most important and most controversial theological statement ever made about the sacraments. Others elaborated it as the *ex opere operato* doctrine, that is, that God operates simply through the work being done independently of the human agent. Augustine's great contribution is to make clear that the source of sacraments is divine agency, not human.

If the Donatists had genuine baptism, they had it contrary to the Catholic church's laws and without baptism's benefits. Remaining obstinate in schism, they could not profit from the love and charity of the community into which baptism initiates one. Augustine does not draw these conclusions to their precise definition, but implicit here are the germs of much later distinctions: sacraments as **valid** (that is, conveying grace) or **invalid**; **regular** (that is, according to church law) or **irregular**; and **efficacious** (that is, beneficial) or **inefficacious**. But once Augustine bent the twig in this direction, it was bound to grow into an important branch of sacramental theology and canon law.

Let us sum up what can be learned from the early church about the sacraments. The number of sacraments was indeterminate and how they operated was undefined. More concern was expressed about who could receive the sacraments and who could perform them, though even here there seemed to be considerable imprecision. What was to become a juridical encrustation of the sacraments in theology and canon law had hardly developed. But what was apparent and characteristic was that Christians experienced in the sacraments God's self giving and rejoiced in these sign-acts. Much later, John Calvin was to say of the eucharist: "I shall not be ashamed to confess that it is a secret too lofty for either my mind to comprehend or my words to declare. And, to speak more plainly, I rather experience than understand it."[4] That could also serve as a summary of much of the early Christian witness to the sacraments.

The medieval period shows a slow move to more definitions and new terminology, a process speeded up greatly in the twelfth and thirteenth centuries. Most of our approaches to the sacraments today are so heavily colored by these late medieval developments that it is hard for us to go behind them. The lateness of these developments is extraordinary. A debate over the nature of the eucharist flared up in the mid–ninth century between two monks of the Abbey of Corbie, in Northern France, **Paschasius Radbertus** and **Ratramnus**. In the eleventh century, **Berengarius** found out, to his consternation, that there were some limits to what were acceptable boundaries to beliefs about the eucharist. He was forced to retract his unpopular views of a purely symbolic approach, but even then considerable latitude was still possible. As late as the twelfth century, the number of sacraments was a subject of varying opinions. In 1140, **Hugh of St. Victor** listed such diverse things as the blessing of palms, the receiving of ashes, bending the knee, or reciting the creeds as sacraments, and the Third Lateran Council in 1179 spoke of "the institution of priests, . . . burying the dead" as sacraments. In short, from Augustine to the twelfth century there was still considerable latitude about many sacramental doctrines.

Meanwhile popular practice and piety had continued to change. The practice of penance underwent a radical shift from the seventh century onward, changing from a public office only for gross offenders to a private office for everyone. Slowly but surely the rites of initiation were pulled apart in the West. Even more slowly, the church tightened its grip on the marriage ceremony. Healing became associated almost exclusively with death and was known as extreme unction. Eucharistic practice moved ever more to celebrating the mass as an awesome spectacle with the people rarely receiving communion and little, if any, participation by the laity. Even ordination underwent changes as accessory ceremonies came increasingly to dominate the rite.

The twelfth century was a time of synthesizing scripture and the fathers, summarizing what had been learned thus far, and dividing such knowledge into manageable segments. Sacramental theology showed a meteoric development. Most influential was the work of

Peter Lombard, professor and (briefly) bishop at Paris, whose *Four Books of the Sentences* was completed around A.D. 1150 and became the basic textbook for Christian doctrine for almost five hundred years. It is the funnel through which all preceding developments of any significance passed on to future elaboration in the West. In a key passage Lombard tells us:

> Let us now come to the sacraments of the new covenant; which are baptism, confirmation, the blessing of bread, that is the eucharist, penance, extreme unction, ordination, marriage. Of these some offer a remedy for sin, and confer helping grace, as baptism; others are merely a remedy, as marriage; others strengthen us with grace and virtue, as the eucharist and ordination.[5]

Within half a century, this became the standard list of sacraments and was made dogma by subsequent councils.

Lombard summarizes earlier teaching on each of these seven sacraments. Following Augustine, he distinguishes between sacraments of the old covenant (such as circumcision) "which only promised and signified salvation" and those of the new covenant which "give it."[6] Using language originally used by Augustine, Lombard defines a sacrament as "the sign of a sacred thing (*res*)." But Augustine's distinction between the *sacramentum* (that which is apparent to our senses) and the *res* (thing, that is, fruit of the sacrament), is refined further by Lombard to a threefold distinction between the *sacramentum* itself (the outward and visible), the *res* (the inward fruits), and the *sacramentum et res* (the two combined, that is, both sign and reality). An indication of future developments occurs in Lombard's statement that "a sacrament is properly so called, because it is a sign of the grace of God and the expression of invisible grace, so that it bears its image and is its cause."[7] Thus a sacrament sanctifies as well as signifies, and the following century was to pursue this in detail.

At another point, Lombard looks backward rather than forward. With the coming of the thirteenth century, it was taken for granted that a sacrament could only be instituted by Christ, an addition to the definition as a "visible form of an inward grace" that was to cause an explosion at the Reformation. But Lombard, while clear that Christ instituted baptism and the eucharist, apparently follows earlier belief that the apostles instituted the rest and relates that unction of the sick was "instituted by the apostles."[8] Lombard and the past were not followed at this point.

Other problems were tackled by thirteenth-century theologians, the **Scholastics**, especially the questions of proper ministrants, recipients, and the effects and operation of grace in the sacraments. In a period of brilliant theological activity, the church's experience of the sacraments was reduced to words. The clarity of language so formulated has endured, and until recently, all subsequent discussions were tied to the terminology devised in this period. The councils of Florence and Trent in the fifteenth and sixteenth centuries did little more than place an official cachet on the theological work done during the thirteenth century.

The most convenient summation of all this work occurred in the **Decree for the Armenians** published by the Council of Florence in 1439 and based on a thirteenth-century treatise by Thomas Aquinas, "On the Articles of Faith and the Sacraments of the Church." The "Decree for the Armenians" began by listing what had by then become the conventional list of seven sacraments which "both contain grace and confer it upon all who receive them worthily."[9] Three things are necessary for each of these sacraments: the proper **matter** (objects such as water), the correct words or the **form** (such as the baptismal formula "I baptize you . . ."), and the person of the designated **ministrant** who must have "the **intention** of carrying out what the church effects through him," that is, he or she must intend to do exactly what the church does in the sacraments (such as baptize). That means a priest does not perform a sacrament while acting in a play or by using the proper matter and form for some purpose other than that which the church designates. "Three of these sacraments—baptism, confirmation, and ordination—impress indelibly upon the soul a **character**, a certain spiritual sign, distinct from all others, so they are not repeated for the same person."[10] The Council then specifies for each sacrament the proper matter, form, minister, and the benefits conferred upon the recipient.

It is all very neat and coherent, a far cry from Augustine's imprecision about even the number of the sacraments. What had happened was that the sacraments had become a system, a carefully worked out way of life in which every important human journey or passage was ministered to with an appropriate sacrament. Birth, growth, marriage, ordination, and sickness were each marked by sacraments. One was nourished in the eucharist and recovered from falling through penance. The effects of each sacrament were carefully worked out so that those who received it with proper **disposition**, that is, without imposing an **obstacle** to its operation, could be assured of receiving the designated grace.

What are the results of these late medieval developments? The church, at last, made up its mind about what it experienced in the sacraments. For better or for worse, it had the tools of Aristotelian philosophy and could give a rational accounting of what it experienced. But this is also its weakness. What we perceive in the scholastic theologians of this period is a rationalism of the right, fully orthodox but more a matter of rational categories than experiential ones. The definition of the miracle of the eucharist in terms of localized substance is an example of this, although the term "substance" in the thirteenth century was a far more experiential term then than it is today.[11] One cannot help feeling in these neat distinctions about the operation of grace a danger of knowing too much, a forgetfulness that one is dealing with heavenly mysteries, not with that which is susceptible to philosophical solution.

The **sacramental system** embracing all of life was a brilliant product of human ingenuity dealing with all aspects of pastoral care. That was its problem. There are limits to human ingenuity when reality breaks out in unexplained ways not comprehended in our philosophy. Too neat a system led Roman Catholicism, especially after the Reformation, to treat the sacraments in excessively juridical ways and to overemphasize the question of validity, an obsession reaching its peak in the eighteenth century. The necessary concern with affirming the sacraments' dependence on God *ex opere operato* could sometimes be diverted from its proper affirmations to a mechanical, almost quid pro quo, concept of grace. Far more free were the **sacramentals**, an indeterminate number of pious practices such as table blessings, use of holy water, almsgiving, and so on, whose benefits were contingent upon the inward disposition of the performer *(ex opere operantis)*. Furthermore, the whole sacramental system was tied very heavily to the ministry of the ordained clergy. Only baptism and matrimony could be administered by the laity and, in the West, usually only bishops could confer confirmation and ordination. Women could only perform emergency baptisms and join a man in marriage.

Still, even those who question the sacramental system cannot but admire its comprehensiveness and thoroughness in caring for human needs, although they may question as well the wisdom of knowing too much about how God acts. Problematic, too, may be the late medieval restriction of the number of sacraments to seven, the belief that all seven were instituted by Christ, and the entire structure of such a tightly interlocking system. When one is dealing with so sublime a subject as how God acts in self giving, neat scholastic divisions and distinctions may not be an adequate substitute for awe and wonder.

Rebellion against such a finely conceived system finally exploded in the person of Martin Luther. Luther's most vehement blow at the sacramental system was struck in his *Babylonian Captivity of the Church* (1520) in which he successively breached the walls the Romanists had erected to protect the mass. Written in white-hot anger, it was no logical exposition but a forceful blast at the whole sacramental system. It is hard to overestimate its force; it shaped all subsequent Protestant thought on sacraments. Except for small groups such as the Quakers and the Salvation Army (which dispute the need for outward sacraments at all), all major Protestant groups accepted Luther's final conclusion that only two sacraments were instituted by Christ, and therefore, there are only two sacraments. Luther drew the restrictions even closer than his late medieval predecessors had done by declaring that the only sacraments are those for which explicit words of Christ are recorded in the New Testament, that is, those with **dominical injunctions** in which Christ clearly commands sacraments. Even Luther had trouble with penance, for which John 20:23 comes close to a dominical injunction. If Luther had had the freedom that prevailed as late as the twelfth century to accept institution other than by Christ alone, the Reformation would have taken another course, but Luther is captive himself to the thirteenth century qualification that a sacrament must have been "instituted by Christ." He simply took this medieval qualification to its logical conclusion by asking "where?"

The force of Luther's attack led the Roman Catholic **Council of Trent (1545–1563)** to assert in defiance: "If any one says, that the sacraments of the New Law were not all instituted by Jesus Christ, our Lord; or that they are more, or less, than seven . . . let him be anathema."[12] Trent (wisely) did not go into details about where all seven were instituted or the contrasting opinions of the fathers. Protestants, just as stubbornly, maintained that only two sacraments had divine authority. Unfortunately, it was no longer possible to agree that the number of sacraments was unknown or that some could have been instituted by the apostles following Christ's own practices. Late medieval definitions had closed those doors for Protestants as well as for Catholics.

The shattering of the sacramental system may not have been what Luther wanted—although he certainly deplored its clericalism, its Aristotelian philosophy, and its works righteousness—but shatter it he did, and the pieces have never gone back together within Protestantism. Luther and his contemporaries knew less about the early church than they thought they did and far less than we think we do. And in their zeal to reform the system they sometimes overlooked its humane side, its ability to minister to the deepest human needs from birth to deathbed. Granted, the system was not without flaws, but it provided pastoral care in a comprehensive way to deeply felt human needs that are permanent.

Pressure on one portion of the sacramental system was sure to distort other parts. When the sacrament of penance was abolished, how could the contrite sinner find the same concrete assurance of absolution that this sacrament had guaranteed? The result was to push the eucharist into being a penitential sacrament, too, a process already strongly developed in late medieval piety. Ever since the Reformation, the Protestant eucharist has done double duty as a sacrament of both penance and thanksgiving. After all, the deep human need to be forgiven did not disappear simply because the sacrament of penance had been abolished; it simply overloaded the eucharist. It is perhaps more accurate to say that Protestantism has two and a half sacraments: baptism and a penitential eucharist.

The dethroning of confirmation as a sacrament was equally problematic. Instead of being reunited to baptism, the Reformation changed it into a didactic experience expressed as a graduation exercise for those who had mastered the catechism. Much of Christian education has been built on such a dubious resolution. Medieval rationalizations of confirmation's effects were not much better but at least Catholicism considered confirmation a gift of God rather than an act of human education.

Matrimony was retained but not as a sacrament. It can be debated whether, in reality, ordination ever ceased being treated as a sacrament. Even John Calvin might have considered it a sacrament had it been for all Christians. Most Protestants treat ordination as imparting an indelible character and do not re-ordain clergy who return to ordained ministry after secular work. Ironically, Protestantism never developed a similar rite of passage for entrance into secular vocations.

Protestants paid a penalty for the loss of healing as a sacrament, partly by the outcropping of bizarre and spectacular efforts to minister to a basic human need: the desire for God's help in restoring health. Recent years have seen a gradual recovery of this form of sacramental ministry.

What did the Reformation accomplish with regard to the sacraments? Many of its results were not intended, especially that of pushing sacramental worship from the center to the periphery of the Christian life. Recoveries came only much later in early Methodism, the Disciples of Christ, and the Oxford Movement. Luther suggested some profound insights on baptism as lifestyle that have never been done justice even by his successors. Calvin succeeded better than his contemporaries in fusing reason, biblicism, and a sense of awe before holy mysteries. In this he came closest to the early church's understanding and left a legacy to which John Wesley resonated. The attempt of most Reformers to restore frequent communion to the laity would have been a tremendous gain had it not been too radical a change from the late medieval practice of infrequent reception of the sacrament. The Reformers were children of the late–Middle Ages, too, but they did achieve clear gains in sacramental worship through simplified vernacular rites, more congregational participation, congregational song, a well-catechized laity, and new emphasis on preaching of the word.

Perhaps the Reformation was overly dramatic for, despite the outbursts, much more of the Augustinian and medieval apparatus of thinking about the sacraments was retained than discarded. Even in railing against transubstantiation, Luther was committed to thinking of the eucharist in terms of a spatial presence. And many of the Reformers preserved the essence of *ex opere operato* in thinking of the sacraments as acts of God. For them, God is the chief actor in the sacraments and humans are the recipients of what God chooses to do for our benefit through sacraments. Calvin saw the sacraments as "visible signs best adapted to our small capacity" in which Christ acts "giving guarantees and tokens."[13] This approach is frankly sacral in insisting that God uses the physical objects and actions of this world to accomplish God's will for us. The efficacy of the sacraments does not depend on us but is a gift of grace. God makes the sacraments happen, although humans are free to receive or to refuse God's gift in them.

The eighteenth century saw a more subtle change but one that was even more drastic than that of the Reformation in sacramental theology. It came about in the desacralizing tendencies of the **Enlightenment** which found repugnant the very notion that God would intervene in present time or use physical objects and actions to accomplish the divine will. Slowly, for some Protestants, these views eroded the traditional Catholic and Reformation view that God acts to accomplish God's purposes through sacraments. The desacralizing tendencies played down God's role in the sacraments and magnified humanity's. Biblicism was still firm enough that Christians accepted two sacraments as required by Jesus' teaching.

For a vast segment of Protestantism, the two sacraments became simply pious memory exercises. The sacraments were occasions for humans to remember what God had done in times past. They were credited with immense practical value in stirring up humans to greater moral endeavor. Remembrance of God's past actions was looked upon as a strong incentive for leading a better life. But the emphasis in desacralized Protestantism was not on God acting now but in remembering what God had done in times past. The agency is human; we remember, we act.

There are premonitions of these developments in Ulrich Zwingli's treatise *Of Baptism* in 1525, though they are less apparent in his understanding of the Lord's Supper. Zwingli still lived in a sacral world in which God intervened in worship. But the real split that opened up as the eighteenth century progressed was between those who followed the traditional Catholic and Reformation concept of God as acting in the sacraments and those for whom the sacraments had become basically pious memory exercises. The latter included a wide variety of Protestants ranging from Anglican bishops to frontier Baptists. Even Ben Franklin indulged in some prayer book revision, making show of the practical benefits of remembering Jesus for amending one's character. This is the rationalism of the left. If the rationalism of the right encrusted medieval piety in a shell of Aristotelian philosophy, then that of the eighteenth century created a rigidly desacralized universe in which nothing was more than its outward appearance.

God no longer made sacraments happen; that depended on humans. It was far more constricting because all depended upon human fervor in generating the ability to remember. Frequently, that ability failed to produce an enduring fervor for remembering God and adjusting behavior. This was a Gethsemane-type of piety ("If Christ did, . . . can't you at least?"), and its fervor was often fragile. The result was a great drop in sacramental worship in Protestant traditions such as that of the Lutherans, which, in some places, had maintained a weekly eucharist until late in the eighteenth century.

The value of the *ex opere operato* doctrine is clear; if the sacraments are only pious memory exercises, then they have little chance of being the center of a vital worship, but remain only a legalistic survivor because Jesus once said "do this." Traditionally, the purpose of the sacraments was not to induce good ethical behavior but to give humans access to God (which, in turn does indeed change behavior).

Today there is a real split in Protestantism between those who follow Luther, Calvin, and Wesley in the traditional view that God acts in the sacraments, using them as a means of grace for divine self giving, and those who follow the desacralizing tendencies of the Enlightenment which saw the sacraments as something humans do in order to stimulate memory of what God has already done. This split is at least as great as was that between the

Reformers and their Roman Catholic contemporaries. Fortunately, neither approach is frozen in ice, and there are signs that both are beginning to change. Today, we see more clearly the divine self giving that occurs in the sacraments, and we are also discovering more about their human side as this relates to communication. And there are clear indications of a sacramental revival now going on in many portions of Protestantism.

NEW UNDERSTANDINGS OF SACRAMENTS

In recent years, great changes have occurred throughout Western Christianity in the ways sacraments are understood. These changes have swept across denominational boundaries and changed both faith and practice in vast segments of the Christian world.

The most obvious changes in practice have been in Roman Catholicism since Vatican II, but change has been underway since the beginning of the twentieth century when receiving communion weekly began to be common for Roman Catholics for the first time in more than a millennium. The **Liturgical Movement** brought further changes in the direction of increased biblical study, more congregational participation, and a firm grasp of the church as community. Vatican II accelerated this process with important advances in the presentation of doctrine (especially with regard to the church and sacraments) and in broad changes in worship. The post–Vatican II revision of the liturgical books brought important changes in the outward form of each of the sacraments though most conspicuously in penance and healing. Less obvious has been a move away from treating the sacraments in legalistic juridical terms (especially those of validity and regularity) to more concern about the fruits (efficacy) in people's lives.

Within Protestantism, changes of equal significance may be detected in the widespread growth of a deeper sacramental piety. Recent years have seen more frequent communion services, progressing from quarterly to monthly to weekly in many congregations. The emerging recovery of the eucharist as a norm for Sunday worship has also been accompanied by more concern with baptism as a congregational act. Less detectable, but even more significant, is the gradual shift away from regarding worship simply as an intellectual experience of instruction or as an emotional outlet, to the realization that worship encompasses our total being—body, emotions, and intellect. Among all Christians, a greater sensitivity has arisen to the crucial role sign-acts play in relations between humans and in the encounter between God and humans. Many have discovered that such a heavily emotional sign-act as the imposition of ashes at Ash Wednesday is as much a part of worship as the doctrinal sermon. Probably the impact of these changes reflects something broader than worship alone: We are discovering more about what it means to be fully human. Revived interest in the sacraments simply shows how deeply anthropological the sacraments are, that is, how closely they reflect what it is to be human.

This new concern has brought focused attention on the **sign value** of the sacraments, that is, how well they communicate. One can baptize with a medicine dropper if all one is concerned about is validity, that is, what is the least one can do and still have a genuine sacrament. But if one is concerned with sign value, baptism will obviously communicate far more about cleansing and washing if a considerable amount of water is seen, heard, and even felt vicariously. For those responsible for the conduct of worship, a new concern is apparent, namely the **quality of celebration**. How well does what we do communicate in human terms what God is doing? In this sense, no detail is insignificant if it heightens the sign value of what we do in the sacraments. The very humanity of the sacraments is shown in how closely they follow normal human forms of communication and relating to others. This places a heavy responsibility on those leading worship to be fully sensitive to all they communicate by voice and body.

Changes in sacramental practice have often reflected new ways of understanding what is experienced in the sacraments. The most significant breakthrough in this century began with the German theologian **Odo Casel**, Benedictine monk of Maria Laach Abbey in Germany. Casel's **mystery theology** stressed that Christian worship is basically a time mystery in which the reality of past events is again offered to us through our reenactment of them in worship. He avoided many of the scholastic terms from the thirteenth century and concentrated on showing how, through the church's corporate recalling of salvation history, each Christian can appropriate these events and live "our own sacred history."[14]

Post–World War II theological developments in the Netherlands and Belgium associated with the names of theologians Piet Schoonenberg and **Edward Schillebeeckx** led to further significant breakthroughs. Schillebeeckx's *Christ the Sacrament of the Encounter with God*[15] was the most influential work on sacramental theology of the Vatican II years. In it, Schillebeeckx presents Christ as the primordial sacrament through whom we encounter God. The visible sacraments are means through which we can experience gracious personal relationship with God. The categories Schillebeeckx uses are personal human relationships, not static and juridical terms. At points, some of the insights of Calvin seem to appear; at others, modern phenomenological philosophy comes to the forefront.

A variety of factors have shaped the new approaches to the sacraments. Biblical studies have greatly illuminated our understanding of the richness and complexity of the biblical witness to the sacraments, and historical studies have traced the slow development of the Christian experience of and reflection on sacraments. Ecumenism has made each branch of Christianity willing to share its particular experience and to appropriate those of others. Old controversies have been bypassed, frequently on the basis of better understanding of the common heritage of the New Testament and the early church. Modern communications theory, anthropological studies, and sociological research have clarified the human content of the sacraments and led to more profound understanding of how humans relate to one another and to God.

Given all these factors, how can we best express the role of sacraments in the life of a Christian today? Practice and theory as well as experience and understanding must all come together. It is not easy to concoct a clear teaching in this short space any more than it is simple to weave a coherent pattern of many disparately colored and textured threads. But this portion of this chapter will attempt, in terms as concise as possible, a contemporary statement of what the sacraments can mean for the Christian of today. We shall speak of all sacraments here. Not all comments apply equally well to each sacrament. Besides having much in common, sacraments obviously differ. Only a few Christians receive ordination, nearly all receive baptism. The generalizations of this chapter must be tempered by the specifics of following chapters.

It should be clear by now that I regard the number of sacraments as indeterminate, just as most Christians did in earlier centuries. The number seven is just as arbitrary as two, and the possibilities that the first twelve Christian centuries entertained seem far richer than those the last eight have selected.

First of all, it would seem that any satisfactory understanding of the sacraments must start with the belief that *God acts in the sacraments*. That is to say, the sacraments depend upon what use God makes of them, not on human moral character, ability, or intentions. The outward, visible form is shaped by humans and may vary in detail from generation to generation but the inward grace depends on God. The *res*, the thing or fruit of the sacrament, depends upon God, although humans can impose an obstacle to what God offers. In this sense we can speak of the objectivity of divine grace in the sacraments.

These, of course, are the concepts Augustine used so forcefully in his debate with the Donatists. The sacraments are not contingent upon the moral character of the celebrant but depend on God alone. Humans are freed from the need to make the sacrament happen; only God can do that. Thus the alternative, the desacralizing position, is profoundly unsatisfactory for it makes the sacraments depend upon human agency and forces their fruitfulness to rest on the degree of fervor with which the sacraments are approached. This confuses the roles of God, the giver, and humans, the recipients. Some form of the *ex opere operato* doctrine seems essential to safeguard the crucial sense of divine activity though this must not be pushed so far as to make grace irresistible or to leave humans completely passive.

Sacraments, as Calvin saw so clearly, are God's idea, designed by God to lead us to God. "Our merciful Lord," Calvin says, "so tempers himself to our capacity that . . . he condescends to lead us to himself even by these earthly elements, and to set before us in the flesh a mirror of spiritual blessing."[16] God knows us best and knows the need to strengthen our faith. The Creator knows best how to address us as creatures. Sacraments then, are God's way of acting. The sacraments are far more than pious memory exercises, for in them, Calvin continues, God "imparts spiritual things under visible ones."

Second, *God acts in the sacraments in self giving*. God takes the initiative in the sacraments. What is given is not some abstract idea of mechanical infusion of energy but a gracious personal relationship, God's life entering ours. We receive God's gift of self. Christianity proclaims that God is love and the very nature of love is to be self giving. In various ways in different sacraments, God acts in self giving to us in forms appropriate to the time and occasion—as forgiveness and reconciliation in one sacrament, as acceptance in another. Gifts are the human way of giving ourselves to others. God does no less in the sacraments. Indeed, because God is given to us in the sacraments, we are able to give ourselves to others in broader and deeper ways. When God acts in self giving, say in the eucharist, we are made one with other worshipers and enabled to serve all the world. Thus the sacraments have the power to change all that we do through power based on God's initial self giving.

God's self giving is by no means confined to sacraments. The whole Old Testament and New Testament are chronicles of ways God has been given to humans in times past. Frequently these have taken on unexpected forms, ways of giving, not to the proud and mighty but to the meek and lowly. God is given to us in creation, in law and prophecy, and in the life together of a chosen people. God is given to us in the human Jesus, who "emptied himself, taking the form of a slave" (Phil. 2:7). Scriptures are a record of God's self giving in the past.

The sacraments are a third testament of God's self giving. Through them, God's self giving occurs as present reality in our own here and now. The reality of past events is made present to us in reading and expounding the scriptures, but the reality of continuing action is imparted to us in the sacraments. They form yet another testament to the self-giving nature of God. All three testaments—old, new, and sacraments—make known to us God's will to give of self for our benefit.

Third, *through the sacraments, God's self giving occurs as love made visible*. For Christians, God's self giving is perceived as the giving of God's love, "and those who abide in love abide in God, and God abides in them" (1 John 4:16). There is no love that does not make itself manifest in some way. Any human emotion as powerful as love is reflected in the way we relate to the loved one. Love is constantly seeking sign-acts by which to reveal itself to the object of our love. It may take such affectionate forms as hugs and kisses, it may crop out in giving a gift, or it may manifest itself in doing the dishes for someone. One writes letters or visits the hospital or telephones as a visible manifestation of love. These visible sign-acts are identified with love. We know another one loves us because of how she or he acts toward us.

This is not an abstract principle, this is simply how people are. We need to be shown. In Jesus Christ, God showed us the fullness of divine love. But we need to be shown this love again and again. In the sacraments, God continues in present visibility what God has already done in self giving in the historical visibility of Jesus Christ. Love manifests itself in various ways according to our varying stages and circumstances of life. God as love is given to us to uphold us in making a lifelong pledge to love another. Another form of self giving is witnessed to as the community prays for our return to health. Love is made visible as the community rejoices in the gifts that someone has received for ministerial leadership.

In these and other ways, the love of God is made visible to us through actions. Just as we depend on the handshake, the kiss, and the embrace to express our love so others can recognize it, so we depend upon sacraments to know the love of God. We make human love visible by acting it out; divine love is no different. Distinctions between the act and love itself soon disappear. The kiss becomes love itself, the act is part of the emotion. The loving deed is love made visible. The sacraments are God's love made visible.

Fourth, *God's self giving as love is made visible through relationships of love within the community*. Although the sacraments involve a vertical (God to human) relationship, they also involve horizontal (human to human) relationships. The sacraments are social through and through. Everywhere in the biblical narrative, God chooses to act within a community of faithful people. The sacraments function within the community, enabling Christians to build one another up in love, faith, and hope.

The sacraments are visible vehicles of love within the community in two ways. They establish new relationships of love, and they maintain and nourish existing relationships of love. When two persons give themselves to each other in marriage, God acts through the community to strengthen the couple's relationship of love by support and blessing. An ordination without the community of faith would come close to travesty. In baptism and confirmation, we move into a new relationship of love within the community as God incorporates us into Christ's Body. In sickness, God enables the community to surround us by its witness of caring love. Death marks yet another transition in which, by God's grace, we pass into the church triumphant from the church militant. Throughout life's journey, God is offered to us. The eucharist nourishes us, and reconciliation raises us when we stumble. In all these sign-acts we are built up in love, faith, and hope through the establishment of new relationships of love or the maintenance of existing relationships of love within the church.

In either case, it is God who acts within the actions of the community to make these relationships of love fruitful. The community of faith acts to perform the outward and visible forms of the sacraments. But it knows that the *sacramentum* is meaningless without the *res*, that inward giving of God's love. The sacrament and the reality are experienced together as the community gathers to receive God's gift of self expressed as love in visible form. This we experience within the community, which is itself a visible manifestation of God's love. By its sign-acts, the church nurtures our love through new or renewed relationships of love. Of course, such love spills over in mission to God's entire world. Just as God uses the words of a preacher to make God's word audible, so God uses the sacraments to make God's love visible. In the sacraments, God acts in self-giving love made visible through relationships of love in the community.

Much of this will become more clear as we explore the sacraments one by one in subsequent chapters. Although we shall explore in some detail the outward form of each sacrament, the essential concern is not what we do but how the reality of God's love is made manifest in each case. We shall need to remember, when we become preoccupied with the intricacies of matter, form, and ministrant, that what ultimately matters is not what *we* do with each sacrament but what *God* does with it.

SACRAMENTALITY

The practical consequence of all of this is the need to see ministering through the sacraments as employing a special language in which objects and actions provide a new vocabulary. In other words, one needs a sense of sacramentality in order to celebrate the sacraments well. The opposite of this is a form of sacramental minimalism in which the bare minimum necessary to have a valid sacrament is performed. Yes, one can baptize with a medicine dropper, if necessary, and it will be a valid baptism, but any dramatic representation of God's cleansing act of forgiveness will be almost totally absent.

One must begin by observing how humans relate to one another in nonverbal ways. Love, in its demand for visible expression, is our best guide. In this sense, we are dealing with the humanity of the sacraments. There must be an integrity between what we say and what we do. Thus to say "Because there is one loaf, we, who are many, are one body" and then to use precut cubes of bread is a visual contradiction of our words. The act of breaking bread in the eucharist is one of the most significant forms of proclamation of the unity of the Body of Christ. This act gave one of the earliest names to the eucharist (Acts 2:46). One way to visualize this is to think of how one might celebrate the eucharist without spoken words but by dramatizing all the verbs. This is definitely not recommended with congregations, but it might be a good exercise for seminarians. Or how would one preside over the marriage of a couple who were deaf and mute?

Behind all this is a deeper sense of what William Temple called a "sacramental universe."[17] Poets have often caught this better than theologians. George Herbert wrote

> Teach me, my God and King,
> In all things Thee to see,
> And what I do in anything,
> To do it as for Thee.

For that which God doth touch and own
Cannot for less [than gold] be told.[18]

Elizabeth Barrett Browning exclaimed, "Earth's crammed with heaven,/ And every common bush afire with God."[19] And Gerard Manley Hopkins found God in "dappled things." The sense of a sacramental universe means that many experiences of ordinary life can be moments of revelation of God's love, but only if we have a sensitivity to sacramentality.

Above all, we must be certain that when we preside at sacraments that the full sign value is expressed rather than blocked by what we do. The minister's body becomes a means of grace. When we give communion it must be a genuine act of giving, not a quick snatch from someone's hand. Usually this implies a hand to hand touch in the process just as when one gives a gift. The presider must be constantly aware of what his or her body is saying. Above all, it must say this is an important act of God's love. One can learn much from professional dancers who have to have a heightened body consciousness at all times.

Thus the fullness of sign value is paramount. Baptism by immersion is the fullest witness to a life changing event. Persons immersed are dramatically and visually changed by being drenched and all their clothes transformed. God's love is no less if we merely sprinkle or pour, but the witness to it is certainly far less graphic. In dealing with the humanity of the sacraments we have to take very seriously what humans perceive as well as what God does. And this is not merely a matter of the intellect but the perception of the senses—all the senses. Sacramentality, then, is basically taking fully seriously our full humanity. The psalmist wrote: "taste and see that the LORD is good" (Ps. 34:8). That sounds very physical, but it seems to be our God's way of relating to us.

CHAPTER EIGHT

CHRISTIAN INITIATION

o one is born a Christian. One becomes a Christian through becoming part of a community with a distinctive way of life involving definite ethical and creedal commitments. This change in our being is marked by sacraments that proclaim what God is doing to bring us to faith.

In this chapter, we shall survey how Christians experience and understand the ways God acts to initiate us into the community of the faithful. God's love made visible in Christian initiation involves a variety of stages and sign-acts. These may include those relating to the **catechumenate** (period of instruction, catechesis, and examination), those that surround the actual washing of **baptism**, a ubsequent act variously known as **confirmation**, **chrismation**, **affirmation**, or **public profession**, and the final stage, **first communion**. The entire ritual process of the making of a Christian will be referred to as **Christian initiation**, and the individual portions will be named as encountered.

It is not always easy to draw a line between practice and the understanding of it, between rite and reason, between liturgical studies and sacramental theology, but that is the course we shall attempt in this chapter. First we shall survey what Christians have done and are doing now in Christian initiation. Then we shall examine their understandings of these various acts. Finally, some conclusions for pastoral use will be drawn.

THE DEVELOPMENT OF CHRISTIAN INITIATION

Current changes in the practice of initiation are only the latest chapters in a long history of development. Once again we must look for roots in Judaism. The sources lie deep in prophetic symbolism and the use of acts and objects for encountering God. The Jewish belief that the material can affect the spiritual is central to these sacraments.

The most conspicuous Jewish antecedent of initiation was **circumcision**, a sign-act that placed males within the covenant relationship between Israel and God. This sacrament of the old law (as Christians saw it) brought the eight-day-old Jewish male into lifelong relationship with a people with whom God had covenanted to be God and king. Even when Christian writers denied that circumcision could do any more than promise and signify salvation, the concept persisted that one was engrafted into God's people through a sign-act.

More questionable is whether first-century Judaism practiced **proselyte baptism**, that is, of male and female Gentile converts. We know that Judaism eventually did baptize converts, and it seems unlikely that such a practice would have been copied from Christianity. The first-century Qumran community practiced daily ritual washing as a sign of spiritual cleansing. Washing with water is, after all, the obvious natural sign of cleansing, as 1 Peter 3:21 recognizes: "baptism . . . [is] not as a removal of dirt from the body, but as an appeal to God for a good conscience." Acts 22:16 echoes this: "be baptized, and have your sins washed away, calling on his name."

There is no question, though, of the influence of **John the Baptist** who baptized Jesus and many others. Paul interprets: "John baptized with the baptism of repentance, telling the people to believe in one who was to come after him, that is, in Jesus" (Acts 19:4). That sums it up fairly well: John's baptism was a baptism of repentance and a baptism of eschatological expectation of the coming Messiah. It was ethical and anticipatory. The church could never forget that Jesus himself submitted to John's baptism as a part of conforming "in this to fulfill all righteousness" (Matt. 3:15). Thus the weight of Jesus' own act in receiving baptism and in allowing his disciples to baptize (John 4:2) gave paramount authority to baptism. Furthermore, Jesus identified his baptism with his own passion and death (Mark 10:38 and Luke 12:50). Thus baptism became an image of Christ's sacrificial death. Both birth and death are represented in baptism.

Other acts the church appropriated were the **laying on of hands** and **sealing** or **anointing with oil**. Both acts signified the transmission of power and blessing (Isaac blessing Jacob in Genesis 27 or Jacob blessing his grandsons, Genesis 48), or the certification of power (Samuel anointing David in 1 Sam. 16:13). Priestly or royal power seems associated with the use of oil. Both anointing and laying on of hands signify the reception of the gifts of the Holy Spirit for those initiated into the "royal priesthood" (1 Pet. 2:9; Rev. 5:10). The association of "anoint" and the words "Christ" and "Messiah" is clear in Greek or Hebrew.

Much more dubious is the influence of the initiatory rites of the various pagan mystery religions popular in the Roman Empire during the days of the New Testament. Certainly there were conspicuous parallels to Christian initiation in the initiatory rites of some secret sects, but that was probably more a cause of embarrassment to the church than a source of ideas. Justin Martyr dismissed the pagan rites as imitations by "wicked demons" of authentic Christian rites.

The New Testament itself gives us only tantalizingly brief glimpses of actual initiatory practices. But what we see there has become determinative for all subsequent developments. Easily the most detailed account of a baptism is Philip's baptism of the Ethiopian eunuch in Acts 8:35-38. Verse 37 (bracketed here) is absent in some texts but present in others. The whole is worth repeating.

Then Philip began to speak, and starting with this scripture, he proclaimed to him the good news about Jesus. As they were going along the road, they came to some water; and the eunuch said, "Look, here is water! What is to prevent me from being baptized?" [And Philip said, "If you believe with all your heart, you may." And he replied, "I believe that Jesus Christ is the Son of God."] He commanded the chariot to stop, and both of them, Philip and the eunuch, went down into the water, and Philip baptized him.

We begin with a form of catechesis, Philip instructing the eunuch. Then comes a profession of the eunuch's faith in which he gives the correct creedal statement. Whereupon they go down "into" *(eis)* the water and Philip baptizes the eunuch. It is essentially the core of baptism as still practiced today.

The creedal statement focuses on the second member of the Trinity, not the whole Trinity. There are other texts that indicate that the earliest Christian baptisms were "in the name of Jesus Christ" (Acts 2:38; 8:12 and 16; 10:48; 19:5; 22:16). Paul makes a short creedal statement in Romans 10:9: "if you confess with your lips that Jesus is Lord" and repeats it in Philippians 2:11: "and every tongue should confess that Jesus Christ is Lord." Consequently, it is all the more problematic that Matthew 28:19 gives a baptismal formula that is clearly trinitarian and which says literally: "baptizing them in the name of the Father and of the Son and of the Holy Spirit." Very likely this represents a second stage of development in actual liturgical practice and was read back into the words of the Lord by the evangelist. This is corroborated by the *Didache* which uses exactly the same baptismal formula. Virtually all baptismal rites since have used the same trinitarian formula.

The witness to the laying on of hands is far more perplexing. The Ethiopian eunuch story makes no mention of it, but this act occurs repeatedly in ambiguous and conflicting passages in Acts. For moderns, this raises questions about the relation of reception of the Holy Spirit to baptism. Acts 2:38 links repentance, baptism, the forgiveness of sins, and the gift of the Holy Spirit. But at Caesarea, the Holy Spirit was poured out before baptism (Acts 10:47); whereas in Samaria, the newly baptized did not receive the Holy Spirit until they received the laying on of hands (Acts 8:17). At Ephesus, after baptism "when Paul had laid his hands on them, the Holy Spirit came upon them" (Acts 19:6). Two things seem likely from these accounts: the Holy Spirit and baptism are directly and intimately related and the laying on of hands or sealing (anointing) (2 Cor. 1:22, Eph. 1:13 and 4:30) seems to testify to this link by emphasizing the presence of the Spirit in those being baptized.

There has been speculation on whether 1 Peter is a baptismal sermon. It addresses its audience as "newborn infants" (2:2 NEB) who "are now the people of God, who once were not his people" (2:10

NEB). The waters of Noah's flood are seen as prefiguring baptism (3:21), an allusion echoed in baptismal rites down to the present. And baptism is compared to a clean conscience (3:21).

Practical problems began to emerge as the church started to age. Hebrews raises the question of apostasy by those who have been baptized: "For it is impossible to restore again to repentance those who have once been enlightened, and have tasted the heavenly gift, and have shared in the Holy Spirit . . . and then have fallen away" (6:4-6). This problem has vexed the church ever since: how to deal with the backslider. The *Shepherd of Hermas*, from the second century, is a bit more lenient. Acknowledging that some deny any repentance beyond baptism, the author concedes that "after that great and holy calling [baptism], if a man be tempted by the devil and sin, he has one repentance, but if he sin and repent repeatedly it is unprofitable."[1]

In modern times, the most troubling problem has been whether the New Testament accounts are compatible with the **baptism of infants (pedobaptism)**. There is explicit evidence neither for nor against the baptism of infants in the New Testament. Those who practice infant baptism are apt to be convinced that the *oĩkos* (household) passages which speak of the baptism of whole households (Acts 16:15 and 33; 18:8; 1 Cor. 1:16) are likely to have included children of the family or of resident slaves. Since the father usually determined the religion of the whole family, it is likely, they argue, that baptism was applied to all within the household as a matter of course. Those who do not practice infant baptism are prone to argue against such practice on the basis that the demands for repentance and faith on the part of those to be baptized (Mark 16:16; Acts 2:38) preclude baptism of infants.

On historical evidence alone, we must agree with Kurt Aland that "infant baptism is certainly provable only from the third century,"[2] though there are some theological grounds for asserting that it was practiced in New Testament times.[3] The earliest irrefutable historical evidence is in very early third-century passages of Tertullian, who deplores the baptism of "little children," who may later embarrass their sponsors, and in a contemporary passage of *The Apostolic Tradition*, which speaks of baptizing the "little children" *(parvulos)* first—some of whom apparently cannot yet "speak for themselves." The document, obviously, is speaking of a practice long familiar but for how long? Is it apostolic or not? We have no proof either way. By the fifth century, infant baptism was widespread. Ever since, most Christians have practiced the baptism of infants.

The second-century church fills out more details of initiation practices beyond the hints the New Testament accounts give us. The *Didache* forbids those unbaptized "in the Lord's name" from eating and drinking the eucharist. Those about to be baptized are to fast. Baptism is preferably in cold running water but, lacking this, water is poured "thrice upon the candidate's head in the name of the Father, Son, and Holy Spirit."[4] Justin Martyr gives slightly more detail (c. 155). The catechumenate involves instruction, the promise to "live accordingly," prayer, and fasting. Baptism is at a place "where there is water," and candidates are washed in the name of the Trinity. Those baptized are then led to where the church is assembled and share, for the first time, in common prayer, the kiss of peace, and the eucharist.[5]

Much more information appears in the next century in Tertullian's treatise *On Baptism* (c. 200) and scattered throughout his other writings. Tertullian indicates a rigorous discipline for those about to be baptized involving "prayers, fasts, and bendings of the knee, and vigils all the night through."[6] The most solemn occasion for baptism, he tells us, is the Pascha. The Day of Pentecost comes second though any moment is possible. The normal administrant is the bishop, if present, then authorized presbyters and deacons, but "even laymen have the right, for what is equally received can be equally given."[7] Just before baptism comes **renunciation** of "the devil, and his pomp and his angels." Candidates are "thrice immersed" after "interrogations rather more extensive than our Lord has prescribed"[8] and then "thoroughly anointed with a blessed unction" such as Moses used to anoint Aaron into the priesthood. Next, "The hand is laid on in blessing, invoking and inviting the Holy Spirit as Jacob blessed his grandsons."[9] Yet another Old Testament image appears in the act of giving the newly baptized "a mixture of milk and honey," a symbol of the promised land (Exod. 3:8).

The Apostolic Tradition corroborates all of this, giving us extensive detail, particularly on a long and rigorous catechumenate which could last as long as three years. During this strenuous period, catechumens are **hearers of the word**, attending the service of the Word, but they cannot pray with the faithful, give the kiss of peace, or remain for the eucharist. Advanced and suitable candidates (the elect) are set apart each year and their conduct examined (eventually ritualized as the **scrutinies**). They undergo a period of intense preparation with daily exorcism. The candidates fast on what is probably our Good Friday and Holy Saturday.

The climax of the initiation process, presumably, occurs on Easter morning after an all-night vigil of scripture reading and instruction. At cockcrow, prayer is made over the water, the candidates undress, and the bishop prepares oils of exorcism and thanksgiving. Then, after the renunciation of Satan, each candidate is anointed thoroughly with oil of exorcism, goes down into the water, and is asked three questions, which are virtually the words of the **Apostles' Creed** (which, to this day, the West uses as the baptismal creed). Each time, after affirming belief in a different member of the Trinity, the candidate is baptized. After the third washing, he or she comes up out of the water and is anointed with the oil of thanksgiving "in the name of Jesus Christ." Then, after dressing, the newly baptized go to meet the assembled church where the bishop lays hands on each, asking God to "make them worthy to be filled with Thy Holy Spirit."[10] The bishop then pours holy oil and lays his hands on the heads of each. Finally, the bishop seals each in the name of the Trinity, making the sign of the cross on their foreheads (**consignation**), and gives each the kiss of peace.

The new Christians now join the congregation for the first time in prayer, the kiss of peace, and the eucharist. On this paschal occasion, there are three cups: water ("a token of the laver"), milk and honey (the promised land), and wine. As can be seen, the whole rite has a variety of actions, all involving a strong sense of touch: anointings, washing, laying on of hands, signing, embracing (the kiss of peace), and eating and drinking.

Other pre-Nicene materials add a few details. The third-century *Didascalia Apostolorum* stresses the need for a "woman deacon" to "anoint the women . . . for the ministry of a woman deacon is especially needful and important,"[11] especially given the practice of baptism in the nude. Egeria tells us that in late–fourth-century Jerusalem at the beginning of Lent the names of those to be baptized that Easter (the *competentes*) are given in.[12] After inquiry into their lifestyles, three hours of daily catechizing and exorcism takes place. After five weeks, they are given the creed to learn, which they must recite back after seven weeks, one by one, to the bishop who examines their understanding. Egeria noted nothing much unfamiliar in the paschal vigil but mentions the eight days of Easter week when the newly initiated have interpreted to them all the sacraments that they have just experienced for the first time.

Fortunately, several examples of this method of **mystagogical catechesis** on the meaning of the sacraments of initiation have survived in the forms of lectures given by Ambrose in Milan, Cyril (or his successor) in Jerusalem, and John Chrysostom and Theodore of Mopsuestia in Antioch. Ambrose tells the new Christians the meaning of the *ephphatha*, the ceremonial opening and blessing of the ears and nostrils (Mark 7:34). Then: "Thou wast anointed as Christ's athlete; as about to wrestle in the fight of this world."[13] After baptism, there is a foot washing, though Ambrose is aware that Rome does not do this.

Cyril gives us much more detail and elaborates on symbolic meanings: "Ye were stripped, ye were anointed with exorcised oil, from the very hairs of your head to your feet, and were made partakers of the good olive tree, Jesus Christ."[14] Theodore adds other details such as the role of the sponsor and clothing the newly baptized in a radiant garment. John Chrysostom gives us the **adhesion** or pledge after the renunciation, "And I enter into thy service, O Christ." He also uses the typical passive Eastern baptismal formula: "_____ is baptized in the name of the Father, and of the Son, and of the Holy Spirit," in contrast to the active form the West adopted subsequently: "_____, I baptize you . . . ." Chrysostom also tells us the candidate's head is thrice lowered into the water and raised.[15]

The most perplexing part of these rites is the variety of anointings and signings. **Anointing** tended to be originally a covering of the body with oil much as soap is used in bathing today, thus suggesting a preliminary to the bath of baptism or preparation for an athletic contest. **Signing** or marking with the sign of the cross (sometimes with oil) is a form of sealing or giving definite identity to the newly baptized. It is all the more puzzling since early Syrian rites knew only a pre-baptismal anointing, conveying the meaning of priesthood, kingship, and gift of the Spirit. As early as the fourth century, in some places, these post-baptismal acts had become associated with the gift of the Holy Spirit. Ambrose speaks of the "spiritual seal, . . . when, at the invocation of the priest, the Holy Spirit is bestowed" and lists the sevenfold gifts given (Isa. 11:2f).[16] Cyril calls anointing "the emblem of the Holy Spirit."

In summation, the early church's rites of initiation involved the whole community. The full rites of initiation came at Easter at the end of a long catechumenate and consisted of a variety of acts at the Easter vigil: anointings, ethical renunciation, creedal profession, washing, laying on of hands, sealing, and eucharist. Post-baptismal catechesis followed. The whole process of conversion, from first inquiry to final and complete commitment, all became ritualized and was eventually tied directly to the celebration of the resurrection.

Much of this was to change with the advance of the Middle Ages. In the East, the whole process of initiation was kept together by having the priest perform the whole rite using **chrism** (olive oil and balm) consecrated by the bishop for the final anointing. This portion of the Eastern rite is known as **chrismation**. It corresponded to the laying on of hands for confirmation, which the West insisted must be done by a bishop. But the West saw a slow movement toward fragmentation and privatization of the whole. The disintegration of the unity of the rite was long and unconscious, not really complete until the end of the Middle Ages. (As late as 1533, the future English Queen Elizabeth I was baptized and confirmed three days after birth, a practice soon made impossible by the 1549 *Book of Common Prayer*.) Unfortunately, most of these changes came about for nontheological reasons. In Italy, there was a bishop in every sizable town, and it was possible to have initiation with all its parts at one time (Easter) and place (a baptistery such as those in Pisa, Parma, or Florence). But as Christianity spread into the geographically vast tribal dioceses of northern Europe, it became impossible to bring everyone to the bishop for his part in the rite. What worked in Italy did not work elsewhere and the bishop's portion of initiation was simply postponed though there was experimentation in allowing priests to do the complete rite in Gaul, Spain, and Ireland.

The origins of **confirmation** are problematic although Ambrose used a verb form of it in the context of sealing in *Of the Mysteries*. In the fifth century, "to confirm" applied to the post-baptismal anointing and hand laying by the bishop, but not until the ninth century did it "become the normal term to use of this part of the initiatory rite."[17] Slowly its meaning changed from that of "to complete" to that of "to strengthen."

Other factors brought about changes too. A catechumenate made no sense for infants. The pressure of Augustine's theology and the fear of infants dying unbaptized, and thus being excluded from the Kingdom (John 3:5), brought about the custom of having infants baptized within a few days of birth. Even so, as late as the thirteenth century, people in some places waited until the paschal season for baptism.

Other factors separated the various parts of initiation. First communion followed baptism for infants well into the Middle Ages. As late as the twelfth century, infants were still communicated by receiving in their mouths the priest's little finger dipped in the wine. Fear of spilling the consecrated wine eventually led to suspending reception of the wine by all laity of whatever age. Children were denied communion until they reached the age of reason but "infant communion . . . was not finally abolished in the West until the Council of Trent."[18] Confirmation was gradually postponed until the years of discretion, which came to mean at least seven years of age. For vast numbers of medieval people and long after the Reformation, this meant that the practical difficulties of meeting a bishop rendered confirmation an unlikely event. Confirmation was desirable, but unlike baptism, not a necessity for salvation.

By the late–Middle Ages, infants were baptized within eight days after birth by being dipped in the font in their parish church in a private ceremony. Then, they might be confirmed after reaching the age of seven (usually in a private ceremony, too) if they chanced on a bishop. And at this age they could receive communion, whether confirmed or not. The whole corporate and paschal character of initiation had been shattered along with its unity. Dipping of infants was slowly yielding to pouring as the Middle Ages ended.

The Protestant Reformers made two significant advances with baptism. They insisted that it be made a public office and in the vernacular. The 1549 and 1552 *BCP* insist that it be administered on "Sundays and other holy days, when the most number of people may come together." The Reformers also simplified the ceremonies. Unlike his first (1523) rite, Luther's 1526 *Order of Baptism Newly Revised*[19] omitted breathing on the child, the giving of salt, the first exorcism, the *ephphatha*, the two anointings, and the lighted candle, though he retained the white robe. It is a severe pruning of accessory ceremonies, but Calvin went even further, "abolishing them, so that there might be no more impediment to prevent the people from going directly to Jesus Christ."[20] Calvin added, instead, didactic exhortations.

The Church of England at first preserved most of the medieval ceremonial. Retained were an exorcism and procession into the church to the font (both abolished in 1552), dipping the child thrice in the font so as to cover the entire body, the chrisom robe and anointing (both abolished in 1552), and the sign of the cross (which became a stumbling block to the Puritans). John Wesley followed the same rite with considerable modifications. In his early years, he insisted on dipping the infant but late in life gave sprinkling as an alternative mode.

The most radical changes came about among the **Anabaptists** who insisted that the only proper candidates for baptism were adult believers. They maintained that baptism should be given only to those of known purity of life and doctrine. They preferred the pure church, consisting of believers, to the state church consisting of everyone. Anabaptists were no less adamant on reconciliation; the **ban** was imposed on any fellowship with baptized backsliders, who could only be reconciled after a period of public ignominy.

The earliest Anabaptists practiced baptism chiefly by pouring. Eventually, some groups, such as the English Baptists, came to demand immersion, although some Anabaptists, such as Mennonites, practice pouring. Some Roman Catholics and Protestants continued to baptize infants by dipping, but this had virtually disappeared by the eighteenth century. Current efforts to revive the practice are making only slow progress, partly due to insufficient fonts.

An early Anabaptist baptismal order by **Balthasar Hübmaier,** "A Form for Baptism," indicates that candidates must first be examined about faith by the bishop, then presented to the congregation. The rite involves prayer for the Holy Spirit to fill the candidates' hearts, creedal questions based on an amended Apostles' Creed, renunciation, questions on willing obedience and desire to be baptized, baptism, prayers, laying on of hands, and welcome into "the fellowship of Christians."[21] Though rejecting infant baptism, some Anabaptists, such as Hübmaier and Pilgram Marpeck, advocated a public service of infant dedication.

At first, English Baptists practiced laying on of hands at baptism.[22] Since only believers were baptized, Anabaptists and Baptists alike had no need for a separate rite of confirmation. Christian initiation was complete at one event, as it had been in the early church.

Quakers took an even more radical step. They eliminated any outward act, insisting that the Bible commanded none but commended, instead, an inward "baptism in the Spirit." Twentieth-century Pentecostals distinguish between the two. Water baptism they practice (usually) for adult believers and usually by triune immersion, but baptism of the Spirit is a separate manifestation of charismatic gifts.

Confirmation was a problem for the Reformers. Luther did not draw up a rite but did not object "if every pastor examines the faith of the children . . . lays hands on them, and confirms them."[23] Martin Bucer cast the die for subsequent Reformed and Anglican developments by tying confirmation to an examination of the child on his or her knowledge of the catechism. Partly as an antidote to Anabaptists, Bucer probably introduced in Strasbourg a confirmation service that was more an examination and graduation ceremony than anything else, although the pastor does conclude by stretching his hands out over the children with a blessing.[24] Calvin followed suit after a diatribe about confirmation "doing injustice to baptism." He preferred "a catechizing, in which children or those near adolescence would give an account of their faith before the church."[25] The Church of England agreed in restricting confirmation to "such as can say in their mother tongue, the articles of the faith, the Lord's Prayer, and the ten commandments" (1549 *BCP*). The bishop was the minister, making the sign of the cross on the forehead (1549) and laying his hand upon their heads (1549 and 1552). Confirmation was made requisite for admission to communion, thus ratifying the late medieval end to centuries of infant communion.

The unfortunate consequence of these developments was that confirmation came to be contingent upon human knowledge—the learning of the catechism. The sacramental sense of the laying on of hands as a gracious act of God became dissipated in favor of a graduation exercise. The Reformers' misreading of church history led them to salvage confirmation in a way that caused new problems. Later, the Puritans devised an act of **profession of faith** as a substitute. This had no sacramental overtones, it was simply a public profession of one's belief, often linked to acknowledging the covenant on which a local congregation was based.

All in all, the Reformation saw more subtraction than addition in the rites of initiation. Recent years have seen new directions with Roman Catholics and several Protestant traditions often converging.

The most common move has been toward recovering the **unity of the initiatory rites**. The most striking instance of this occurs in the Roman Catholic *Rite of Christian Initiation of Adults* (R.C.I.A.). This represents a recovery of the extended catechumenate, which ritualizes the whole process of conversion so that the congregation shares in the individual's growth in faith. The catechumenate is spread out over months, or even years, in three stages or gateways. It begins with the inquirer reaching the state of acceptance as a catechumen, continues when the catechumenate nears completion with election or enrollment of names at the beginning of Lent, and concludes with reception of the three initiatory sacraments at Easter. Lent is used as a period of enlightenment or illumination, marked on three Sundays by scrutinies, exorcisms, and presentation and recitation of the Apostles' Creed and Lord's Prayer. The whole is a recovery of primitive practice refined to fit the life of a missionary church in the world today. The "Rite of

Baptism for Several Children" and "Rite of Confirmation within Mass" have been simplified, congregational participation has been increased, and a greater emphasis has been placed on the use of scripture. The baptism of children now testifies to greater responsibility on the part of parents.

A different course has been taken by Lutherans, Episcopalians, United Methodists, and Presbyterians in stressing the unity of the initiatory rites. These downplay confirmation as a separate and distinct rite but introduce subsequent occasions of **affirmation, reaffirmation,** or **renewal** of baptismal promises by all the congregation. The new Episcopal service advocates that the bishop be the normal celebrant as far as possible. There is a laying on of hands on all those being baptized, and chrism may be used in making the sign of the cross. The service may continue for others with confirmation, reception ("into the fellowship of this Communion"), and reaffirmation. The whole is to be set normally in the context of the eucharist. The Lutheran rite contains the laying on of hands and consignation immediately after baptism. A separate service, "Affirmation of Baptism," provides possibilities of confirmation, reception into membership, and restoration to membership. The 1989 United Methodist "Services of the Baptismal Covenant" also combine water baptism and laying on of hands and provide for confirmation and other reaffirmations of the baptismal covenant in addition to reception into The United Methodist Church and reception into a local congregation. The central prayer, the thanksgiving over the water, is recovered after a sixty-year absence. The whole congregation is encouraged to participate annually, especially at Easter, Pentecost, All Saints, or Baptism of the Lord, in reaffirmation of their own baptism. The Presbyterian reforms are similar.

Mention should also be made of the "Renewal of Baptismal Promises" now part of the Easter Vigil among Roman Catholics. The "Renewal of Baptismal Vows" occurs on the same occasion among Episcopalians and Lutherans. A service of covenant renewal at the start of the new year is an alternative practice among United Methodists.

A common note in most of the new initiatory rites has been concentration on the essential actions: the ethical change expressed by the renunciation, the creedal change expressed by the trinitarian affirmation, the blessing of the water, the washing of baptism, the laying on of hands or sealing, and the first eucharist. Accessory actions such as multiple anointings, the *ephphatha*, the giving of salt, the white garment, and the lighted candle tend to be optional or have been eliminated. The recent reforms include recovery of many early practices and a critical approach to later developments.

THEOLOGY OF CHRISTIAN INITIATION

Baptism in the New Testament is in an eschatological context, beginning with the baptism of John the Baptist in the urgency of his preaching for repentance: "Repent, for the kingdom of heaven has come near" (Matt. 3:3). Baptism is done in the expectation of the nearness of the kingdom. Occasionally, entire families were baptized as a unit so that none would be left behind (1 Cor. 1:16; Acts 16:15, 33; 18:18). Baptism gives entrance to the kingdom: "no one can enter the kingdom of God without being born of water and Spirit" (John 3:5).

As the rites changed over the centuries, there were equally important shifts in the ways Christians understood what they experienced in initiation. We cannot understand the rites themselves without examining the concepts they gave expression to and how the rites were instrumental in shaping ideas about themselves in turn.

The New Testament witness to initiation is fascinating and complex. A vast array of hints and metaphors is thrown out on what initiation meant to the first Christians, but no systematic exposition of these ideas appears in scripture. Nevertheless, these biblical metaphors are the foundation of all subsequent attempts at understanding what God is doing through the rites of initiation.

For the sake of convenience, we can identify the principal **five New Testament metaphors of initiation**. This should not blind us to the fact that there are other minor themes in the New Testament relating to initiation; naming the name of Jesus, sealing, salvation from eschatological doom, and entering the royal priesthood are some of them. But these five chief metaphors or themes seem to be used most frequently and to have had the most influence on both faith and practice. They are union with Jesus Christ, incorporation into the church, new birth, forgiveness of sin, and reception of the Holy Spirit.[26]

We shall begin with the metaphor of initiation as bringing one into **union with Jesus Christ**. Paul expresses it thus:

Do you not know that all of us who have been baptized into Christ Jesus were baptized into his death? Therefore we have been buried with him by baptism into death, so that, just as Christ was raised from the dead by the glory of the Father, so we too might walk in newness of life.

For if we have been united with him in a death like his, we will certainly be united with him in a resurrection like his. (Rom. 6:3-5)

The same idea recurs in Colossians 2:12. Baptism conveys to each one baptized both the death of Jesus and the possibility of resurrection through him. What Christ has done is done for the individual named in baptism. It is a personalizing and internalizing of the climax of history as holy events are given to individuals through union with both the person and the work of Christ. We become priests with him and die and rise with him. The ancient practice of designing baptisteries so as to suggest a going down into and rising from a watery grave is a way to make literal this sharing in Christ's death and resurrection.

Very closely related to this theme is that of **incorporation into the church**, Christ's Body. Paul says, "For in the one Spirit we were all baptized into one body" (1 Cor. 12:13). Probably the most egalitarian statement in all of scripture is Paul's assertion that for those "baptized into Christ . . . there is no longer Jew or Greek, there is no longer slave or free, there is no longer male and female; for all of you are one in Christ Jesus" (Gal. 3:27-28; see also 1 Cor. 12:13). Baptism is the sign-act of entrance into the church no matter at what age it is practiced. Hence fonts are often placed near the entrance to church buildings and some rites involve an entrance procession into the midst of the building and people.

Initiation is also the **new birth**. Closely tied to union with Christ in death and resurrection and to joining a new body, the church, the Johannine image of new birth appears in Jesus' discussion with Nicodemus: "no one can enter the kingdom of God without being born of water and Spirit" (John 3:5). Implicit in this image is being a new creature in Christ Jesus, having put one's past, the Old Adam, behind one. Titus 3:5 ("He saved us . . . through the water of rebirth and renewal by the Holy Spirit") uses the key word, *paliggenesía,* or regeneration. This term has often been the source of controversy. New birth is the most feminine of images, and some fonts have been designed to suggest a pregnant woman. Baptism is spoken of as both womb and tomb.

The most obvious thing about baptism (so obvious it is often overlooked) is the cleansing action of water representing the **forgiveness of sin.** In Acts 22:16, Ananias commands: "be baptized, and have your sins washed away" (see also 1 Cor. 6:11). Both 1 Peter (3:21) and Hebrews (10:22) compare baptism with an outward washing and the inward cleansing. The relation of baptism and forgiveness is clear in Acts 2:38: "Repent, and be baptized every one of you in the name of Jesus Christ so that your sins may be forgiven." It became dogma in the Nicene Creed: "one Baptism for the remission of sins." The act of washing in baptism and the pre-baptismal anointing with oil are the most obvious enactments of forgiveness. The giving of a new white garment after baptism reinforces the idea of a newly clean conscience, and the putting on of Christ (Gal. 3:27).

Reception of the Holy Spirit is a complex metaphor partly because the eventual splintering of the rites of initiation in the West has raised questions about the role and timing of this reception. When this metaphor is seen in conjunction with incorporation into the church, some of these problems disappear. The church is the environment of the Holy Spirit's activity. One cannot be a part of the Spirit-filled community and not receive the Holy Spirit. *The Apostolic Tradition* repeats the refrain, "in the Holy Spirit and the holy church," suggesting where the Holy Spirit is known and experienced. The Acts 2:38 passage quoted above continues "and you will receive the gift of the Holy Spirit." Jesus' own baptism has a theophany of the Holy Spirit visible as a dove (Matt. 3:16). Sometimes, as we have seen, the coming of the Spirit seems manifested most clearly by one portion of initiation, the laying on of hands (Acts 19:1-7). Other images seem to refer to the activity in initiation of the Holy Spirit: "illumination" or being "enlightened" (Heb. 6:4) or being "sanctified" (1 Cor. 6:11). The giving of salt (wisdom) or a lighted candle (preparedness) to those just baptized and the visual symbol of the dove underscore the Spirit's work in initiation.

The most important witness in the New Testament accounts is that initiation is far deeper than any single interpretation of it. Our problem is to obtain a balanced understanding that does justice to all five chief metaphors. All subsequent developments are to be held accountable to this standard of balanced understanding. Initiation is a jewel with many facets. We do not sense its full brilliance until we see all facets reflecting the light.

Probably as concise as possible a statement of these five metaphors occurs in Justin Martyr's two short accounts of initiation in his *First Apology*. He speaks of being "made new through Christ," being led into and greeted by the Christian assembly, the "rebirth by which we ourselves were reborn," the repentance of sins and being "washed in the water," and the "washing which is called illumination."[27] Irenaeus combines several of these themes by speaking of baptism as the water without which "dry flour cannot be united into a lump of dough, or a loaf . . . so we who are many cannot be made one in Christ Jesus without the water which comes from heaven."[28] Clement of Alexandria favors the theme of "enlightenment"; others of the Fathers have their favorites but taken together there seems to be a fair degree of balance. What a person does not find in one is likely to appear in another.

Unfortunately this balance was always a fortuitous matter and always subject to extraneous pressure. In this case, it came about in a most unintentional fashion. Augustine, who made a fairly balanced use of these metaphors himself, as a result of the controversy with Pelagius pushed the church very strongly in the direction of looking at baptism as the remedy for two kinds of sin: original, that is, the guilt we all inherit from Adam's sin, and actual, that which we commit ourselves.[29] It is a bit ironic that Augustine himself was not baptized until fairly late in life, but the consequence of his systematic development of existing concepts of original sin was to hasten the baptism of infants for fear that children dying unbaptized would be brought by the guilt of original sin to the gates of hell.

The whole medieval development tilted emphasis in the direction of the forgiveness of sin, especially that of original sin in the case of infants. As we have seen, the paschaltide portrayal of union with Christ was underplayed, while incorporation into the church, when that was equivalent to civil society itself, was of relatively little account. The sense of new birth lost much of its drama when only infants were baptized. The teaching of the work of the Holy Spirit was undernourished in the West, and baptism was a good example of such malnutrition. Peter Lombard has much to say about baptism, but it boils down to one word: "remission."[30] The forgiveness of sin is an important part of the biblical witness to initiation, but when it became so dominant that it crowded out the other themes we cannot but feel that a one-sided understanding of what God does in initiation had occurred.

One of the saddest of the medieval developments was in the understanding of confirmation. We have seen how this portion of initiation was segregated in the West because of conservatism in limiting it to a bishop. Throughout its whole subsequent history, confirmation has been a practice looking for a theology. Peter Lombard could find very little to say about confirmation (two pages), but he said all the early medieval church had provided: "The virtue moreover of the sacrament is the gift of the Holy Spirit for strength, who is given in baptism for remission." Lombard goes on to attribute to Rabanus the statement that one is strengthened through the laying on of hands "to proclaim to others that which he has attained in baptism."[31] Lombard also suggests that confirmation is needed "to be complete Christians." A sermon of the fifth-century Faustus of Riez had apparently first suggested the terminology that "after baptism we are confirmed for combat," leading "to confirm" to be identified with "to strengthen." These are the raw materials, and practically the only raw materials, the scholastics had with which to build their systems.

The 1439 *Decree for the Armenians* sums up the late medieval development (or lack of it) by telling us: "In this sacrament the Holy Spirit is given to strengthen us, . . . that the Christian may confess boldly the name of Christ."[32] The matter "is the chrism made from oil . . . and from balsam . . . blessed by the bishop. The form is: 'I sign with the sign of the cross and confirm thee with the chrism of salvation, in the name. . . .' " The normal ministrant is the bishop though occasionally a priest can administer it with chrism blessed by a bishop. Shorn of connection to baptism, confirmation became a dangling participle.

By the time of the Reformation, baptism, confirmation, and first communion had become almost everywhere detached entities. The Council of Trent simply solidified late medieval practices and beliefs. Baptism was not a strong point of controversy between most Protestants and Roman Catholics, though a lively debate developed within Protestantism over it. The Reformers do not sort out conveniently as to our five New Testament metaphors of initiation, though we can point out certain centers of gravity among them. The fear that infants dying unbaptized could not be saved troubled them less so that forgiveness of sins tended to recede from dominance. But new considerations, such as the doctrine of election, brought new pressures.

Luther shows some of the most profound insights, insights that still have not yet been fully appropriated. Luther's special stress is on baptism as a "promise" in which, as he says, "Christ is given us." What ensues is a lifelong covenant relationship of faith whereby our baptism is victorious over doubt and sin, for "baptism is in force all through life." Indeed, in moments of deepest despair Luther could assert that "I am baptized, and through my baptism God, who cannot lie, has bound himself in a covenant with me."[33] And in a famous line he exclaims, "There is no greater comfort on earth than baptism."[34] Luther suggests the possibility of looking at the whole Christian life in terms of a baptismal spirituality, that is, as a lifelong living out of one's baptism. Luther comes close to stressing union with Jesus Christ and forgiveness of sin as his dominant images.

Zwingli introduced a new concept altogether: that baptism is merely a dedicatory sign. He bases his argument on the Romans 6:3-5 passage, which he interprets figuratively. Baptism, for Zwingli too, is union with Christ, but he is leery of physical signs for "it is clear and indisputable that no external element or action can purify the soul." "Hence," he concludes, "water-baptism is nothing but an external ceremony, that is, an outward sign that we are incorporated and engrafted into the Lord Jesus Christ and pledged to live to him and to follow him."[35] Zwingli's concept of baptism as badge of profession, as pledge, or as covenant sign, tends to make of it an external matter of record rather than the source of a warm inward relationship, as in Luther. Zwingli also sets the precedent for thinking of infant baptism as a dedication rite, a theme popular among some American Protestants.

Calvin deplores Zwingli's view of baptism as simply a "token or mark" of profession. Calvin stresses baptism's power to save through forgiveness or cleansing and union to Christ. But the predominant metaphor for him seems to be that of being "received into the society of the church, in order that, engrafted in Christ, we may be reckoned among God's children."[36] He is concerned to refute the Anabaptist critique of infant baptism. Infants too, Calvin insists, are within the covenant and members of the church.

The Anabaptists, of course, insisted that "young children are without understanding and unteachable; therefore baptism cannot be administered to them without perverting the ordinance of the Lord, misusing His exalted name, and doing violence to His holy Word."[37] Clearly, for them, baptism was to be contingent upon human faith and repentance. Only those already reborn could join the baptismal covenant. Although the Anabaptists' concepts of the church are quite different from Calvin's, incorporation into the company of regenerate believers is probably their dominant theme. For many of them, baptism involved not only water and spirit but also their own blood of suffering and martyrdom (1 John 5:6-8) during constant persecution. They taught and lived as if all of life was a baptism.

The Anglican prayers in the 1549 and 1552 baptismal services achieved a remarkably good balance of the biblical metaphors partly because they tend to collect biblical images. The "Articles of Religion" called baptism "a sign of Regeneration or new Birth," a phrase that caused controversy in the nineteenth century about whether baptism caused or merely signified regeneration. Anglicans retained confirmation, but by 1552 it had become more a rite praying for strengthening than an objective conferring of grace.

John Wesley added further complications by placing an emphasis on **conversion** as a necessary part of the Christian life after infant baptism. For reasons not entirely clear, he omitted confirmation while retaining most parts of the Anglican rites of baptism. Nineteenth-century Methodists instituted a service of **Reception of Members** after a period of probation for those already baptized. This was eventually replaced by calling those baptized as infants "preparatory members" until they were received as "full members" or (after 1964) confirmed. This distinction is now the subject of controversy.

The recent past has seen some important developments in efforts to understand Christian initiation. It has become a center of much controversy and some enlightenment. A storm was stirred up by a lecture given by **Karl Barth** to Swiss theological students in 1943 and first published in English five years later as *The Teaching of the Church Regarding Baptism*.[38] In it, Barth contended that infant baptism "is necessarily clouded baptism" and that only adults capable of understanding the event should receive baptism. Essentially Barth's approach was a cognitive one; baptism is a "representation" or "message" to the one baptized. By contrast, another Swiss theologian, **Oscar Cullmann**, replied that baptism is causative in that it places a person within the community where faith becomes possible rather than simply informing that person of something. Cullmann insisted that, potentially, Christ has died for all and that this is made actual when one is incorporated into the church and receives the possibility of growing up in an environment of faith.[39]

The fray was also joined on strictly historical grounds by two New Testament scholars, Joachim Jeremias and Kurt Aland.[40] The debate is by no means resolved, as *Baptism, Eucharist, and Ministry* clearly shows.[41] All Christian bodies from Baptists to Roman Catholics currently express doubts over their own practices and teachings. Baptists have misgivings about treating children as outside the church; Roman Catholics fear that all too often many baptized children never become part of the church's life.

Much of the debate over infant baptism versus believer's baptism seems to be a shortcut around more basic questions about the nature of sacraments. If a sacrament is a self-giving act of God, cannot infants or anyone else receive its benefits? If, on the other hand, we are speaking of an ordinance that is basically a high-level bit of religious education, a pious memory exercise or representation, then can it be appropriate for a person who has not reached an age of reason? Thus most pedobaptists and those baptizing only believers can never agree because they begin with two entirely different concepts of sacraments, an act of God or a human act.

In recent years, the whole question of the unity of Christian initiation has also become an important issue. This is resolved, of course, in believer's baptism because the ritual event is a single one, but it increasingly seems an anomaly for those who baptize infants not to welcome them into the fullness of the family of God by sharing in communion. In some denominations, this has resulted in making initiation complete at one age, with baptism, laying on of hands, and communion coming together at whatever age. Infants receive a small amount of communion wine. To refuse communion to baptized children now seems to make membership in the Body of Christ contingent upon the ability to think conceptually. The more we learn about child development the more questionable such a restriction becomes.[42]

Practical questions cannot be settled apart from study of the whole issue: What is initiation itself? Here the chief way forward seems to be by recovering the richness of all the biblical images with a clear sense of balance. Initiation is forgiveness of sin but it is also incorporation into the church and other themes as well. The new initiatory rites are hopeful signs that this biblical balance is being recovered.

PASTORAL ASPECTS OF CHRISTIAN INITIATION

Numerous pastoral possibilities arise out of the current ferment in initiation rites and theology. We shall mention three prime practical concerns. First and foremost is that initiation is **evangelism**. This was obvious to the early church, which grew by initiation. It was a lesson the modern church has been slow to learn despite the great missionary expansion of the last few centuries. Initiation is how the church grows.

There are several practical implications from this. Initiation must cease to be "promiscuous," that is, unrestricted and indiscriminate. Strangers who call to have the baby "done" or unfamiliar people who troop down the aisle for "walk-in" baptisms must be politely told that the pastor will be glad to call on them to begin the process of catechesis. At least, a pastoral visitation with parents or prospective candidates must always precede baptism and could often accomplish much afterward, too. For the unbelieving parents, it means that the church has to say "no," but in the process of explaining the demands of initiation the pastor has perhaps the only opportunity for witnessing to what Christians believe. For the adult inquirer, it means enrollment in some kind of catechumenate. *The Apostolic Tradition*'s three-year catechumenate was a bit rigorous but those who had been through it were willing to die (and frequently did) for their faith. The Roman Catholic "Rite of Christian Initiation of Adults" and similar rites are worth serious study by all Christians. Not only does this process give the inquirer the full support of the community during his or her growth toward full incorporation, but it also causes the congregation to reexamine the basis of its own faith.

Baptizing and teaching belong together (Matt. 28:19-20). The church year gives opportunities to preach on the meaning of initiation, especially at the Baptism of the Lord, Easter, Pentecost, and All Saints. It is no wonder that most Christians are confused about initiation; they have never had any kind of mystagogical catechesis to explain it to them. But they deserve to know more so that, whenever they serve as witnesses to initiation, they can be put in mind of what God has already done for them. Baptism builds up the church from within as well as from without.

The second point is the importance of the **sign value** of what is done in initiation. Initiation is basically signifying actions; something happens for which words alone cannot suffice. The actions must be allowed to speak and not be muffled by indifference or lack of sensitivity to their sign value.

Initiation is a communal act, and the community must be present. The whole congregation is a sponsor. How can one marry by proxy without losing much that is meaningful? How can one be incorporated into the Body when the community is absent? Many Protestants insist that initiation always occur in the Sunday service with the whole congregation present. Other traditions are now moving in this direction. The community itself is the foremost sign of incorporation, not a vacant church building.

Baptism is washing. It is a highly tactile act that demands that water be seen, heard, and (in effect) felt by the whole congregation. Those churches that immerse have a deeper sacramental sense in this case. Under present practices, in many Roman Catholic and Protestant congregations, the facilities and practices are both defective. Baptism often looks more like a dry run than a vigorous cleansing and has been lampooned as "dry cleaning." If one's concern is to communicate the life-giving flood in which God acts, abundant water communicates this best. Clearly, this means that baptismal bowls are insufficient and that most modern fonts will not do. Medieval and some post-Reformation fonts were large enough for dipping a baby. That was the mode Luther clearly preferred, that the Church of England's rubric has always specified (though ignored for the last two hundred years), and that the new Roman Catholic and Episcopal rites suggest first. But it does imply facilities and practices different from those that most pedobaptist churches now have.

If our concern is to show forth by actions what God does, then **sprinkling** (more commonly simply moistening) with a few drops of water is most insufficient (unless we have a very anemic doctrine of God). **Pouring** is somewhat better if the water can be seen and heard as it splashes. **Dipping** (infants) or **immersing** or **submersing** (children and adults) is clearly best. If we are willing to let the act speak for itself, we will not bury it under verbiage but actually wash people. Above all, we should avoid making it an act of Christian cuteness; the center is God, not the baby.

Laying on of hands and anointing are dramatic actions which must be allowed to make their own witness. They should be made as personal as possible with the use of the Christian names of all those involved. Each candidate should be touched individually. When the entire congregation participates in baptismal reaffirmation or renewal, sprinkling of the whole congregation (without suggesting rebaptism) is greatly to be desired. In no way a repetition of baptism, reaffirmation or renewal is a vivid recalling of what God has already done for us in baptism. Once a year is frequent enough but annual services of renewal or reaffirmation are widely appreciated now.

The third point is the need to make visible the **unity of the whole process of initiation**. Ideally, all portions of the rites ought to be performed at the same time on Sundays or at Easter in the midst of the congregation, as many new rites suggest. In churches with bishops, when possible, the bishop should be the minister of the whole integrated rite, thus clearly manifesting the universal church.

Baptism, laying on of hands, and first communion ought to come together. Anything that implies halfway membership or preparatory membership is unbiblical and a contradiction in terms. When God acts, it is not halfway or preparatory. God's acts are unqualified self-giving. We may reject them eventually, but God remains faithful to God's promise of acceptance offered to us in initiation. The unity of the initiatory rites should witness to this. Certainly baptism and the eucharist belong together. The early church was right in understanding the eucharist as the only part of initiation that is repeated. Those who have received baptism and the laying on of hands or anointing ought immediately to be welcomed to the Lord's Table, no matter at what age they have come. If anyone is old enough to become a part of the Lord's Body, he or she is old enough to be welcome to the Lord's Table.

CHAPTER NINE

THE EUCHARIST

The eucharist is the most distinctive structure of Christian worship. It is also the most widely used form of worship among Christians, being celebrated daily and weekly in thousands of congregations and communities all over the world. In chapter 6, we examined the service of the word, which, since early times, has formed the first half of the eucharist. We now turn to the second half, the acted sign.

Various groups use a variety of names for both halves combined: "eucharist" (that is, thanksgiving) or "Lord's supper" (1 Cor. 11:20), "break bread" (Acts 2:46; 20:7), "divine liturgy," "mass," "holy communion," and "Lord's memorial." The second half by itself also is sometimes called the "eucharist," "mass of the faithful," "offering of sacrifice" (Tertullian), "service of the table," "sacrifice," "offering," or "anaphora" (in a broad sense). Since the end of the first century, the term "eucharist" has been used. It is the most descriptive term available and the one we shall use most frequently.

Whatever the name, the content throughout Christianity is the same: a sacred meal based on Jesus' actions at the Last Supper. Despite all the diversity in practice throughout the Christian world, there is also remarkable constancy in the form the rite takes. All churches profess loyalty to following what the writers of the New Testament interpreted to be Jesus' words, actions, and intentions.

The widespread similarity in eucharistic practices throughout Christianity witnesses to the imprint Jesus left on this type of worship. No wonder, then, that despite strong Jewish roots, the eucharist is the most distinctive form of Christian worship. It bears the authority of direct connection with Christ himself.

In this chapter, we shall examine very quickly the eucharistic practices of Christians across time, their understanding of what they experience in eucharistic celebrations, and the consequences for pastoral action. There is much to cover, so we may not linger long over any topic, however important, but must sketch only the bare outlines of historical, theological, and practical matters.

THE DEVELOPMENT OF EUCHARISTIC PRACTICE

Nowhere else are the Jewish roots of Christian worship so important—or so complicated—as they are in the eucharist. Every type of Jewish public worship made a contribution to the Christian eucharist almost as if Jesus and his followers had deliberately sought to build on the foundations the Jewish people had laid. We now realize that whenever these Jewish foundations have been forgotten, the eucharist has been distorted in practice and misunderstood in experience. Understanding the Jewish contributions can hold Christians true to their own eucharist. Three locations for Jewish worship are particularly important in this regard: the temple cult, synagogue worship, and family meals.

Since the seventh century B.C., Jewish **sacrificial worship** had been nationalized in the **Jerusalem Temple**. The whole sacrificial cultus had developed as a communal means of relating to God as a nation and of achieving communion with God as individuals. Sacrifice was a way of life, and the daily morning and evening sacrifices of the Temple (Exod. 29:38-39) were remembered in the prayers of devout Jews everywhere. Sacrificial imagery is picked up in the very narratives of the institution of the Lord's Supper ("my blood of the covenant, which is poured out for many") (Matt. 26:28) and recurs throughout the New Testament, especially in Hebrews.

Psalms sung daily in temple worship became part of the eucharist. Conspicuous examples are the entrance song, "I will go up to the altar of God, / To God, the giver of youth and happiness"

(Ps. 43:4, Latin version) and the *Benedictus qui venit*, "Blessed is he who comes in the name of the Lord" (Ps. 118:26, Latin version). Responsorial psalmody also forms an important part of the Christian service of the word.

We have already seen how the **synagogue service** evolved into daily public prayer and the service of the word, but its contribution does not end even with all that. Synagogue worship involved prayer, prayer which came to have a specific form and content. The form was that of blessing God for what God had done, especially as narrated in the readings. Blessing God and thanking God are equivalent terms, largely a recital of the *mirabilia Dei*, God's mighty acts for God's people. Such prayers have a creedal function. God is blessed by reciting those acts one wishes to recall, thus making prayer also a form of proclamation. A similar mentality operates in Jewish table prayer for the home, blessing God by reciting acts for which one gives thanks, for example, "we thank (or bless) you, who did. . . ."

It is only a natural evolution to turn from those works of God already accomplished to beseeching God to bring about those yet hoped for in the future: "Restore thy *Shekinah* [glory] into Zion thy city, and the order of worship into Jerusalem" (after A.D. 70). Supplication for further mighty works is the sequel to proclamation of what God has already done. Much of the form and content of synagogue prayers was simply adopted as the pattern for Christian eucharistic prayer, especially the framework of blessing (thanking) God through creedal prayer.

The same understanding of prayer as thanksgiving also appeared during **family meals,** but there, actions were equally important. The Last Supper was obviously a sacred meal, but so were all those many other meals Jesus shared with his disciples. Each Jewish meal is a holy event shared only with family or close friends. If the Last Supper was the Passover meal, as the Synoptic Gospels insist, then Jesus was transforming the most solemn occasion of the Jewish year (the festival when the Jews hoped and prayed the Messiah would appear). Jesus used the specified words and actions of a familiar pattern to state that the Messiah had come, indeed. Jews, who do not agree the Messiah has come, continue to perform the **Passover Seder** (sacred meal) to this day; Christians, who agree that Jesus was the Messiah, celebrate the eucharist (thanksgiving) instead.

Jesus deliberately used the climactic occasion of the Jewish year to establish the new covenant, but he did it in terms of the old worship. According to the Synoptics, at the Last Supper Jesus followed the conventional reenactment of the original passover meal as commemoration of deliverance from captivity in Egypt. It is a liberation saga, mandated in Exodus 12:25-27. Normally, children ask, "What do you mean by this observance?" (v. 26). Replies of interpretation (*haggadah*) are given. This is the model for the words with which Jesus instituted the eucharist. But just as important are the actions: special food is eaten, bread is broken, and cups of wine are shared at the Passover. Words and significant acts help to make present the saving power of God's acts culminating in the great event of liberation and look forward to God's future works of deliverance. Throughout, God is blessed for past events, which are once again made present in their ability to save, and God is implored to confer future benefits. Eating and drinking, as well as thankful remembering and anticipating, all go together.

The New Testament gives several accounts of the institution of the eucharist as well as fleeting glimpses of it as celebrated in Jerusalem, Troas, and Corinth. There are also stories of meals of Jesus, his disciples, and multitudes before the resurrection and of Jesus with his disciples after the resurrection.

Two parallel sets of **institution narratives** appear in the New Testament: Mark 14:22-25 and Matthew 26:26-29 are quite similar, and 1 Corinthians 11:23-26 and Luke 22:15-20 have strong similarities. The Lucan account is unique (in some texts) in mentioning two cups. The slight differences between the accounts may be explained by the theory that what we have in these texts is a description of what was being said and done by several local churches in different places when celebrating the eucharist. They all would have understood themselves as following the intentions, words, and actions of the Lord himself at the Last Supper. The churches, after all, had been celebrating the supper from Pentecost onward, long before any written accounts were made. Thus our links to the Last Supper itself through the narratives of its institution are actual eucharistic celebrations. Even so, the German New

Testament scholar, Joachim Jeremias, was of the opinion that one can come close to discerning the eucharistic words of Jesus himself. Jeremias considered the Marcan account the closest with the most likely wording resembling:

> This is my body/my flesh
> my blood of the covenant
> the covenant in my blood
> which . . . for many.[1]

The **words of institution** have important dimensions. In their context, they are sacrificial in speaking of a covenant made in blood. All accounts, especially the Lucan, are oriented in an eschatological direction (as was the Passover itself) in looking forward to the coming kingdom of God. In giving interpretations, albeit new and shocking interpretations, to the food and actions of the meal, Jesus was simply following convention. Jeremias believed that Jesus' word about not eating (Luke 22:16) was in the form of a vow (such as Paul's attackers took in Acts 23:12) and may indicate that Jesus did not partake himself.

A key word in the Pauline and Lucan accounts is the word *anámnesis*. No single English word conveys its full meaning; remembrance, recalling, representation, and experiencing anew are all weak approximations. *Anámnesis* expresses the sense that in repeating these actions one experiences once again the reality of Jesus himself present. In recent years, this concept has been a key term in ecumenical discussions of the eucharist as memorial with nuances of sacrifice and presence.

The actions of institution are no less important than the words. English scholar **Gregory Dix** made much of the "**four action shape**" which determines the "shape of the liturgy."[2] Mark 14:22 reads: "he *took* bread, and having *said the blessing* he *broke* it and *gave* it to them" (NEB, emphasis added). The same actions are used over the cup except there is no breaking. These same actions are listed elsewhere: in the miracle of the five loaves and two fish (Mark 6:41), the Emmaus road account (Luke 24:30), and even among a shipload of pagans (Acts 27:35). The foods used at the Passover meal involved symbolic actions as well as utilitarian ones (dipping in bitter herbs, eating unleavened bread). Dix's most lasting contribution has been to remind us that the eucharist is basically action. He considered four actions central: taking, giving thanks (blessing), breaking, and giving. Of these four, the giving of thanks and giving of bread and wine are now seen as the more significant.

John's Gospel does not give details of the actual meal at the Last Supper except for words exchanged with Judas. It does give, however, a unique description of another sign-activity, **foot washing** (John 13:3-17). Apparently the early church understood this not as an imperative but as an acted parable; we have no evidence of it as apostolic practice. The act of foot washing became part of the initiation rite in Milan and, eventually, part of the eucharistic celebrations of various Protestant groups such as the Church of the Brethren,[3] some Pentecostals, some Baptists, and Seventh Day Adventists. Since 1955, it has been recovered in the Maundy Thursday services of many churches.

The dating of the Last Supper is an unresolved controversy. The Synoptic Gospels present the Last Supper as the Passover meal whereas John says it was "before the festival of the Passover festival" (13:1), or on the day (beginning with nightfall) on which the lambs were slaughtered in the Temple (cf. also 18:28). In John's chronology, the sacrifice of the lambs coincides with the crucifixion. Probably the majority of New Testament scholars follow the Johannine dating of the Last Supper on the evening before the Passover, though many others do present the Last Supper as the actual Passover meal. Given John's penchant for symbolism, it does not seem unlikely that he could have combined the sacrifice of the lambs and the crucifixion for symbolic effect.[4] In any case, the climactic events of Christ's passion and death occur in the context of the Passover festival and are heavily colored by its celebration of past deliverance from captivity through blood and its anticipation of imminent future liberation by divine action.

The New Testament gives us only quick glimpses of first-century eucharists. Acts 2:46 says the Jerusalem church "broke bread at home and ate their food with glad and generous hearts." A phrase in Paul's stern warning to First Church, Corinth, against unworthy partaking of the "Lord's Supper" links the eucharist to proclaiming "the Lord's death until he comes" (1 Cor. 11:26). Paul threatens with sickness and death those guilty of eating and drinking unworthily, that is, without discerning the Lord's body in the community. It is also clear that the Lord's Supper is just that, a full meal. Some scholars have tried to discover two kinds of eucharist in the New Testament and early Christian literature, a joyful one and a somber type.[5] These theories now seem highly unlikely, for the death of the Lord is both a sobering memory and a source of joy.

We catch a fleeting view of another eucharist as Paul prepared to leave Troas (Acts 20:7-12) where Eutychus slept through Paul's preaching, but we learn little else about the eucharist itself. A unique reference occurs in the Epistle of Jude where there are problems apparently similar to those in Corinth. "These are blemishes on your love-feasts [*agápais*], while they feast with you without fear, feeding themselves" (v. 12). The **agape** or **love feast** was a full meal but somehow distinct from the eucharist. *The Apostolic Tradition* goes to pains to distinguish it from the Lord's Supper. At what time the Lord's Supper stopped being a full meal is unknown; apparently one could still be a glutton and a drunkard when Paul wrote. There is slight evidence in an early (c. A.D. 112) letter from Pliny, a pagan Roman governor in Bithynia, to the Emperor Trajan. This letter can be interpreted to mean Christians in Bithynia were accustomed to an early Sunday morning eucharist and an agape in the evening but had given up the agape under persecution. For *The Apostolic Tradition*, the agape was an occasional church supper put on by private benefactors with clergy present. Leftovers were sent to the poor. Too easily, the agape degenerated into abuse and was proscribed by councils in the fourth century. The blessed (but not eucharistic) bread, the **antidoron**, distributed after the liturgy in Eastern Orthodox churches may possibly be a survival. The love feast was revived among eighteenth-century Brethren, Mennonites, and Moravians and still flourishes.[6] John Wesley borrowed the practice and introduced it into Methodism in 1738. The agape has been used on ecumenical occasions when a eucharist is not feasible.

It is tempting to read back into the New Testament period the information we have on eucharistic practices in following centuries. Yet this is risky and we must admit that our knowledge of the first-century eucharist is very limited. Much more evidence appears in the second and third centuries. The *Didache* may contain prayers from either a eucharist or an agape. It includes a strict warning about not giving communion to the unbaptized, instructions to be reconciled to one's brother or sister before "offering your gift at the altar" (Matt. 5:23-24), and a famous line: "As this piece [of bread] was scattered over the hills and then was brought together and made one, so let your Church be brought together from the ends of the earth into your Kingdom."[7] This and a subsequent phrase have a strong eschatological flavor. Prophets, we are told, may "give thanks in their own way." *Didache* 14 and Justin's *Dialogue with Trypho* 41 quote Malachi 1:11 about a "pure" sacrifice and specifically refer to the eucharist in sacrificial language.

In Justin's *First Apology*, we find our first outline of the eucharist. In one case it follows a baptism, but ordinarily it would come after the service of the word:

> On finishing the prayers [petition and intercession] we greet each other with a kiss. Then bread and a cup of water and mixed wine are brought to the president of the brethren and he, taking them, sends up praise and glory to the Father of the universe through the name of the Son and of the Holy Spirit, and offers thanksgiving at some length that we have been deemed worthy to receive these things from him. . . . When the president has given thanks and the whole congregation has assented [with an "amen"], those whom we call deacons give to each of those present a portion of the consecrated [literally, "eucharistized"] bread and wine and water, and they take it to the absent.[8]

The **kiss of peace** (Rom. 16:16; 1 Pet. 5:14) is a sign of love and unity that concluded the intercessions and led to the offertory (as in *Didache* 14). It retains this position in the East but lost it in the West until the recent revisions in some churches. Apparently the wording of the central prayer of thanksgiving by the president (bishop or presiding presbyter) is still fluid at this stage. Justin, in this second account (ch. 67), tells us the president "sends up prayers and thanksgivings to the best of his ability." A century later, Cyprian saw the mixture of water and wine as a symbol of the unity of people (water) and the blood of Christ (wine). It was probably originally utilitarian. The deacons carry bread and wine to those sick and in prison, setting a very early precedent for extended communion and eventually **reservation** of the consecrated elements in churches between eucharistic celebrations. A collection is also taken up for the benefit of the needy.

Our most important source of information about the early eucharist is, once again, *The Apostolic Tradition*. This conservative document, trying to stem liturgical experimentation in the third century, has sparked much innovation in the twentieth. The wording of the eucharistic prayer after the ordination of a bishop has been widely copied by Protestants and Roman Catholics alike. It is the basic source for the Roman Catholic Eucharistic Prayer II. Readers are advised to study the actual text to accompany the following discussion.[9]

As soon as a new bishop is ordained, all offer him the kiss of peace. Then deacons bring the offering (bread and wine) and the bishop "laying his hands on it, with all the presbytery" begins the thanksgiving.[10] Deacons bring the offering but the presbyters share (here silently) in the prayer, a practice known as **concelebration**. The **great thanksgiving (eucharistic prayer, canon, anaphora, prayer of consecration)** begins with a dialogue between chief celebrant and the congregation. The dialogue includes the *sursum corda*, today rendered "Lift up your hearts," and invites the congregation to join in the thanksgiving, which the bishop speaks. This is the way most eucharistic prayers still begin. All share in it though one person speaks the words.

Most subsequent liturgies move on eventually to the *sanctus* ("Holy, Holy, Holy"), based on Isaiah 6:3 and Revelation 4:8. *The Apostolic Tradition* does not mention the *sanctus*, either because it was not in use, occurred elsewhere, or was not considered necessary to mention. The **post-*sanctus*** continues thanksgiving for what God has done in Jesus Christ, recites Christ's works, and concludes this section with the **words of institution**. Then, a section known as the *anámnesis*-**oblation** summarizes what is being recalled and offers the bread and cup to God. *The Apostolic Tradition's* final portion is an invocation of the Holy Spirit or *epiclesis* in which the Holy Spirit is invoked to make fruitful the communion of those who partake. Some rites have either a consecratory or preliminary *epiclesis* (usually before the words of institution), or a communion *epiclesis* after the *anámnesis*-oblation or both. *The Apostolic Tradition* cites benefits desired from the Holy Spirit. It is a short step from this to **intercessions** for others, both living and dead, just as synagogue prayers had easily moved from thanksgiving by recital to supplication for further action. *The Apostolic Tradition* had not moved in that direction, but it was a natural development and it soon followed. The whole prayer then concludes with a trinitarian **doxology** of praise and an **Amen**.

Now why is all this so important? What *The Apostolic Tradition* gives us is the prototype of the central prayer of the central act of Christian worship. The eucharistic prayer was for several centuries the most common theological statement of the Christian faith. In thanking God, the church followed the Jewish custom of summing up its faith in what God had done. The prayer is largely a recital of the *mirabilia Dei*, God's saving acts. It is proclamation and creed rolled into one. The structure is basically Trinitarian: thanking God the Father, commemorating before God the Father the works of God the Son, and invoking God the Father to send God the Holy Spirit. The whole is then concluded with a doxology praising all three members of the Trinity. The form is thoroughly Jewish: praising God by reciting of God's past acts and invoking their continuation. The contents are thoroughly Christian: the recalling of what God has done in Jesus Christ and continues to do through the Holy Spirit.

The ability to lead in this central prayer demanded a person who could faithfully represent the beliefs of the Christian community. *The Apostolic Tradition* even says: "It is not at all necessary to recite the same words we have prescribed . . . in giving thanks to God, but let each one pray according to his ability, . . . only let him pray what is true praise [*orthodoxia*] (sometimes translated sound doctrine)."[11] One of the most important functions of the ordained ministry is the ability of presbyters and bishops to sum up the faith of the whole church and proclaim it in prayer. No wonder second-century Ignatius of Antioch limited presiding at the eucharist to being "by the bishop or by someone he authorizes."[12] Each pastor is a theologian for the congregation—to them is entrusted the statement of the community's faith through its supreme expression, the eucharistic prayer.

Slight changes occurred after *The Apostolic Tradition* in the eucharistic prayer, chiefly in an expansion of the words calling to give thanks after the *sursum corda*. This is called the **preface** and is a beginning of the recital of thanks. In the West, it could vary according to the season or occasion and formed a **variable preface**. In Eastern rites and some Protestant rites, it is fixed and unchanging. The *sanctus* comes next and often the *benedictus qui venit*: "Blessed is the one who comes in the name of the Lord" (Ps. 118:26, Matt. 21:9). In some rites, a **preliminary** *epiclesis* occurs in the early part of the post-*sanctus*. The final *epiclesis* can give way to quite extended intercession. Protestant rites, in general, have avoided the preliminary *epiclesis* and the intercessions at this place. Once one has mastered this particular pattern of eucharistic prayer, it is possible to improvise them in many different ways just as one can write sonnets in the specified form. The pattern of most eucharistic prayers adopted in the West since Vatican II includes:

dialogue
preface
sanctus and *benedictus*
post-*sanctus*
(preliminary *epiclesis*)
words of institution
anámnesis-oblation
epiclesis
(intercessions)
doxology
Amen

But, as *The Apostolic Tradition* hints, not all "have the ability of praying at length in solemn form." Shortly we begin to find more or less fixed texts coming into use. One of the earliest comes from the hand of **Sarapion**, bishop of Thmuis, Egypt, about the middle of the fourth century. The most distinctive element is an *epiclesis* directed to the second member of the Trinity.[13] A generation or more later, comes a very lengthy text in book eight of the *Apostolic Constitutions*. Though probably never actually used, it represents the victory of prescribed forms over the freedom expressed by the *Didache* and Justin.

The Apostolic Tradition's ordination eucharist contains rather obscure references to the offering of and giving thanks over oil, cheese, and olives. In its paschal eucharist, milk and honey, water (symbol of baptism), and wine are given after the bishop has broken the bread (the **fraction**) and distributed the fragments with the words: "the bread of heaven in Christ Jesus." The three chalices are given with a Trinitarian form to which each recipient responds "Amen." The service ends abruptly as all leave, and "each one hastens to do good."

In the post-Nicene era, a variety of eucharistic rites developed scattered around the perimeter of the Mediterranean. (See diagram 2 on p. 36.) All have common characteristics. By the sixth century, the service of the word and the eucharist had been wed for the next thousand years. The fourfold actions, foreshadowed in the New Testament accounts, in Dix's famous words, "constituted the absolutely invariable nucleus of every eucharistic rite known to us throughout antiquity."[14] However much the form of words may vary, the basic contents of the second of these acts—the giving of thanks or eucharistic prayer—function in remarkably similar ways. In the fourth, fifth, and sixth centuries, important divergences in style and wording appear, witnessing to the diversity of peoples yet retaining constancy of purpose. The comparative study of these is a vast science; we can only suggest here a little of the richness of diversity present by following these liturgical families around the Mediterranean in a counterclockwise direction.

The characteristic **Alexandrian** or Egyptian eucharistic prayer is typified by that named after **Mark** who, tradition has it, ministered in Alexandria. In these rites, the preface often has a long recital of God's works of creation and redemption derived from the Old Testament (noticeably absent in much of the Western tradition of eucharistic prayer). This moves into intercession (including prayer for the rising of the Nile) and the **diptychs** (list of those for whom offering is made, dead and living). Then follows the *sanctus*. Characteristically the post-*sanctus* begins "Full in truth are heaven and earth." A consecratory *epiclesis* leads to the institution narrative. After the *anámnesis*-oblation comes another *epiclesis* both consecratory and communion in intent and a concluding doxology.

Further East, we encounter the **Antiochene** or **West Syrian** family with important documents from Antioch and Jerusalem and the best known example is the liturgy of **St. James**. This is familiar to many as the source of the hymn text, "Let all mortal flesh keep silence." Characteristic of this family is the preface with its celestial roll call. The post-*sanctus* picks up on the word "holy"—"holy you are"—in a recital of old and new covenant works. A series of acclamations and amens by the people have recently been copied in the West. A long series of intercessions for the living and dead follows the *epiclesis*, each petition beginning, "Remember, Lord." The language is florid, poetic, and never brief. The **Armenian** rite is probably ultimately derived from this family though with later Byzantine influence.

Easily the most puzzling family is the **East Syrian**, originating in Edessa as the liturgy of **Sts. Addai and Mari**. Isolated by heresy and Islam, it has continued in use relatively untouched by other influences. As such, it has early roots, perhaps reflecting third-century practice in that region. The most controversial aspect is an apparent lack of words of institution, which would make it unique among Christian liturgies. The *epiclesis* comes last after the intercessions.

To the family of **St. Basil of Caesarea** in Asia Minor we owe an early version known as the **Alexandrian Basil** since it may have been brought to Egypt by Basil himself, around A.D. 357. This has been widely admired in recent years and forms the basis for various recent denominational eucharistic prayers. A later version, probably revised by St. Basil himself is filled out with more scriptural references. It is used by the Orthodox churches of the world on ten days of the year, chiefly in Lent. Structurally both versions are of the Antiochene type, but the latter liturgy of St. Basil has a detailed post-*sanctus* recital of creation, fall, and redemption.

Somewhat dependent upon it is the liturgy of **St. John Chrysostom** or the **Byzantine liturgy**, the second most widely used eucharistic rite in the world today. It, too, reflects Antiochene structure. John Chrysostom had been bishop in Antioch at the end of the fourth century. The post-*sanctus* and intercessions are relatively short and the whole prayer appears condensed in comparison with most of those already mentioned.

Turning westward, we momentarily pass over the Roman family

to note an assortment of non–Roman Western rites known collectively as **Gallic** and subdivided into **Ambrosian** (or **Milanese**), **Mozarabic** (from Spain), **Celtic** (originating in Ireland but scattered where Celtic missionaries traveled), and **Gallican** in the narrow sense of Frankish-German. There are connections between these rites and those of the East, although the exact derivation is uncertain. The Ambrosian rite is still in use in the Archdiocese of Milan and the Mozarabic in one chapel in Toledo Cathedral in Spain. A common characteristic is florid language and eucharistic prayers which, except for the *sanctus* and words of institution, change entirely according to the day or season, providing extraordinary variety.

For two centuries following *The Apostolic Tradition*, there is a blackout of material regarding the **Roman rite** although Ambrose foreshadows much that emerges in Rome, and the few surviving North African fragments show some similarities. The mists lift in Rome when we discover several early **sacramentaries**, collections of the priest's prayers for the various masses of the year including initiation and ordinations and various **ordines**, collections of rubrics. Of the oldest sacramentaries, the **Leonian** has preserved proper prayers from more than three hundred masses, many of which may actually go back to Pope Leo I (440–461). The older version of the **Gelasian** may contain opening prayers and prefaces shaped by Pope Gelasius I (492–496) who seems to have polished the canon itself. The **Gregorian** was named for Pope Gregory I (590–604) who reformed the Roman rite and anchored the **Lord's Prayer** at the end of the canon.

Various sacramentaries were in circulation in the early medieval West. Charlemagne sought standardization for purposes of imperial unity and requested a copy of an authentic Roman sacramentary. Pope Hadrian I (772–795) transmitted one to imperial headquarters at Aachen, but it turned out to be sorely incomplete for parochial purposes. One of Charlemagne's ecclesiastical advisors, probably **Benedict of Aniane**, added a "Supplement" of materials drawn from the various Gallican rites then in use throughout the Empire. Any distinction between the mandatory official rites and the optional "Supplement" soon eroded, and the two were conflated. Two centuries later, the combined sacramentary was brought to Rome and imposed on Rome itself by Germanic emperors.

Consequently, the Roman rite assimilated a variety of Gallican propers including additional **prayers over the gifts**, prefaces, and **prayers after communion**. These complemented those developed in Rome previously. In the West by the fifth century, the kiss of peace had been relocated after the eucharistic prayer.

Throughout the Middle Ages, the eucharistic prayer remained stable. But increasingly it and the other central action, the giving of bread and wine, were surrounded by subjective **apologies** or prayers about the unworthiness of clergy and people. These tended to be penitential and introspective in tone. Accessory actions, such as censing the altar-table and washing the hands of the priest, joined private prayers of the celebrant at the offertory. The *Agnus Dei* ("Lamb of God") was introduced in the late–seventh century at the fraction as was **commixture** (mixing a particle of bread in the wine, a remnant of a symbol of unity of the pope and churches of his diocese). Individualistic prayers surrounded the giving of bread and wine. The **ablutions** (ceremony of cleaning the vessels and hands of the celebrant) developed as a reflection of late medieval scrupulosity about each drop and crumb of the consecrated elements. The late–Middle Ages also added a last Gospel (John 1:1-18), and a modern pope attached a few concluding prayers. These anticlimactic elements quickly disappeared after Vatican II.

The resulting Western eucharistic rite is charted in simplified form in diagram 10 with each period's contributions. Elements which moved or were removed are in parentheses.

Diagram 10 shows the structure the Reformers inherited. Long lost had been any grasp of the original function of the eucharistic prayer as the great thankful summation and proclamation of the church's faith. Inasmuch as this occurred at all, it had been relegated to the creed as part of the service of the word (in the West) or as a prelude to the anaphora (in the East). The medieval subjective devotions, which had crept in before and after the eucharistic prayer, became the minor that the Reformation majored in. The Anglican Prayer of Humble Access ("We do not presume to come to this thy table") is a good example of this type of piety. Its apology, "we be not worthy so much as to gather up the crumbs under thy table," may be the most graphic image of the Reformation.

The Eucharist

Apostolic Tradition	Fourth to Sixth Centuries	Medieval
(kiss of peace) offertory		
		offertory prayers and ceremonies
	prayer over the gifts	
eucharistic prayer	preface, *sanctus*, inter- cessions Lord's Prayer kiss of peace	
fraction		*Agnus Dei* commixture priest's prayers "Lord, I am not worthy"
giving bread and wine	communion song	
		silent prayer ablutions
	prayer after communion blessing with dismissal	
		(last Gospel)

Diagram 10

The Reformers did, however, take some very important positive steps although none of them caught the ancient significance of the eucharistic prayer. They put the mass into the vernacular, simplified it, and (except for Zwingli and the Anabaptists) tried valiantly to restore frequent communion. But, for a laity accustomed to receiving communion rarely, or only once a year, frequent communion proved too radical a departure to win widespread success except in some Lutheran areas.

Luther gave the strongest, if not the earliest, impetus to reforming the mass with his Latin rite, the *Formula Missae* of 1523 and his vernacular *Deutsche Messe* of 1525.[15] Luther is conservative until he comes to the canon, "that mangled and abominable thing gathered from much filth and scum," which he simply slashes down to the words of institution and *sanctus*.[16] In one stroke, he out-medievalizes the Roman Catholic Church, which had located the moment of consecration precisely at the words of institution. Luther advocated the addition of vernacular hymnody. His German mass retained much ceremonial including the elevation of bread and wine and instructions that the "German *sanctus*" or other hymns be sung during the distribution of the bread and hymns or the *Agnus Dei* during the giving of the cup.

Zwingli's 1523 *Attack on the Canon of the Mass* substituted four of his Latin prayers for the canon. In 1525, Zwingli produced his *Action or Use of the Lord's Supper*, which made Luther's reforms look tame. Gone were virtually all ceremonial and music. What remained was an austere commemoration and fellowship meal, practiced four times a year.

Martin Bucer's work in Strasbourg underlies much of Calvin's liturgical efforts and with Zwingli's rite helped mold the Reformed eucharistic tradition. Bucer was anticipated in Strasbourg by Diobald Schwarz and Calvin in Geneva by Guillaume Farel. Calvin's *Form of Church Prayers*, Geneva, 1542, represents the work of his predecessors brought to a definitive shape for the Reformed tradition. It was transmitted through John Knox's *The Forme of Prayers*, Geneva, 1556, and subsequent Scottish editions to the English-speaking world. Characteristic of the Reformed tradition, the eucharist is excessively didactic and includes a reading of the words of institution outside the eucharistic prayer as a

warrant for the eucharist's observance. The fencing of tables (reflecting 1 Cor. 11:27-32) forbade evildoers from communicating.

Practices varied greatly among the Anabaptists: Extreme simplicity characterized their celebrations, elaborated only by a highly developed hymnody. Among the English Puritans, fixed liturgies were by no means avoided in the late sixteenth and early seventeenth centuries, but the *Westminster Directory* of 1645 eventually substituted *ordines* for sacramentaries and rubrics for rites, though it outlined a model eucharistic prayer. The Quakers, of course, insisted on silent and inward feeding on Christ while avoiding outward sacraments.

The **first Anglican Book of Common Prayer,** that of **1549,** carried a vernacular communion rite which was recognizably a conservative blending of the **Sarum** rite of southern England with Reformation theology. Much of the 1549 *BCP's* eucharistic theology was deliberately ambiguous, permitting both Catholic and Protestant interpretations. Three years later, this rite was replaced with one that removed most ambiguity and involved drastic restructuring. The canon was cut in two. The oblation was placed after communion so as to eliminate any traditional sense of sacrifice. Despite minor changes in 1559, 1604, and 1662, what is basically the 1552 rite is still in official use in England though later largely replaced by *Common Worship*. The American prayer books (1789, 1892, 1928) utilized a much richer Scottish eucharistic prayer.

John Wesley followed the 1662 *BCP* eucharistic rite in his *Sunday Service* of 1784, only abbreviating it slightly. Wesley's two great contributions were a eucharistic revival with weekly celebrations and (with Charles Wesley) a magnificent collection of 166 eucharistic hymns. These contain a rich variety of sacrificial, eschatological, and pneumatological emphases that was absent from Protestant eucharistic piety for many centuries, but Wesley's strong eucharistic discipline and eucharistic hymns were eventually lost by his followers. An abbreviated form of his rite continued in use in America.

Pentecostals vary greatly in the use or non-use of set forms for the Lord's Supper. They do concur that the Holy Spirit must be free to break into any pattern through spontaneous elements. Frequency of eucharists varies from weekly to rarely.

Recent tendencies in many churches center on restoration of many practices of the ancient church. It is generally agreed that most of the medieval developments were distortions, although we may be as prone to romanticize the early church as Victorians were the medieval church. Many of the changes have been the result of historical studies of comparative liturgiology. The results of such studies are made more appealing in that the church in a post-Christian era has much in common with a pre-Constantinian church. The results of liturgical revision are so similar that in many cases it is often hard to tell which tradition has produced a new eucharistic rite if the title page is lost.

Basic to most rites since the Church of South India rite first appeared in 1950 is structuring around the fourfold actions of which Dix wrote. Rediscovery of the centrality of the eucharistic prayer as the church's supreme faith statement has spurred revision of existing eucharistic prayers and composition of new examples. American Lutherans recovered such a prayer in 1958. The eucharist itself is being observed more frequently in most Protestant churches, advancing from quarterly celebrations to monthly, and then to weekly. The same increase in frequency had occurred among most Anglicans in the early twentieth century.

A common development has been the move to a variety of eucharistic prayers. This reflects the most significant of new developments, a forthright acceptance of pluralism as a positive good and consequent efforts for flexibility and adaptation. As a result, the Roman Catholic Church, after being restricted to a single canon for a millennium and a half, now has five eucharistic prayers for use on any occasion and (in the United States of America) other prayers for masses with children and at times of reconciliation. A rich assortment of prayers over the gifts, prefaces, and prayers after communion are provided.

Pluralism is reflected in the 1979 Episcopal *BCP* by the inclusion of two entire rites: one with Elizabethan language and two possible eucharistic prayers and another in today's language with four choices. A third outline rite also contains two eucharistic prayers.

The 1978 *Lutheran Book of Worship* provides three complete musical settings, which can be used with any one of the three eucharistic prayers: a traditional scheme, the institution narrative alone, and a brief form concluding with the institution narrative. Three other eucharistic prayers appear in the Ministers Desk Edition.

Significant changes have developed in the United Methodist rite as approved for the 1989 *United Methodist Hymnal*. These include four versions of "A Service of Word and Table," the chief difference in the first three being the degree of completeness of texts. The acts of confession and pardon follow the sermon and lead into the peace and offering. Five musical settings are provided for the great thanksgiving. Service IV is in the traditional terminology of the 1552 *BCP*, reinstated by Wesley, with the John Merbecke musical setting of 1550. In Service IV, after nearly four and a half centuries, the two portions of Cranmer's eucharistic prayer have been reunited. A new feature for United Methodists is the provision of twenty-four approved eucharistic prayers in *The United Methodist Book of Worship*, 1992. These prayers change completely according to the festival (Pentecost Day), season (Advent), or occasion (Christian Marriage), much as the early Gallic liturgies did. New developments among American Presbyterians are found in *Book of Common Worship*, published in 1993. This provides a normative Sunday pattern of eucharistic celebration, although in practice that is still exceptional among most Presbyterians. The book contains twenty-five eucharistic prayers with a variety of proper prefaces for various occasions. The basic structure is: gathering, the word, the eucharist, and sending.

A similar fourfold division appears in most other service books, especially the understanding of gathering in Christ's name as an act of worship in itself, the emphasis on a full service of the word with three lessons and psalmody, a variety of eucharistic prayers, and the sending forth into service to the world.

UNDERSTANDING THE EUCHARIST

As was the case with baptism, the context of the eucharist in the New Testament is highly eschatological. The words of institution at the Last Supper indicate the imminent coming of the kingdom: "until it is fulfilled in the kingdom of God" (Luke 22:16). Even the kingdom is seen in terms of table fellowship: "so that you may eat and drink at my table in the kingdom" (Luke 22:30). There is a strong sense of the imminent return of the Lord and the beginning of the kingdom of which the Lord's Supper is a foretaste and anticipation. Each celebration invokes and advances the coming of the kingdom both by prayer and anticipation.[17]

Christians have understood the eucharist in a variety of ways. Indeed, to reduce what Christians experience in the eucharist to a single interpretation would be to miss much of the eucharist's power, although such reductionism has often been too tempting to resist. The method we shall follow here is to trace six metaphors that Christians have used to explain what they experience in the eucharist.

We shall use the terms of Yngve Brilioth, formerly Lutheran Archbishop of Uppsala, Sweden, though we shall apply them somewhat differently. In *Eucharistic Faith and Practice*, 1926, Brilioth identified **five New Testament metaphors of the eucharist**. They are eucharist or thanksgiving, communion fellowship, commemoration or the historical, sacrifice, and mystery or presence. To these, in view of subsequent history, we would add another: the eucharist as the work of the Holy Spirit.

These metaphors, and possibly others, appear in fragmentary form in the New Testament, which is even more elusive in revealing the meaning of the eucharist for first-century Christians than in disclosing its form. But clearly one of the central acts in the Lord's Supper, as in its Jewish antecedents, is **thanksgiving**. All four institution accounts speak of Jesus as giving thanks or blessing God. It is hard to imagine thanksgiving as absent from the joyful action that bubbled over as the Jerusalem church broke bread "with glad and generous hearts" (Acts 2:46).

Paul makes the sense of **communion or fellowship** apparent in such passages as 1 Corinthians 10:16-17: "The cup of blessing we bless, is it not a sharing *(koinônía)* in the blood of Christ? The bread that we break, is it not a sharing *(koinônía)* in the body of Christ? Because there is one bread, we who are many are one body, for we all partake of the one bread." The church built on the Jewish concept of the unity of those eating together. In its sharing, the community receives Christ and the one bread becomes a sign of the unity of the communicants.

The focal point of Jewish prayer is a "think-thank" process of **commemoration** with thanksgiving. The key phrase used by both Paul and Luke, "in *anámnesis* of me," is an underscoring of this process. To remember, recall, know again, or experience anew is certainly one of the main purposes for practicing the eucharist (Luke 22:19 and 1 Cor. 11:24-25). Commemoration is now seen as including not just the incarnation but all the works of Christ beginning with creation, including both testaments, and looking forward to Christ's coming again (1 Cor. 11:26).

The words of institution use the language of **sacrifice** in recalling a covenant established by the pouring out of blood. Hebrews is particularly rich in sacrificial imagery, comparing Christ to both high priest and victim who "offered himself without blemish to God" (9:14). The church's early appropriation of Malachi 1:11: "a pure offering," shows how natural such imagery was to apply to the eucharist. Hebrews 13:15 also speaks of "a sacrifice of praise," though there is no unambiguous relating of sacrifice and the eucharist in Hebrews. More important is Paul's understanding of Jesus' whole life and ministry as having "emptied himself, taking the form of a slave" (Phil. 2:7). This obedient sacrifice is memorialized by the eucharist.

In the words of the Last Supper, Christ states his **presence** by identifying bread and wine with his body and blood. Paul, in words quoted above, identifies eating and drinking with sharing in the body and blood of Christ. Some would cite the John 6:51 passage as eucharistic ("The bread that I will give for the life of the world is my flesh").

The eucharist as a locus of the **Holy Spirit's work** is not explicit in scripture but appears in early Christian literature and plays a major role subsequently. A fairly good balance of these basic themes appears in the early church, never worked out into full theologies, never precisely balanced, but mentioned frequently enough to show that these concepts were current in the understanding of why Christians gathered to "do this." Even Justin's short accounts in the *First Apology* speak of the eucharist in which the president "offers thanksgiving," and gives evidence of fellowship as all salute "each other with a kiss," share in the "amen," and partake together. The scriptures are read and the eucharistic action is introduced as being done "for my memorial." A realistic (that is, identifying bread and wine literally with body and blood) concept of presence is suggested in calling the bread and wine "the flesh and blood of that incarnate Jesus."[18] The *Didache* prays eschatologically: "Let your Church be brought together from the ends of the earth into your kingdom."[19] Sacrificial references appear very early; the *Didache* compares the eucharist to the "pure" sacrifice of Malachi 1:11, and Clement's First Letter speaks of those who make offerings *(prosphorá)* or gifts *(dôra)*, presumably as ministers of the eucharist.[20]

Ignatius of Antioch gives us one of the strongest images of presence in speaking of the eucharist as "the medicine of immortality" and insists against the Docetists that "the Eucharist is the flesh of our Saviour."[21] He is equally firm that the fellowship of the church is centered in the bishop. Irenaeus declares the presence of Christ in the cup, which "is his own blood," and the bread, which "is his own body."[22] Cyprian speaks of fellowship in poetic terms: "As many grains, collected, and ground, and mixed together into one mass, make one bread; so in Christ, who is the heavenly bread, we may know that there is one body, with which our number is joined and united."[23]

The work of the Holy Spirit is expressed by *The Apostolic Tradition* which, in its eucharistic prayer, invokes the Father to send the Holy Spirit on the offering of the holy church and to fill those gathered so as to strengthen their faith in truth. This activity is defined more explicitly more than a century later in Cyril of Jerusalem's mystagogical catecheses. He tells the newly initiated that in the eucharist "we call upon the merciful God to send forth His Holy Spirit upon the gifts lying before Him; that He may make the bread the Body of Christ, and the Wine the Blood of Christ; for whatsoever the Holy Ghost has touched, is sanctified and changed *(metabébletai).*"[24] This suggests the direction the Orthodox churches subsequently took in understanding the function of the Holy Spirit in making holy and transforming the eucharistic elements. Cyril is a portent of an approach that became highly important in the East though neglected in the West until recently.

We, aware of later developments, find puzzling the way early Christians spoke of the presence in terms both realistic and symbolic. Cyril speaks in the same lecture of the bread and wine as the "sign *(antitýpon)* of the Body and Blood of Christ." Augustine uses language that sounds realistic at times and, at other times, obviously symbolic. Unfortunately, such ambiguity is no longer a possibility for us, but it is refreshing to see the latitude of expression still possible in the fourth century. The boundaries of acceptable terms were wide.

Augustine gives us insights into the theme of sacrifice. Building on the concepts of Christ's eternal sacrifice (Heb. 9:14) and the Christians' union to Christ, Augustine says, "This is the sacrifice of Christians; we being many, are one body in Christ. . . . [The church] herself is offered in the offering she makes to God."[25] Thus the eucharist is a joining of the church's worship with Christ's own eternal offering on its behalf. This concept of sacrifice was overshadowed in subsequent centuries.

The first thousand years of Christianity is characterized by the absence of tight theological distinctions about understanding the eucharist. Even the vocabulary for technical theological discussion of the eucharist is lacking. A variety of terms are used, each author choosing what suits his purpose best. A portent for the West appears in the suggestion of **Ambrose** that it is the recitation of the words of institution that accomplishes consecration: "And by what words and whose sayings does consecration take place? The Lord Jesus's. . . . So the word of Christ accomplishes this sacrament."[26] But the early period has a marvelous freedom in expressing what it experienced in the heart, not what had to be defined in the head. The church experienced the eucharist rather than debated it.

Two monks started the debate in the West, **Paschasius Radbertus** and **Ratramnus**, both from the Abbey of Corbie, France, in the ninth century. Paschasius, trying to compress into words Christ's presence experienced in the eucharist, used language we would call literal or realistic; shortly later Ratramnus tried to express the same experience in more spiritual or symbolic language. Two centuries later, controversy again erupted, this time much less friendly. Flatly rejected were the efforts of **Berengarius** to express in symbolic terms the experience of the presence of Christ in the eucharist. A crude confession was forced on him, affirming that the Body of Christ is handled and broken by the priest's hands and crushed by the communicant's teeth. From the eleventh century onward, the eucharist became the subject not just of devout experience but also of intellectual speculation.

There is nothing wrong in this, but unfortunately the more controversial themes came to the forefront and others quietly withered away both in piety and in doctrinal development. A penitential and introspective piety prevailed rather than a joyful spirit of thanksgiving. The mass had come to focus almost entirely on the passion, death, and resurrection with the sorrowful mysteries predominating in the West. As the rite became increasingly clerical and communion became a rare or once-a-year affair, any strong sense of communal celebration was dissipated. The Old Testament lessons were gone, and no references to creation and the rest of the old covenant salvation history appeared in the Roman canon. Thus commemoration of Christ's work was severely curtailed. The eschatological dimension had long since disappeared, and the Roman rite simply overlooked any statement of the Holy Spirit's eucharistic activity.

Left were two areas for debate: how Christ was present and how the eucharist was a sacrifice. Late medieval theologians devoted their attention to these two areas. The most significant development was agreement on the word that described the experience of bread and wine as conveying the reality of Christ. As we have seen in Berengarius's case, the church was groping its way toward realistic language of a spatial variety. But the word **transubstantiation** arrived late, long after the idea had been striving for expression. It was not used definitively until 1215 when the Fourth Lateran Council spoke of "the transubstantiation of bread into body and wine into blood."[27] The term itself has undergone changing meaning in subsequent history. Using the best of philosophical tools available, especially Aristotle, the scholastics described this miracle so that it could be expressed, "the substance of the bread is turned into the body of Christ and the substance of the wine into his blood."[28] The **accidents** (what is perceptible to the senses) remain unchanged, but the **substance** (inner reality) is miraculously transformed contrary to all else in the natural world where all accidents and substance conform to each other. This triumph of rationalism tried to explain the mystery rather than merely accepting and adoring it.

Hand in hand with such theological definitions went practices which increasingly removed the sacred elements from contact with the people except for a dramatic showing at the **elevation** when the bread and cup were raised for all to see. The doctrine of **concomitance** made it clear that the whole Christ is present in every drop and crumb of the consecrated elements, so it was no longer considered necessary for the laity to receive the cup with all the dangers of spilling Christ's blood that this entailed. With infrequent communion, the laity's role was minimal. The priest offered mass on their behalf in a language few people understood.

Thought about the eucharist as sacrifice also developed so that the mass was seen as propitiatory, being performed to bring about desired purposes. Sophisticated explanations that the mass was a memorial and not a repetition of the unique sacrifice of Calvary too often were lost on most people. Current theories of the atonement focused almost exclusively on the death of Jesus as satisfying the Father's scheme of justice, and the eucharist dovetailed all too neatly into this scheme of things. Too easily, this narrow concept of sacrifice made the eucharist a means of securing God's favor instead of a proclamation of such favor already accomplished for all eternity.

Presence and sacrifice were aspects highly developed by the late medieval period but this spurt of doctrinal construction was at the expense of a balanced interpretation. If ample concern had been given to the eucharist as the proclamation of thanksgiving, the sacrament of unity, the commemoration of all salvation history, the present work of the Holy Spirit, or the foretaste of the messianic banquet, then doctrinal developments would have been far different. At least, so it seems from a modern perspective.

A reshuffling of priorities occurred in the Reformation with a limited success achieved in some instances in restoring a balanced eucharistic understanding. Unfortunately, the Reformers themselves had been so thoroughly formed by late medieval penitential piety that they brought this attitude to their rites. There were few things the Reformers were unanimous about, but rejecting late medieval approaches to understanding presence and sacrifice was one of them. The Reformation (facilitated by the use of the vernacular) saw tremendous gains in recovery of a sense of fellowship, some improvement in the breadth of commemoration, and reforms in the concepts of presence and sacrifice. Brilioth says, "The rediscovery of the idea of communion [fellowship] is the greatest positive contribution of the Reformation in regard to the eucharist."[29] Accomplishments in recovering a joyful sense of thanksgiving were mixed, acknowledgment of the work of the Holy Spirit was recovered by Calvin, and eschatological perception was rare except among Anabaptists suffering persecution.

Luther, who discarded the canon of the mass because it reeked of sacrifice and who saw sacrifice as the "third captivity" of the mass, was able to accomplish little that was positive about sacrifice.[30] He did, however, wrestle with the concept of presence and though rejecting the idea of transubstantiation ("the second captivity"), did insist that the bread and wine became the substance of Christ's body and blood, though still retaining the natural substances of bread and wine just as a red hot iron can be both iron and fire. Since Christ is everywhere present by his divine nature (ubiquity) and all the powers of his divine nature are communicated to his human nature, Christ can be present on a thousand altar-tables simultaneously. This solves some problems though it still states the concept of presence in spatial terms: Christ is present "in, with, and under" bread and wine. Even in rebellion, Luther is captive to medieval concepts of the presence. Luther recovered much congregational participation in the restoration of the chalice to the laity ("the first captivity"), the use of vernacular, and rich congregational hymnody.

Surely the greatest single tragedy of the Reformation was the conflict between Luther and Zwingli over the concept of presence, a fight which culminated in the **Marburg Colloquy** (1529). Zwingli, impatient with any concept that the physical could convey the spiritual, repudiated Luther's teaching on presence with the view that Christ is only present spiritually by his divine nature. Zwingli's strength was emphasis on fellowship and the spiritual union of the participants together confessing their faith, a transubstantiation of people rather than elements. Luther was caught between the rationalism of the right (scholasticism) and the left (Zwinglian humanism), so the two Reformers split over the sacrament of unity. Clearly they were, indeed, of a "different spirit."

John Calvin's role was something of a mediator between the two, but he added much that was his own, or rather, recovered something of the early church. God, who knows us best, uses outward signs in self-giving. Because of our sin and lack of faith, such signs are necessary; because of God's love for us, they are effective. We feed on Christ in the eucharist, but it is made possible only through the operation of the Holy Spirit who raises our souls to heaven. The means of feeding on Christ is a "mystery, which plainly neither the mind is able to conceive nor the tongue to express."[31] In stressing the role of the Holy Spirit and the sense of mystery, Calvin picks up some authentic early Christian strands that medieval developments had overlooked. Calvin also stresses that the Lord's Supper implies mutual love or fellowship: "For what sharper goal could there be to arouse mutual love among us than when Christ, giving himself to us, not only invites us by his own example to pledge and give ourselves to one another, but inasmuch as he makes himself common to all, also makes all of us one in himself."[32] His spatial location of Christ in heaven is crude, nor does Calvin contribute much that is positive on concepts of sacrifice, thanksgiving, commemoration, or eschatology. But Calvin's theology recovers the centrality of the work of the Holy Spirit.

Among the Anabaptists an intense sense of fellowship thrived, reinforced by the **ban** against fellowship with baptized believers who had lapsed. The pure church was also a church under persecution—a reality reflected in their hymnody. Under the threat of persecution and conscious of their martyrs, Anabaptist celebrations were typified by a vivid eschatological fervor.

There has been much controversy over Cranmer's eucharistic doctrine as expressed in the first two *BCPs*. In general, his position is seen as somewhat similar to Zwingli's but with a stronger view of the value of frequent communion. "Yet he is distinguished from the Zurich reformer in esteeming the Lord's Supper more highly and in emphasizing that its faithful observance is accompanied by the operation of God's grace."[33] Zwingli's feelings for fellowship are present too, as well as a rather strong dimension of commemoration, though like most of the Reformation materials this focuses narrowly on the passion.

John Wesley had the advantages of living in a time after the

Reformation controversies and possessing a deep knowledge of patristics. Though close to Calvin in many aspects, Wesley achieved a balance that even the Genevan reformer lacked. This is reflected in the divisions of John and Charles Wesley's *Hymns on the Lord's Supper*: "As It Is a Memorial of the Sufferings and Death of Christ," "As It Is a Sign and a Means of Grace," "The Sacrament a Pledge of Heaven," "The Holy Eucharist as It Implies a Sacrifice," "Concerning the Sacrifice of Our Persons," and "After the Sacrament."[34] At last, a strong positive Protestant statement of eucharistic sacrifice occurs in Wesley, coupled with a patristic-Calvinistic sense of presence as mystery. The eschatological and pneumatological aspects are vividly present, too, as is fellowship, though commemoration and thanksgiving still focus only on Christ's passion and death.

The late–twentieth century saw extraordinary developments in new understandings of the eucharist, especially for a more carefully balanced approach. Brilioth's book, used by such Roman Catholics as Louis Bouyer, has been itself a contributor to this process, but much has come about through broader ecumenical contacts and greater study of the biblical, historical, and theological aspects of eucharistic theology. The problem areas of presence and sacrifice have received the most attention, but in all areas our understanding has been greatly increased.

Vatican II made a notable contribution in restating the whole question of presence by declaring that Christ is present in the mass not in one but in a variety of ways: in the person of the minister, in the bread and wine, in the sacramental action, in the word, and in the congregation (CSL, par. 7). More recently, the presence of Christ in the poor in our midst has been realized as another mode of presence. How different history might have been had these insights come a thousand years sooner!

Catholic theologians have picked up another trail in developing the concept of **transsignification** in which emphasis is on the meaning or purpose of the sacramental signs in the eucharist.[35] Earlier, Odo Casel had opened new possibilities in portraying the mass as a time mystery rather than a spatial one. According to the concept of transsignification, if the meaning of something is a principal component of its very being, it can be said that the bread and wine undergo an ontological change in the eucharist by coming to signify the body and blood of Christ. By analogy, a box of chocolates becomes a gift through the sign-act of giving and then is no longer simply candy but a means of self giving. These newer concepts, which virtually equate meaning with being, admit the insights of recent phenomenological philosophy and sometimes seem to reflect Calvin's understanding of God's use of signs as a way God accommodates to human capacity. Such new approaches are far from being unanimously accepted by Roman Catholics but have had great appeal to many Protestants as the basis for common understanding. The degree to which this has become possible is shown in the 1982 ecumenical document, *Baptism, Eucharist, and Ministry.*[36]

Our understanding of sacrifice has broadened immeasurably by equating it, not with just the passion-atonement aspect, but with the whole incarnation of Christ, who emptied himself of being God to take the form of a slave (Phil. 2:7). The presence of sacrificial terminology in the New Testament and early church has been more widely recognized. Recovery of such images as Augustine's picture of the church in union with Christ in Christ's eternal offering for us have made a more positive approach possible without undercutting the unique character of Christ's work already accomplished. Currently, sacrifice is also seen as the memorial of Christ's work, all that Christians have or could hope to have to offer God. Commemoration and sacrifice are thus closely related.

Commemoration is now seen in its broadest aspects as encompassing all the work of Christ from creation to final judgment. Important new liturgical developments are the inclusion of Old Testament lessons and psalmody in the Lord's Supper once again and the recovery in Western eucharistic prayers of recital of the saving works of God in the Old Covenant. Commemoration is far broader than recalling just Good Friday and Easter.

Thanksgiving has been expressed abundantly in many modern liturgies concurrent with a broadened understanding of commemoration. Eucharists have once again become joyful occasions of praise. Part of this is due to contacts with the Eastern churches, which have always maintained that one comes to church primarily to praise God for what God has done, not to tell God what sinners we are. Even the sorrowful mysteries of Christ's suffering and death are ultimately joyful.

The Eastern churches, too, have made Westerners aware of how vital is the understanding of the eucharist as the work of the Holy Spirit. Virtually all new eucharistic prayers have a distinct *epiclesis*. Pentecostals, operating primarily from experience rather than theological reflection, have cherished these insights since the beginning of the twentieth century.

Evidence of new value for fellowship is abundant, as is seen in the post–Vatican II reform of a vernacular liturgy, communion in the hand and in both species, and efforts for full congregational participation. As have Roman Catholics, the churches of the Reformation have regained the kiss of peace as a congregational act.

It is not quite so apparent but there has also been increased concern with the eucharist as anticipation, looking in an eschatological direction to the heavenly banquet that will mark the completion of all things in Jesus Christ. Many new eucharistic prayers explicitly state this aspect of Christian faith. An acclamation, recovered by Roman Catholics and Protestants alike, is one sign of this: "Christ will come again."

There is much in which to rejoice in these new understandings of what the church experiences at the Lord's Supper. These interpretations bring Christians not only closer to the witness of the Bible and early church, but also closer to each other.

PASTORAL CONCERNS

Pastoral practice should reflect how the church has grown in understanding in recent years so that one can exercise the fullest ministry in this area. There is a close relationship between theory and practice for those responsible for planning, preparing for, and presiding at the eucharist.

In the first place, the **architectural setting** will dictate many, if not all, of the possibilities open to us. All traditions have moved in recent years to demanding a free standing altar-table so that the priest or minister can face the people across it. This became mandatory in new Roman Catholic churches in 1964, and most

Protestant churches have followed suit. Once one has celebrated facing the people across the Lord's Table it is hard ever again to turn one's back to them.

Not only must one be able to face the people, but also it must be easy for them to come to the altar-table if this is the practice of one's tradition. Some traditions are recovering the action of gathering around the Lord's Table whether to stand, to kneel, or to sit around extensions of it. The very act of coming forward in the company of one's neighbors is a powerful nonverbal sign of fellowship and offering of self. The altar table must be not only visible but also accessible. Increasingly, in many churches even on noneucharistic occasions the altar-table is the focus of acts of prayer and offering while proclamation centers in the pulpit. This implies a single ministerial altar-table, cleared for action, that is designed to be used and is used. It does not indicate a monumental altar-table, conspicuous but used only as a repository for an unused Bible, flowers, or candles.

The Lord's Supper is basically **action** supplemented by words. How careful are we to let the actions speak? An excellent experiment purely as a learning experience is to celebrate the eucharist in silence, forcing the actions, vessels, elements, setting, vestments, and every other available medium of communication, except the audible, to speak for itself.

All the new eucharistic rites are based on the fourfold pattern of actions described above. Does the taking or preparing draw attention to the fact that a meal is to follow and the altar-table and elements must be prepared? Do we use our hands as well as our voice to express that we are giving thanks to God over the elements? Is the breaking of bread a clear sign of the unity of the one loaf broken for many? Is there an actual touch of hands as the bread is given into the hand of each recipient? All these acts call for careful attention so that their sign value is expressed,·not concealed. Good communication demands sensitive preparation.

God works through presider and people, but the presider has the responsibility to make the communication as clear as possible. We would not mumble while preaching the sermon; we should not underplay actions while acting the eucharist. These sign-acts are not decoration; they are a vital part of ministry in bringing people to communion with God. At the Lord's Table, we understand how completely God knows and loves people as full human beings. The glory and majesty of God's being is accommodated to our humble human capacity. Thus what we do with our hands, bodies, and voices in leading the eucharist is a vital ministry that demands sensitivity to how humans relate and communicate. There is a body language as well as a vocal one, and we must learn to speak both with eloquence.

The **bread and wine** themselves are also an important part of the action. It was sometimes said it took more faith to make Roman Catholic school children believe that communion wafers are bread than to believe the bread becomes Christ's body. Real bread they had seen. The use of common food is at the heart of the eucharist. Christ did not choose nectar and ambrosia, the food of the gods, but bread and wine, the food of humans. The signs must not be fake. Much of the sign value is lost when the bread becomes cardboard wafers, plastic "fish food," or anything other than what bread appears, tastes, and smells to be. The same is true of wine. Nonalcoholic wines are now available; at least the fruit of the grape must be used, not something artificial that has never seen a vineyard. The bread must be bread that can be broken easily, neither too fresh nor too stale. The act of breaking it can be one of the most meaningful parts of the service if carefully done. The act of giving is important, too. Giving a gift can be a real art; giving bread and wine are no exceptions.

Particular problems apply to giving the cup. Certainly the highest sign value of unity is in giving the wine from a common chalice, but people in most segments of American culture believe most devoutly in germs, although few have seen one. The American Medical Association has stated that when a chalice of wine is turned and wiped after each communicant, such practice "seems to remove any danger."[37] But for those with overwhelming anxieties, these fears may be escaped by dipping the bread in a common chalice (**intinction**), pouring from the chalice into individual cups, or giving the wine already poured in individual cups. Until modern times, the amount of bread and wine consumed was not tiny crumbs and drops but somewhat more generous portions, certainly with a higher sign value.

Special problems arise in ministering to the sick. The Roman Catholics have devised a system of **extraordinary ministers** (laypeople) who are trained to bring consecrated bread to the sick and elderly, sometimes daily. Another arrangement is to have several persons from the congregation join the minister or priest in a sickroom celebration, abbreviated to be sure, but nevertheless a real common service of discerning the Lord's body. Some churches now have eucharistic rites for use in the sickroom. The bringing of consecrated bread and wine to the sick has been an important ministry ever since Justin Martyr.

Much planning, preparation, and care in conducting the eucharist in all its outward and visible aspects is necessary so that it may best communicate the inward reality of Christ's generous self giving to us in the eucharist.

CHAPTER TEN

OCCASIONAL SERVICES

ife is full of recurring cycles and unique events. One may become ill on numerous occasions, but one has to die only once. We find that Christian worship has ways of ministering to the recurrent cycles and to the events that are unique. Accordingly, we shall speak of the recurrent cycles as journeys and the unique events as passages. Both call for special concern and care on the part of the Christian community through **occasional services** or what we might call **pastoral rites**. These services manifest the Christian community's loving care for its members as they continue their steady journey through life or pass through new and irrevocable experiences.

The journey through life involves, for all Christians, transgressions against what we know as God's will. All Christians by definition are sinners and know it. But Christian worship provides ways of dealing with this aspect of our condition, especially when the burden of sin becomes intolerable. Through various ways, Christians can repent and live with assurance that God acts to forgive sin. Various names identify the process: **penance** or **confession** are the traditional terms; **reconciliation** is the favored word at present. We shall use this last term because reconciliation suggests both the vertical sense of being reunited to God and also the horizontal sense of reunion with one's neighbor.

Reconciliation is often seen as medicine for a sick soul. At the same time, Christianity ministers to bodies that are sick or injured. For some people, sickness is a rare occurrence or something they are spared entirely, but for many people it may be a recurrent cycle.

Ever since the apostles, Christians have been involved in the **healing of the body** as well as sick souls. Ministry to the sick and dying has received more attention in Christian worship in recent years than ever before. Sickness is an important part of many people's life journey, and the church must be present at these times, too.

The mountain peaks and valleys of life are occasions for Christian worship just as surely as the flat plains of day-by-day living are. The crisis points of life are marked when the community of faith gathers around individuals to express its love as people pass through various stages: **marriage** (for most), **ordination** (for some), **religious profession or commissioning** (for some), and **death** (for all). Each passage reflects three stages in varying degrees: separation from a past way of life, transition or movement when one crosses the threshold into a new order of being, and incorporation into a new way of life or death itself. Several are accompanied by transition periods of time (engagement, seminary studies, novitiate, declining health) as well as transitions in space (a new home, new place for ministry, new community, the cemetery).

For Christians, none of these passages is a purely private moment but rather a concern shared by the whole Christian community. A wedding signals the formation of a new family and potentially adds to the body of Christ. Even the loneliness of dying is mitigated by the belief that death does not remove one from the church but only transfers one into the larger portion, the Church Triumphant. As communal concerns, these intensely personal moments are usually celebrated in the midst of the Christian community. The community of love surrounds and supports us both in the joys of marriage, ordination, profession or commissioning, and in the sorrows of death.

God reaches out through the human community to establish new relationships of love at these special times. These new relationships are expressed in varying ways in different relationships and various kinds of love, such as conjugal or for the bereaved. The eucharist can be an important part of the church's ministry of love in these moments of passage.

Except for ordination and religious profession or commissioning, these passages are by no means uniquely Christian but affect all people. In the ways life crises are observed, we see more clearly than anywhere else in Christian worship the influence of local culture. A great variety of customs and local practices function at these moments, occasionally in conflict with Christian faith, sometimes concurring with it, and frequently indifferent to it. Christians have no monopoly in commemorating such passages as marriage or death, but they are certainly influenced by the ways others observe such events. It is important to know what is the distinctive Christian witness on such occasions and what is culturally determined so that one can make informed decisions in dealing with specific situations. Strangely enough, the more marginal one's relationship to a Christian community may be, the more important Christian passages such as marriage and funerals often are. Indeed, they may be one's sole contact with the community of faith. Thus these passages are important contacts in the evangelization of marginal Christians.

We shall consider first the services for life's journey—reconciliation and healing. Then we shall look at Christian marriage, ordination, religious profession or commissioning, and care of the dead. Each deals with effective ministry in a moment of deep human need. Our survey will be quick but will indicate some contemporary directions of faith and practice in each area.

RECONCILIATION

Not everyone needs healing of the body; everyone needs healing of the soul. Jerome speaks of baptism and reconciliation as planks to which we may cling after the shipwreck of sin. Reconciliation has certain parallels to baptism just as to physical healing. Baptism has been compared to marriage, which makes visible the establishment of a permanent relationship based on love, but even in such a relationship there come times of conflict and the need to "make up," to be reconciled. Thus, unlike baptism, which is not repeatable, reconciliation is a recurring event.

It is surprising that the New Testament tells us little about baptized sinners. Paul threatens he "will not be lenient" in Corinth (2 Cor. 13:2) and a notorious sinner is to be handed "over to Satan" (1 Cor. 5:5). Ample precedent was available in the Old Testament for the penitential practices of supplication, fasting, mourning, and wearing sackcloth. In light of the important role the text played in subsequent ages, it is amazing that the early church seems to place little emphasis on the verse that most clearly gives authority to forgive or retain sins, John 20:23. Clearly the return of sinners is sought in the Gospels, and Paul equates bondage to sin with death. Evidence for ritual acts of reconciliation beyond the cleansing of baptism are hard to find in the New Testament.

Tertullian tells us much about the early practice of reconciliation in his early third-century treatise *On Penance*. Sin is not only an offense against God but also a wound of the church for it endangers all Christians (especially in time of persecution). It is far better to acknowledge one's sin and suffer embarrassment before the community than to enter hell after this life. God cannot be deceived. Penance involved a rigorous public discipline of daily deprivation for those guilty of gross sins, such as apostasy. Penitents were excluded from the eucharist until reconciled to the church on Easter just as the newly baptized were being admitted to their first communion. Reconciliation was indeed the plank after a shipwreck for those who had sinned grievously and destroyed the cleansing effects of their baptism. Involving a period of fasting, wearing penitential clothing, and continence, reconciliation was usually practiced once in a lifetime. Tertullian considers it medicinal, a way of healing a wound in the community, just as astringent medicine heals. Thus Easter morning publicly celebrated the reconciliation of lost sheep both to God and to the offended Christian community.

Drastic changes in reconciliation occurred in the Middle Ages. Indeed, no sacrament except perhaps healing has reversed its original form so much. Originally administered by bishops, reconciliation came to be performed by presbyters; from being openly public it became private and secret; from being practiced once or twice in a lifetime, it became yearly at least and weekly in modern times; from being the rare exception it became required of all. Much of the impetus for these changes came about through the dissemination throughout Europe of Celtic **penitentials**, handbooks prescribing penalties for wrongdoings.[1] From the seventh century, the influence of the Celtic books spread, popularizing a type of penance wholly separated from that of the public assembly of the church. Indeed, some of the early Irish confessors were laymen and laywomen, but eventually only priests could be confessors. Late medieval councils decreed that confession was necessary before receiving communion, both of which must be received at least yearly, a fateful link for both sacraments.

Reconciliation was a lost opportunity in the Reformation. Luther drew up "A Short Order of Confession before the Priest for the Common Man" in 1529 and rewrote it as "How One Should Teach Common Folk to Shrive Themselves" two years later.[2] These seek to avoid the artificiality of cataloging one's sins by number and species and to give one the peace that reconciliation can offer. Both forms are for private confession to a priest or father confessor. The other Reformers were content to append penitential prayers to their public Sunday services.

Recent changes in reconciliation have been dramatic. We have seen how the Middle Ages brought drastic changes to this sacrament. Vatican II mandated revision of the "rite and formulas" of penance but gave no hint of such significant changes as those in the three distinct rites that appeared in 1973: those for "Reconciliation of Individual Penitents," for "Several Penitents with Individual Confession and Absolution," and for "Several Penitents with General Confession and Absolution." The most controversial has been the last; its use has been very restricted. In all three rites, there is provision for the reading of scripture. The last two rites dramatize the "relation of the sacrament to the community." All participants share in general confession and praise for God's mercy. The whole represents both a recovery of and an advance beyond early practice in emphasizing the communal nature of sin and our need to be reconciled to one another by God's mercy.

Many Protestant congregations have experimented with various types of **corporate services of reconciliation**. There are signs that the deep human needs reconciliation ministers to are being met. Lutherans now provide services for both "Corporate Confession and Forgiveness" and "Individual Confession and Forgiveness." Episcopalians, following practices recovered in the Oxford Movement of the nineteenth century, make provision for private "Reconciliation of a Penitent." American Presbyterians provide "A

Service of Repentance and Forgiveness for Use with a Penitent Individual."

Most of these churches include penitential elements in most Sunday services, especially the eucharist. The Lutherans now provide an optional preliminary "Brief Order for Confession and Forgiveness" before the eucharist. Episcopalians provide a rather free-floating "Penitential Order" for use at the eucharist and rather strongly hint that, in its absence, a general confession should follow the intercessions. For Roman Catholics and Presbyterians, the introductory rites of the normal Sunday services begin with acts of confession and pardon, a legacy of the Middle Ages.

Increased concern has been shown in recent years for penitential seasons such as Advent and Lent and occasions such as Ash Wednesday. The Puritan Tradition long had special days of humiliation and fasting as well as days of thanksgiving. There is also an old Methodist tradition of watch night services and covenant services. The first *BCP* had a service for Ash Wednesday with the fierce curses from Deuteronomy 27—a service renamed in 1662 "A Commination, or Denouncing of God's Anger and Judgements Against Sinners." Somewhat more mellow observations of Ash Wednesday have become common in many churches with optional imposition of ashes. Much of the value of corporate reconciliation is of an occasional nature and could work best when tied to special times in the church year or civil life.

The Middle Ages saw development of the church's understanding of what it experienced in reconciliation. Lombard has much to say about reconciliation (seventy pages), indicating great development by the twelfth century in the frequent use of this sacrament by all. Most important, he tells us "that by penance not only once, but often, we rise from our sins . . . true penance may be done repeatedly."[3] The process of reconciliation that Lombard discusses in detail is summed up by the Council of Florence as involving three acts of penitence as the matter of the sacrament: "**contrition** of the heart . . . **confession** with the mouth . . . [and] **satisfaction** for sins . . . chiefly by prayer, fasting, and almsgiving." The form was the words of the priest (the minister of this sacrament): "I absolve you."[4]

Reconciliation was not considered a sacrament in any of the

Reformation churches although Luther encouraged private penance, and penitential elements became a conspicuous part of Sunday worship. With all its shortcomings, the medieval practice of penance did enable men and women to live life with the concrete assurance that God had truly acted to forgive them when they had been truly contrite, confessed to a priest, and performed works of satisfaction. The Reformation brought the sense that all Christians could exercise a priestly role to one another in confessing and pardoning one another. But often where power is available to all, it is exercised by none. All Protestant traditions found standards of discipline and judgment necessary, though means of enforcement varied. Calvin tied the disciplinary action of **fencing the tables** (that is, excluding notorious sinners, 1 Cor. 11:27) to the eucharist, and Wesley demanded communion tickets from his class members. Both practices placed an undue disciplinary burden on the eucharist.

The new concepts behind current reforms in reconciliation are actually very old. They focus on the nature of sin as an offense against neighbor as well as God. In various rites, the whole community engages in listening to God's word in scripture, conducting examination of conscience, pleading for forgiveness, and hearing God's will to forgive declared. The corporate nature of sin in such forms as racism, nationalism, sexism, and other injustices which groups practice against others comes in for examination and confession in many of these rites. Thus services of reconciliation are deeply involved in the Christian pursuit of justice.

MINISTRY TO THE SICK

The church's ministry to the sick has involved a variety of cultic acts over the centuries. These have ranged from simple bedside prayer to public healing services. Recent years have seen a strong shift in practice on the part of Roman Catholics and increased interest among Protestants in exploring new ways of ministering to the sick. Both have had to avoid the bizarre and spectacular.

The Gospels are full of accounts of Jesus' healing ministry, and Acts makes it clear that the apostles continued in this work. Mark

6:13 tells us, the twelve "anointed with oil many who were sick and cured them" while Jesus was still with them. Apostolic practice is abundantly chronicled, but the key passage for subsequent developments is James 5:14-16. Several matters stand out in this passage. The elders or presbyters (the council presiding over a church) have a special ministry of healing. Their function is to "pray over" the sick "anointing them with oil in the name of the Lord." The purpose is definitely healing of the body, but it is also accompanied by forgiveness of sins. Therefore all Christians are advised to "confess your sins to one another, . . . so that you may be healed."

The use of oil for healing purposes was widespread in the ancient world and was both used externally for **anointing** and taken internally. For Christians, such use was natural since "Messiah" or "Christ" meant "anointed one." Both human prayer and divine activity are joined: prayer to save and the Lord to raise up. The statement of the power to heal is strong in James 5 though no more so than Mark 16:18: "they will lay their hands on the sick, and they will recover."

The most striking part of the passage, of course, is the link of physical healing to forgiveness of sin. We are inclined to distinguish sharply between these two, but the writer is concerned with full restoration, both bodily and spiritually. Quite clearly the purpose of anointing and prayer is both physical and spiritual healing.

Our next clear insight into anointing of the sick comes in *The Apostolic Tradition*. After the eucharistic prayer, someone may offer oil. The bishop gives thanks over the oil, and God is asked to grant that "it may give strength to all that taste of it and health to all that use it."[5] The oil is obviously meant both to be drunk and to be applied externally for the purpose of healing. More than a century later, Sarapion gives us more detail; he includes a prayer over the oil after the eucharistic prayer: "that every fever and every demon and every illness may be cured through the drinking and anointing."[6] A subsequent prayer in Sarapion's collection is even more explicit in listing the medicinal and exorcistic virtues ascribed to the oil. In these early centuries, anyone in need of healing (or their friends) would bring oil to church, have it blessed, and then drink it or anoint themselves. The Eastern churches were more insistent on having priests perform the act of anointing. The West eventually made it normal for priests to anoint with oil that had been blessed by the bishop.

Well into the Middle Ages, the purpose of anointing the sick was seen as restoration to health, both physical and spiritual. Peter Lombard says it has "a double purpose, namely for the remission of sins, and for the relief of bodily infirmity." The one who receives it properly is "relieved both in body and in soul, provided it is expedient that he be relieved in both."[7] Lombard then launches into a long defense of repetition of the sacrament in case of recurring illness. But the later twelfth century increasingly saw anointing solely as preparation of the dying soul for entrance into heaven, as implied by the name **extreme unction**. This was a drastic change from the earlier conception and practice, which saw anointing as involving healing for both soul and body. Until recently, the scholastics were appealed to in supporting the approach that unction was the "sacrament of consecration for death."

Whereas the earliest method of anointing seems to have been wherever there was pain, by the late–Middle Ages it came to be on the eyes, ears, nostrils, mouth, hands, feet, and loins—all capable of sin. By the fifteenth century, it was determined that it should be given only to those in danger of death. The form was: "Through this holy unction and his most tender compassion, the Lord grants thee forgiveness of whatever sins thou hast committed by the sight," and so on, the matter being olive oil blessed by the bishop.[8] The benefit is "the healing of the mind and, so far as is expedient, of the body also," a rather dubious second thought.

Subsidiary sacraments and sacramentals also grew up as part of the church's ministry to the sick and dying. These included a series of psalms, prayers, lessons, and sprinkling with holy water for use when visiting the sick. Confession might be heard, if possible. Confirmation would be given if not done previously. Communion was to be given (the **viaticum**). An apostolic blessing was provided, and, at death, the soul of the dying was commended to God with the prayer: "Depart, O Christian soul." In all, just as the catechumenate made a ritual of the whole process of conversion, so the rites of the sick made a ritual of the whole process of dying as a Christian.

Little of this survived the Reformation. Calvin denounced

anointing as "playacting, by which, without reason and without benefit, they wish to resemble the apostles."[9] The apostles' gift of healing was a "temporary gift," and Calvin would have none of the current way "these fellows [Catholics] smear with their grease not the sick but half-dead corpses." Cranmer preserved portions of the Sarum "order for visiting a sick man," though abbreviating it greatly. The *BCP* retained a psalm, prayers, an exhortation, the creed in interrogatory form (as at baptism), confession and absolution, psalmody, and anointing, "upon the forehead or breast only." Bucer had problems with the anointing and it disappeared in 1552. But Bucer had no such problem with Cranmer's rite for "The Communion of the Sick," which provided that on communion days some of the elements should be reserved and brought from the church celebration to the sickroom (extended communion). On other days, there was to be an abbreviated celebration "in the sick man's house." Calvin, however, disagreed: reservation was "useless" since the sick could not hear the institution and promises. If these were recited in the sickroom there was "a true consecration," but prior consecration was of no effect.[10] Peter Martyr sided with Calvin, and any mention of reservation vanished in the 1552 *BCP*.

All traditions continued forms for **visitation of the sick**. Most of these involved prayers and confession for those anxious to die well. Early Methodism saw frequent sickroom communion celebrations. Anointing reappeared among the Church of the Brethren early in the eighteenth century. The current rite includes reading of scripture, an invitation to confession, and the anointing with oil on the head thrice, "for the forgiveness of your sins, for the strengthening of your faith, and for healing and wholeness according to God's grace and wisdom."[11]

Within the past century, there have arisen in both Protestant and Roman Catholic circles public healing services. Outside the United States, these are sometimes associated with shrines. Radio and television ministries have spread the popularity of such services enormously. Christian Science provides a healing ministry. All these efforts, though occasionally not above criticism, reflect the persistence of deep human need in this area and the frequent failure of many parishes to provide for it. Some of the most interesting experiments have been performed among charismatics in this country and in new Christian sects in Africa, many of which have mass anointings.

Vatican II gave instructions to broaden the sacrament and rename it the "anointing of the sick" for anyone "in danger of death from sickness or old age" (CSL, par. 73). Today there has been apparent success in reversing the twelfth-century narrowing so that the sacrament is given to the elderly or anyone seriously ill and may be repeated. The new rites include "Visitation and Communion of the Sick," "Rite of Anointing a Sick Person," "Viaticum," "Rite of the Sacraments for Those Near Death—Continuous Rite of Penance, Anointing, and Viaticum," "Confirmation of a Person in Danger of Death," "Rite for the Commendation of the Dying," and assorted texts. Many options are provided to adapt the rites for varying circumstances. For those dying baptized, three or even four sacraments are provided as forms of ministry (reconciliation, confirmation, anointing, and eucharist).

Within Protestantism, there has been a significant recovery of both public and sickroom healing services. The Episcopal Church has renamed and extensively revised its "Ministration to the Sick." Anointing is now provided as an integral (though optional) part of the rite. There is provision for both sickroom celebration of the eucharist or use of the reserved sacrament. There is also "Ministration at the Time of Death" with the traditional commendation "Depart, O Christian soul" and prayers for a vigil. Lutherans provide "Laying on of Hands and Anointing the Sick," while United Methodists now have both a public and a private "Service of Healing." Both services provide for possible anointing and the laying on of hands and may include a eucharist for which there is an appropriate eucharistic prayer. Prayers for especially traumatic occasions are also provided. Likewise, Presbyterians now have available "A Service for Wholeness for Use with a Congregation" and another "with an Individual." Marvelous new possibilities are now available and are being used increasingly.

There are many touchy theological issues involved in the ministry of healing, and the church has not always been willing to deal with them. The late medieval narrowing of anointing to a final catch-all sacrament of reconciliation simplified things considerably but solved nothing. It meant the church tended to lose sight of the unity of spiritual and physical affliction about which the Bible was so realistic. It meant a convenient but unrealistic dualism between body and soul. Though the New Testament is generally careful not to make illness the result of sin, it does show a close relation of the two as when Jesus heals by forgiving sin (Matt. 9:2-6) or in the James 5:14-16 passage. Reconciliation, too, was described in the early church as a healing medicine (Tertullian, *On Penance*). The church's ministry is directed to the healing of both the body and the soul. Christians are called to save people and not just souls. A large part of the ministry of Jesus and the apostles was spent healing people's bodies as well as souls.

There are certainly difficulties in the modern world in making anointing have the sign value it once did in a culture where everyone associated anointing with healing and personal hygiene. But there would seem to be real pastoral value in having such an objective act as part of ministry to the sick in order to do something visible and concrete besides oral prayers. Frequently, the sick cannot hear or understand spoken prayers but can perceive acts such as anointing. Given its biblical roots and long history, anointing would seem to be a most appropriate act.

The problems with regard to the **reserved sacrament** have changed greatly since the Reformation. As early as Justin Martyr, communion elements were sent to those absent (the sick and imprisoned).[12] The fears the Reformation had of adoration of the consecrated elements seem hardly a danger today. Fresh possibilities of ministry have opened up here. A sickroom celebration with a small group of people may seem a fuller sign since the participants are present, but this is not always possible.

A central problem in ministry to the sick is how to express adequately the church's loving concern for both body and soul, the whole person. James 5:16 suggests that all Christians are to participate in confessing and praying for one another "so that you may be healed." Our Christian neighbor, to whom we are united in baptism, has a claim on us, and we on him or her, to share in sustaining health. In this sense, ministry to the sick is an important relationship of love within the community of faith. Healing is a concern in which the whole community of faith makes its love for an ailing member visible. Relationships of love demand honesty and peace of conscience for which mutual confession becomes a part of healing of both mind and body.

Although only a few may have the ministry of anointing or bringing communion, all are called to engage in intercessory prayer for the sick member of the body. Ministry to the sick is by the whole Christian community, though most of it will take place outside the sickroom. Every Sunday service ought to include the sick and injured in the corporate prayers of intercession, and all members ought to engage in this ministry in their personal devotions. Ministry to the sick is an important part of making love visible as God acts through the community of faith.

A few pastoral dimensions are clear. Ministry to the sick involves participation of all the congregation, but much systematic visitation may get left to the clergy. Much could be said about the need for more objective acts of ministry such as anointing and communion. The Church of the Brethren *Pastor's Manual* and the new Roman Catholic and Protestant rites are well worth study. There are many places where actions speak louder than words, and the sickroom is often one of these. One often despairs of saying the right thing but sometimes an expressive gesture can be more nearly adequate. Frequently just one's presence, just being there, is a foremost sign of love. But a general sensitivity to what we do as well as to what we say ought to be cultivated. Taking the patient's hand, placing one's hand on his or her forehead, anointing with prayer, and giving communion are important forms of this ministry. Often these objective acts communicate even when hearing is impossible.

Clergy never engage in ministry alone but share it with the rest of the Christian community. Concern for the sick ought to flow over into both public and private worship. More structures need to be devised to encourage laypeople to visit and bring communion to the sick, many of whom a pastor cannot reach regularly. This is an important part of the ministry of the laity, too important to leave to chance.

Churches need to practice **public services of healing** of body and soul that are not spectacular, that do not make extravagant claims, but do take seriously that God does act in self giving in public worship. Not the least of God's gifts is the gift of healing of body and soul. Public services of healing involving reading of scripture, prayer, laying on of hands, and (perhaps) anointing are becoming increasingly frequent. They testify, after all, to God's will to health and the Church's concern for people's bodies as well as their souls.

We turn now to look at the various unique events or passages through which we pass in this life. We shall consider events that are not recurrent cycles but usually have a once and for all quality about them.

CHRISTIAN MARRIAGE

There are few, if any, occasions more joyful than a wedding. Yet the church's approach to weddings has been a slow and cautious one, always willing to leave most of the festivities outside the church door. Even now the wedding service is a curious amalgam of Christian and pagan elements. The words are an unlikely match of liturgical language and legal jargon. The minister serves as both pastor and civil servant, subject to the canons or laws of both ecclesiastical and civil societies. Weddings are a strange combination of Christ and culture.

The New Testament, though it frequently uses wedding imagery, tells us nothing about Christian weddings. We do have an account of the Jewish wedding feast Jesus attended at Cana (John 2:1-11) where occurred "the first of his signs . . . and [Jesus] revealed his glory," but all we learn is that it was not a somber and sober occasion. The early fathers tell us little more. Apparently the early church was content to allow local customs to persist. These included the Roman betrothal ceremony in which promises for the future wedding were made and a ring given. The Roman wedding rite contained the joining of hands, sacrifice at the family altar, the wedding banquet with a wedding cake, and marriage bed rites. These ceremonies started at the home of the bride and concluded at the new home of the couple. The betrothal vows, joining of hands, and giving of a ring persist in Christian weddings today. The church's role for many centuries seems to have been limited to influencing Christians to marry Christians. Ignatius of Antioch said, "It is right for men and women who marry to be united with the bishop's approval." Christian blessings were substituted for those in the name of pagan deities, and the eucharist might be celebrated in place of pagan sacrifice.[13]

Other pagan rites accumulated as the church converted northern Europe: rice as a fertility symbol, giving away the bride, bridesmaids dressed to confuse evil spirits who might hex the bride (apparently evil spirits were none too perceptive), the wedding veil as a similar protection, and the offering of money. For centuries, weddings continued to take place in homes or taverns, and the church's involvement was minimal. Many weddings today make one envy the church's wisdom then!

The church's encroachment was unintentional. With the growth of legal systems out of chaos, it became increasingly necessary to have written records of weddings to prevent clandestine marriages and to provide for legitimacy of offspring and uncontested inheritances. Wealthy people (cf. Jan van Eyck's portrait of Giovanni Arnolfini and bride) could afford painted portraits as a record; ordinary people needed a written certificate. In most villages, the only literate person was the priest ("clergy" meant learned), and his presence became increasingly necessary at weddings simply to witness and record them legally. A nuptial mass (distinct from the wedding itself) would frequently be celebrated at the parish church after the wedding and the newly married couple blessed just before the fraction.

The legal character of the wedding ceremony is its most distinctive feature. Weddings consist essentially of a public **contract** freely and mutually assented to before witnesses. The traditional language, "to have and to hold," is language still used in conveyance of property. "From this day forward" dates the contract. Then follows the unconditional nature of said contract, "for better for worse." "Till death us do part" terminates the above, and "I give thee my troth" is the pledge of faithfulness to it. All this is lawyers' talk, not liturgists'. Words almost identical to today's vows appear in English in fourteenth-century manuscripts, long before other liturgical documents were translated into the vernacular. The center of this most joyful occasion is a legal transaction.

By the twelfth century, weddings were moving to the church door or porch where most of a village's legal transactions took place in the sight of God. The priest had by now become requisite for the wedding itself. A nuptial mass and blessing inside the church often followed the wedding. The nuptial mass was prohibited in Advent and Lent. Chaucer tells us of his Wife of Bath, "husbands at the church door she had five" and was ready for more. Luther's wedding rite (1529) still took place at the church door and then moved inside for scripture reading and blessing. In the English Reformation, the full wedding service finally (after fifteen hundred years) took place inside the church building.

Eastern Orthodox churches have preserved distinctive symbolic ceremonies such as exchanging the vows and rings in the vestibule (the world), processing inside the church (the kingdom), crowning both bride and groom as a symbol of the kingdom of God (their future family), both drinking from a single cup, and a triple procession around a table in the nave. Theologically, the priest is considered the actual minister of the sacrament. He represents Christ, who acts in this sacrament within his body, the church.

By and large, the Reformation found few changes necessary beyond substituting the vernacular for the entire service and simplifying it somewhat. Wedding rites have always tended to be conservative since society has such an enormous stake in their proper observance. The Church of England continued to require three prior readings of **banns** (public announcements of the forthcoming wedding) thus underscoring society's involvement. The woman's promise in the *Sarum Manuale*, "to be bonere and buxum in bedde and at te borde," was dropped, but much of the medieval service was retained. Psalm 128 asking that they may "see [thy] children's children" and a prayer for the fruitfulness of the union were retained, but the church did not press for a miracle; these items could be omitted "where the woman is past child birth." Rubrics called upon the couple to receive the eucharist "the same day of their marriage."

Puritan objections brought the removal of some ceremonies, such as the giving of rings, but most of them have quietly been restored in subsequent years. The tendency in Protestantism in the past hundred years has been to retain or to recover much of the pre-Reformation shape of the service. Protestants have been reluctant to accept the frankly sexual nature of the rite as it appeared in the Reformation. At least the medieval-Reformation rites acknowledged that marriage involved sex and usually produced children. The Church of England may still use that wonderful line in the vows: "With this ring I thee wed, with my body I thee worship," but that proved too much for eighteenth-century American Episcopalians. From Luther's "Order of Marriage" comes the use of Matthew 19:6, "What God has joined together, let no one separate" and the declaration, "I pronounce them joined in marriage."[14] Cranmer and most Protestant services used these or similar works. English-speaking Protestantism generally follows the medieval-Anglican versions of the vows, including the **betrothal vows** (future tense: "*N.*, wilt thou have . . .") and the **espousal vows** (present tense: "I, *N.*, take thee . . .") and the giving of the rings ("With this ring . . ."). Wesley omitted giving away the bride and the giving of rings; his descendants restored both.

Recent revisions of the marriage rite have so much in common, it is hard to distinguish between them. In most of them, the obligations of the community are underlined, such as the congregation taking a vow "to uphold these two persons in their marriage." Many new versions try to make the wedding rite a full service with hymns, lessons, and other acts of worship provided to make it resemble normal Christian worship. Too often, a fifteen-minute ceremony has sufficed to seal a fifty-year covenant.

There has been a marked shift among Protestants toward suggesting the eucharist as part of the service for Christian couples. Roman Catholics encourage the eucharist for Catholics. Propers for nuptial eucharists are provided in several churches. In most cases, there are numerous options and far greater possibilities for flexibility than ever existed before. Several churches make provision for the blessing of a civil service held previously. A few service books contain materials for wedding anniversaries and the renewal of marriage vows.

Another common characteristic is emphasis on equality. Women no longer promise to "obey him, and serve him," and the giving away of the bride has disappeared in some services, though made an option in others. A positive statement of God's goodness in creating us male and female appears in many rites, though most are still reticent about mentioning the possibility (or current existence) of a family except the Roman Catholic.

Certainly the most noticeable common feature is the espousal vow itself, worded so as to state lifelong intent ("as long as we both shall live"). This is specifically stated in all the chief new official rites and is a clear sign of a split between much of contemporary culture and Christian ideals. A common feature in recent rites is avoidance of the clerical "I pronounce" in favor of a statement such as that of the United Church of Canada: "*N.* and *N.* have made a covenant of marriage before God and in the presence of all of us. . . . Therefore, I declare them to be husband and wife."[15]

An important recent development has been the compilation of *A Christian Celebration of Marriage: An Ecumenical Liturgy*.[16] Prepared by the ecumenical Consultation on Common Texts, the service is designed to be used by Christians of differing traditions. At present (2000), it still awaits approval from the Vatican.

The church's thinking about the wedding service has been greatly influenced by the fact that so much canon law focuses on questions of marriage. This has tended to make reflection on marriage revolve more around legalistic controversies than liturgical ones. Indeed, except for the Reformation debate over whether matrimony was a sacrament, controversies over the rite itself have been almost nil.

Two New Testament passages have been of prominence in the church's thinking about marriage: the sayings of Jesus with regard to the indissolubility of marriage (Matt. 19:9 and 5:32) and Ephesians 5:22-23. The rites of the Western church have ignored the eschatological references to Christ comparing himself to the bridegroom and his disciples as sharing in the wedding feast (Matt. 9:15; 25:1-13), an allusion to the coming kingdom of God. The Ephesians passage calls marriage "a great mystery *(mystérion)* . . . with respect to Christ and the church" (5:32, literal trans.). The church has relied on this passage as indicating the completeness of the union between husband and wife, though it may tell us even more about the union between Christ and Church. *Mystérion* became *sacramentum* in Latin, thus ensuring the eventual inclusion of marriage among the seven sacraments.

The early church had few problems in interpreting marriage in a monogamous culture. Even Tertullian could find little to complain about in the pagan marriage rites as long as Christian blessings and sacrifice were substituted for pagan equivalents.

Peter Lombard puts matrimony last and has little to tell us. He follows Augustine in noting that marriage was the only sacrament instituted before the fall, being initiated originally as a duty and, after the fall, as a remedy against lust.[17] Augustine understood quite well the evils of which he spoke but is hardly positive in recommending marriage as "a remedy for the sick." But Lombard mentions the creation narrative, Cana, and Ephesians 5, to show "that marriage is a good thing otherwise it would not be a sacrament; for a sacrament is a sacred sign."[18] Lombard shows that sexual union is necessary to reflect the fullness of the union between Christ and the church.

Indeed, some medieval theologians came to believe that the actual sexual union was the real matter of the sacrament, an act rather difficult for the church to administer. But the actual giving of the contract "by mutual consent uttered aloud at the spot" came to be considered the true form and matter of this sacrament. Since Christ had left no form, the church was free to change the actual words used but not the necessity of a mutual free consent. The church may forbid marriage because of various **impediments** such as clandestinity, marriage under duress, or simulated consent. The amount of canon law dealing with marriage is complex.

The resulting consensus (in the West) was that the couple themselves are the only proper ministrants of this sacrament, it being the one sacrament a Roman Catholic priest or bishop cannot perform though he may administer a nuptial mass and bless the union.

According to the *Decree for the Armenians*, the purposes of marriage are threefold: "first, the begetting of children and their bringing up in the worship of the Lord; secondly, the fidelity that husband and wife should each maintain toward the other; thirdly, the indissoluble character of marriage, for this typifies the indissoluble union of Christ and the Church."[19]

The chief change the Reformation made was to deny that marriage was a sacrament. Calvin speaks for all the Reformers:

No man ever saw it [matrimony] administered as a sacrament until the time of Gregory [VII]. And what sober man would ever have thought it such? Marriage is a good and holy ordinance of God; and farming, building, cobbling, and barbering are lawful ordinances of God, and yet not sacraments. For it is required that a sacrament be not only a work of God but an outward ceremony appointed by God to confirm a promise. Even children can discern that there is no such thing in matrimony.[20]

The Reformation, however, was almost as conservative in understanding the experience as it was with regard to the rite itself. The first *BCP* tells us the ends of marriage are, first "the procreation of children, to be brought up in the fear and nurture of the Lord, and praise of God. Secondly, it was ordained for a remedy against sin, and to avoid fornication, . . . Thirdly, for the mutual society, help, and comfort, that the one ought to have of the other, both in prosperity and adversity." This is hardly a romantic view of marriage! It was actually the English Puritans who reversed this order and put first mutual "help and comfort." Finally, 1 Corinthians 13 took precedence over 1 Corinthians 7. Modern thought has accepted the Puritan reordering of priorities in the purpose of marriage, although popular culture is prone to stress romantic infatuation. If one had to choose between a purely romantic notion of love, based solely on mutual attractiveness rather than on mutual responsibility, then the medieval-Reformation purposes do not sound so bad. Society's need for procreation in order to ensure survival, though, is far less urgent today.

The most important change in recent years has been a new emphasis on marriage as **covenant** rather than as contract. This represents a return to a biblical and early Christian (and pagan Roman) perspective in which God is seen as acting to witness and guarantee that a covenant will be carried out with all fidelity. The medieval tendency, pursued by the scholastic theologians, to think of marriage in terms of contract instead of covenant, made it easy for the Reformers to deny that matrimony was a sacrament. After all, most contracts deal with impersonal matters in which the action of God is not at all apparent. Rarely do contracts involve love. A covenant relationship, on the other hand, is based on a lifelong ideal of mutual love, not the prudence of a legal contract. It is significant that Vatican II always speaks of marriage in terms of covenant rather than as contract.

Several concerns are prominent in recent thought about the marriage rite. Vatican II mandated that various local "praiseworthy customs and ceremonies" be not only retained but also encouraged (CSL, par. 77). Indigenization is clearly favored as long as there is a clear declaration of lifelong consent in the vows on the part of both parties. The gross inequalities of the old nuptial blessing (which prayed that only the woman "be faithful and chaste" and "fortify herself against her weakness") are changed to "equal obligation to remain faithful to each other" (CSL, par. 78). All churches have become subject to pressures to secularize weddings by the addition of sentimentalities, especially in music. The banalities that have often plagued Protestant weddings are now also a problem for Roman Catholics. In theory, indigenization is an excellent idea, but if it means singing "O Promise Me" or "Sweetheart of Sigma Chi" at church weddings, one may have second thoughts.

The question of whether the church should perform weddings must be raised. After all, for most of its history the church let society do this. The best argument in its favor seems to be that the church as a community of faith has an intimate concern in surrounding a Christian couple with love and in ministering to them. A new relationship of love is established when one enters the marriage covenant just as when one enters the church covenant through initiation. The wedding is a visible sign of this new relationship of love and calls others to nurture this love in the same way the church undertakes in love to nature the faith of a newly baptized infant or adult. In both cases, the relationship of love is a permanent one. Not only does the wedding couple contract with each other, but also the community itself covenants to uphold them. The reading of the banns beforehand and asking if there is any impediment at the start of the wedding help underscore the social nature of marriage. The family, inaugurated at marriage, is in essence a small church modeled on mutual love within the Body of Christ. The eschatological image of the Eastern churches of the family as a foretaste and small model of the kingdom of God is instructive.

The new rites are specifically designed for people of Christian faith. What obligation, if any, do the churches have to minister to the nonbelievers who desire a church wedding? One must ask if this is a necessary social service or simply a surrender to a secular world.

Other problems abound in modern society. How can the church minister to that segment (nearly half) of society who have undergone the agony of divorce? This is especially perplexing in case of remarriage. The Eastern churches make provision for such with integrity. More radical is the question of homosexual unions which the major churches, so far, have officially refused to sanction. Pressures for celebrating such unions have grown. As social structures change, the church will face new problems about the marriage relationship.

One trend seems clear if one can judge from the new rites. The Christian wedding is conceived of as a covenant before witnesses by a man and a woman who, by their free and mutual consent, make unconditional promises of lifelong fidelity to each other with the help of God. There is nothing new or novel about this; it represents an understanding present ever since the New Testament. Luther (and some of the Gallican rites before him) simply reinforced this view by adding Matthew 19:6 to the rite itself: "What God has joined together, let no one separate," words which most of the new rites contain. These words certainly imply a sacramental view of marriage even though Luther repudiated such. They indicate that God works through the church's actions to bring about a new and permanent relationship of love.

Numerous pastoral concerns arise out of the need to show forth this distinctive nature of Christian marriage and the rite itself. Presiding at weddings is certainly one of the most joyful pastoral roles ministers or priests have but also one of the most demanding in complexity.

First of all, this ministry demands considerable time and skill in **counseling** those desiring to be married. The state has its own laws regarding who may be married, and most churches have additional standards. The priest's or minister's role is to be faithful to the standards of his or her church and this involves the ability to say "no." Certainly this must be the case where there is no willingness or time for counseling. Refusing to perform a walk-in wedding is actually performing a service for people, though unlikely to be so understood.

The positive side of counseling, both premarital and after marriage has begun, is the ability to present the church's witness to the meaning of responsible love, so widely made trivial in our society. The pastoral role, of course, is contingent upon having a flock and the congregation's support in upholding a couple's intention of a Christian marriage. We have not just the church's doctrines to present but the church as a living community.

When clergy perform a wedding they also act as unpaid civil servants of the state. That means they are subject to the **laws of the state, province, or country** in which the wedding is performed. Violation of these laws, either through ignorance or knowingly, is a criminal activity for which there are fines and penalties. There is no substitute for making oneself familiar with the laws of the *civil jurisdiction in which the wedding is to be performed*. In the United States, no uniformity exists from state to state about when and where a wedding license is valid, the number of witnesses needed, or the method for filing the wedding certificate. The only way to be sure is to check with the county clerk in the state in which the wedding is to be performed. For example, in some states, the wedding may be performed only in the county issuing the license and sometimes only within a specific number of days.

Due respect for ministerial etiquette ought to be observed when performing a wedding in a parish other than one's own. This ought to be done only at the pastor's invitation, and he or she deserves a letter of thanks from the visiting minister.

All the skills of a diplomat are needed in helping to **plan a wedding**. Various matters, such as the music, can easily get out of hand unless there are standards of excellence and appropriateness to suggest. A general rule is that the pastor should be consulted from the very beginning of making wedding plans. Friendly persuasion can often prevent distortion of the religious meaning of the service and lapses in good taste. Printed materials have some authority in convincing those in doubt. One's denomination can usually supply a list of recommended wedding music. Each congregation ought to publish rules for use of its property for weddings, including such items as who can use the organ, a schedule of fees for use of the church building and janitorial services, where and how flowers and candles may be placed so as not to damage the furnishings or conceal liturgical centers, and rules about photographers. The minister or priest is in a much better position to enforce printed rules passed by the local parish council, vestry, elders, or official board than on his or her own authority.

Most Christian couples are open to suggestions about how to make their wedding the finest possible act of Christian worship. The priest or minister must be familiar with the options available. Most new rites give a number of possibilities and leave much to the clergy's discretion. This is more demanding of pastoral leadership but also provides a better opportunity for ministering. One needs to be familiar with the possibilities (and problems) of celebrating the eucharist with a wedding congregation, some of whom may not be Christians. Since Western Christianity teaches that the couple marry each other and the clergy only preside, this should shape the entire service. Certainly the couple should face each other in saying their vows and in giving the rings.

One would have to be very bold, not to say foolhardy, to try a wedding without a **rehearsal**. If nothing else, the rehearsal ought to build confidence in the couple, who are often very nervous during the actual wedding. The minister or priest should rehearse all the problem areas that nervous people can flub: the entrance procession, the taking of hands, the exchange of vows, the giving of rings, and the recession.

Once the wedding is over and the legal details cared for, there are equally important pastoral responsibilities in marriage counseling and integrating the couple in new ways into the life of the congregation. Most of these are happy responsibilities as one watches the maturing of love. Marriage is indeed a "great mystery" through which God works and clergy are privileged to have a part.

ORDINATION

The majority of Christians have probably never seen an ordination, yet most Christians are served by ordained men and women. In some churches, only bishops perform ordinations, and ministers and priests may rarely be present at an ordination other than their own. Yet nowhere else does the church make so explicit its understanding of the purpose of the church and its ministry. Even though ordination is a rite of passage reserved for the tiny minority of Christians who enter ordained ministry, it ought to be better understood by all Christians.

The witness of the New Testament to the rites of ordination is minimal. It consists in the laying on of hands with prayer after election or appointment by the apostles (Acts 6:1-6, 13:3, 14:23; 1 Tim. 4:14, 5:22; and 2 Tim. 1:6). It is accompanied by fasting and likely includes a charge to those ordained (Acts 20:28). The act of **laying on of hands**, as we have seen in initiation, is a sign of the passing on of power, blessing, or the setting apart of another person by one authorized to do so.

The New Testament tells us of a variety of ministries (1 Cor. 12:28). There is development within its pages of a small and by no means decisive list that hardly distinguishes lay from ordained ministries. The *Didache* speaks of prophets, obviously people of special gifts, and we learn from *The Apostolic Tradition* of confessors who had suffered for their faith, which was considered sufficient consecration without laying on of hands unless one was to become bishop. Readers, subdeacons, and healers were recognized rather than ordained. In *The Apostolic Tradition*, only three receive ordination: bishops, presbyters, and deacons.

Once again we rely on *The Apostolic Tradition* for the first substantial evidence of how ordination took place in the early church. This document gives a full account of ordination of bishop, presbyter, and deacon.[21] Ordination occurs in the setting of the eucharist instead of during the service of the word. Apparently, the new **bishop** is chosen by the people some time prior to the actual ordination, which takes place on a Sunday with other bishops present. The people give their assent, probably by acclamation. Then the bishops lay on hands while one bishop prays the prayer of ordination. The prayer begins by recital of God's saving acts, then invokes that the Holy Spirit be poured out on the new bishop so that he may serve properly in his responsibilities (which are listed). The new bishop is greeted with the kiss of peace and then presides over the eucharist.

For the ordination of a **presbyter,** *The Apostolic Tradition* notes that the bishop lays hands on him while other presbyters also touch him. The bishop prays, perhaps using some of the same language as in the ordination of a bishop but specifically invoking the Spirit for the ministry of a presbyter. The prayer cites Moses'choice of the seventy (Num. 11:17-25; cf. also Luke 10:1-17). The ordinand's new colleagues in the order of presbyters also share in the laying on of hands (though not in reciting the prayer). But, in the case of the **deacon,** only the bishop lays on hands, since, the deacon serves the bishop and is not a member of the council of presbyters. Prayer invoking the Holy Spirit for the work of a deacon is used. For all three orders, the central act is the **ordination prayer** said during the laying on of hands. Other ceremonial is minimal.

The early sacramentaries contain appropriate prayers for the ordination of all three orders: usually a bidding prayer, a collect, and the ordination prayer itself.[22] Usually the last are a catena of scriptural references, beginning with Moses and culminating in invocation of the Holy Spirit for the work of the appropriate order.

In the third century, only three orders were ordained. But the early Middle Ages saw the elaboration of four **minor orders:** **porter, lector, exorcist,** and **acolyte.** At first these were simply instituted by being given the tools of their trade, the *porrectio instrumentorum* or **tradition of instruments** (key, book of lessons, book of exorcism, and candle, candlestick, and cruet). The ceremony of **tonsure** (cutting of hair) marked the pledge of celibacy and entrance into the **major orders,** which came to be reckoned as **subdeacon, deacon,** and **priest.** Rites for each minor order developed with an address, a formula as they were given the symbols of their office, and two prayers of blessing. The subdeacon shares in the ministry of the altar-table, so celibacy was imposed at this stage. Originally these orders were permanent and not stepping stones to a "higher" order. For centuries, bishops of Rome were chosen from among the Roman deacons.

The latest revision of the *Roman Pontifical* (English trans. 1978)[23] abolished the tonsure, the minor orders of porter and exorcist, and the major order of subdeacon. It produced rites of "Institution" of readers and of acolytes and a rite of "Admission to Candidacy for

Ordination as Deacons and Priests." Ordination rites for three major orders follow: bishop, priest, and deacon.

Abolition of several orders is not the only drastic simplification that has occurred in the new *Roman Pontifical*. The Middle Ages saw the accretion of a number of subsidiary ceremonies, largely the result of fusing ninth-century and tenth-century Gallican practices to the more restrained Roman rites. Such newer ceremonies included anointing the hands of the priest, vesting ordinands in the appropriate vestment, and the tradition of instruments. These had found their way, via the tenth-century Romano-Germanic Pontifical, back to Rome itself in the eleventh century. The ceremonies were further elaborated by the great liturgical scholar, **William Durandus,** Bishop of Mende, France, in the late–thirteenth century, by the Roman curia late in the fifteenth, and became part of the *Roman Pontifical*, as revised in 1596. Until recently, the subsidiary ceremonies overshadowed the ordination prayer and laying on of hands. A series of short prayers and an imperative formula had taken the place of the primitive great ordination prayer. That prayer has now been restored to prominence. The ancient role of the people in the election of the candidates and in acclaiming them "worthy" had disappeared but is now recovered, at least symbolically.

The rites the Reformers inherited were of confused priorities. It is not surprising that they had only moderate success in unraveling the historical complexities of ordination. Much of the ceremonial was eliminated. Laying on of hands seems to have been generally maintained though even this was avoided for a time in Geneva and Scotland because of fear of superstition. Minor orders and the sub-diaconate were everywhere abolished. Luther performed one of the earliest Protestant ordinations in 1525, and the rite he eventually devised, though he never published it, became the source of most Lutheran ordinations. His text of 1539 for "Ordination of Ministers of the Word" consists largely of scripture, admonitions, prayer, and the laying on of hands while reciting the Lord's Prayer.[24] The first Anglican collection of ordination rites (the **ordinal**) dates from 1550 and was revised in 1552. The ordination formula is imperative ("Take thou" or "Receive") rather than a prayer and is addressed to each candidate during the laying on of hands.

For many Protestants, the great change was that ordination became an act of the local congregation with election once again a real practice. Frequently ordination was practiced by members of the congregation or by ministers of neighboring churches. Most Quakers, of course, dispensed with ordained ministry altogether.

Recent revisions, both Protestant and Roman Catholic, have shown a return to the priorities of the early Church as witnessed to in *The Apostolic Tradition*. The *Roman Pontifical* and the Episcopal, United Methodist, Lutheran, and Presbyterian services all agree in making the great prayer of ordination the center of the rite with laying on of hands occurring concurrently. These central prayers are modeled on those of *The Apostolic Tradition* and replace imperative formulas with invocation. Most of these rites indicate that ordination should occur in the setting of the eucharist with those being ordained exercising their proper roles in the eucharist. The role of the congregation is magnified with opportunity for acclaiming the candidates or promising support to the ordained. Subsidiary ceremonies are retained in most cases but made clearly secondary to the ordination prayer and laying on of hands. Some churches provide related services for the installation of a pastor. These rites are more remarkable for their similarity than their diversity.

How have Christians understood the rite of ordination as functioning within the life of the church? One could easily develop an ecclesiology from the rites themselves, but our concern is with how the rites function.

It is clear from the New Testament onward that ordination is accomplished through prayer and laying on of hands. Our earliest examples of the central prayer in *The Apostolic Tradition* fall into a familiar pattern: thanksgiving to God for what God has already done in times past and invocation of further work in giving requisite gifts to those now being ordained. Thanksgiving and supplication form this prayer much as they do the eucharistic prayer. The Western church has been much more consistent in testifying to the work of the Holy Spirit in ordination rites than in the case of the eucharist.

The other biblical act, the laying on of hands, signifies the power and authority received by the ordinand to be exercised within the church. Varying views explain how this power and authority relates to continuity and succession whether through persons or through teachings. The variety of gifts that Paul mentions in 1 Corinthians 12 are all given by the Spirit for one purpose: to be used for the edification of the church. *The Apostolic Tradition* speaks repeatedly of the "Holy Spirit in the holy church," and the prayers are for gifts of the Holy Spirit to be used in ministry within the holy church.

The early understanding of ordination got confused in the course of history. The scholastic urge to fit ordination into the same pattern as that of the other sacraments eventuated in the Council of Florence's decree that the matter "for the priesthood is the cup with the wine and the paten with the bread; for the diaconate, the books of the Gospel, for the subdiaconate, an empty cup placed upon an empty paten."[25] The form for priests, it declared, was, "Receive the power to offer sacrifice in the Church for the living and the dead, in the name of the Father, and of the Son, and of the Holy Ghost." Since Christ did not specify the form or matter of ordination, the church could revise practice. In 1947, Pius XII in *The Apostolic Constitution on Holy Orders* reaffirmed that the matter was laying on of hands. The form he prescribed now appears within the ordination prayer in the *Roman Pontifical*.

The Reformers had difficulty accepting the concept that ordination conveys an indelible character. At his most radical, Luther saw ordination as functional in designating one Christian to do what all have the authority to do and, indeed, any could do if stranded on a desert island without benefit of clergy. "We are all equally priests, that is to say we have the same power in respect to the Word and the sacraments."[26] Ordination remained, for Luther, a public calling to "the ministry of the Word." Some churches took this even farther in equating ordination with installation into the pastoral office in a local church. Reordination, however, is rarely practiced when one moves to serve another congregation or when one changes denominations. It is, however, a major problem in church unity talks.

In general, Protestants have avoided the belief that ordination brings specific graces and have looked at it largely as designating people to certain functions. One could argue that the apostolic practice of laying on of hands suggests a higher concept of authority than the words of theologians may concede. On the other hand, election and acclamation by the people certainly show that whatever power and authority are conferred have meaning only as used in ministry for the church. It is vital to recognize that ordination is something done for the church and not just to individuals. Only in recent years have we realized that preoccupation with what the individual receives misses the point and that what the community itself receives is the real focus of this sacrament.

All Christians share in ministry. The ordained represent the local church to the universal church and vice versa. So the ordained may be called "representative" ministers except in churches where only males are ordained.

Ordination functions within the community of faith as a way of making visible a new relationship of love. The congregation rejoices in someone being called by God to serve it through ordained ministry and for the gifts of leadership he or she brings. It is a service of thanksgiving in that ordination acknowledges and thanks God for God's **providential call** of a person to ordained ministry and invokes God's further blessing on that individual. Ordination also functions as a formal **ecclesiastical call** by which the church recognizes that a person has been called of God and is now set aside as one who has suitable gifts and graces to represent the Christian community.

It is indeed strange that Christianity has never devised rites to commemorate entrance into nonecclesiastical vocations. Luther and most Protestants have maintained that every vocation that serves others is a valid priestly vocation. Luther reminds us that the milkmaid has as holy a vocation as the nun. Each and every person in an honest occupation serves his or her neighbor and thus is involved in ministry. But the churches have never developed rites comparable to ordination for those who choose other ways to serve humanity.

Most pastors will not have opportunity to plan ordinations, but there are a few practical matters in most of the new rites that deserve mention. In the first place, since ordination is for people, the people themselves need to have opportunity for active participation. Spontaneous acclamations when the candidates are presented, even applause, ought to be encouraged. Hymns and unison prayers should be shared in fully by those gathered. Representatives of the laity may be involved in some acts, especially in greeting those newly ordained. This ought not be left only to parents and family but, as much as possible, done also by those whom the ones ordained will actually serve.

The ancient use of the eucharist as the setting in which ordination is done has much to commend it. Ordination is almost as joyful an occasion as a wedding; the congregation is almost certainly all Christian, for whom the eucharist is the most suitable sign of joy and thanksgiving. The eucharist also gives those ordained their first public opportunity to exercise important parts of their ministry of word and sacrament.

Much has happened in recent years to make the new ordination rites converge. If the various churches were as close in their understanding of orders and ministry as they are in the practice of ordination, Christians would indeed have reached a happy stage for the reunion of Christianity. But doing sometimes precedes thinking, and use of the new rites is certainly a significant step toward unity. An important statement of ecumenical progress is found in *Baptism, Eucharist, and Ministry* although ministry remains the most controverted of the three topics.[27]

RELIGIOUS PROFESSION OR COMMISSIONING

For a significant number of people, there are religious rites through which they pass into a lifetime of service that may or may not involve ordination. We speak of rites that initiate people into religious communities of sisters, nuns, mendicants, monks, various clerical orders, lay institutes, deaconesses, or missionaries. It is likely that there will be a significant increase in lay ministries in the future, making services of commissioning even more important than now.

Groups organized for ministry have a long history. Already in the first and second centuries we find evidence of Christians living intentional lives of virginity. By the third century, there were in many communities groups of widows and virgins who had distinct roles in church life. The fourth century reveals that these groups had a communal life, and rites of consecration to such a lifestyle soon developed. The history of these rites is quite different for men and for women.

For women, these rites usually involved the bishop giving sanction to the taking of a vow of virginity, receiving a veil, and, eventually, a ring. The chief image for joining women's orders came to be matrimonial, with making espousal promises and receiving a ring as central actions.

Among the earliest men's orders, the central image was originally a second baptism. The offering of self was signified by vows taken at the altar-table or placing a signed document on it and had some of the qualities of martyrdom. The surrender of worldly properties, which might be drawn up in a list and placed on the altar-table, was an important part. Clothing played a significant role as the future monk put aside the clothes of this world and took the habit of his new community. Each item—cowl, scapular, robe, and belt—became symbols of the new life in community. In the later Middle Ages, dying to this world became symbolized by prostration before the altar-table and being wrapped in one's habit as if in a funeral pall. The monk died to self and was raised to a new life in community.

Entering the novitiate, making temporary vows, and taking permanent vows were all ritualized. If one left the community, his own clothing was restored. Thus a variety of images is present in the monastic rites of religious profession: second baptism, martyrdom, and Christian burial.

There also developed a series of rites for the leaders of communities, especially for the "Blessing of an Abbot," and the "Blessing of an Abbess." In many ways, these rites paralleled the consecration of bishops, and mitered abbots received many of the symbols of authority of a bishop though usually without episcopal jurisdiction.

All these rites have been extensively revised in modern times. Various orders and communities have their own distinctive services though with much in common. The current generic Roman Catholic rites are found in *The Rite of Religious Profession*. Usually the local bishop presides at these ceremonies. In the Episcopal

Church, a rite is provided for "Setting Apart for a Special Vocation," which provides for a novitiate, temporary vows, and final or life vows. Each stage involves a request, a sermon, examination, promises or vows, prayer or blessing, and presentation of clothing. Other churches have various formularies for special ministries, such as "Setting Apart of a Deaconess" among Lutherans; United Methodists have "An Order for Commitment to Christian Service," "An Order for Commissioning to Short-term Christian Service" and several other services. Presbyterians provide rites of "Commissioning to Ministry within [or outside] a Congregation."

CARE OF THE DEAD

The final form of ministry to life's passages is care of the dead. This is usually thought of simply as Christian burial, but that is only part of the process. The service of Christian burial is practiced to console the bereaved and to commend the deceased to God. It is a key part of a long process of teaching, pastoral care, and remembrance. This may not seem a cheerful subject with which to end our study of Christian worship, but it does show that the Christian's whole life involves the praise of God from baptism to burial. And the observance of Christian death has much to tell us about the Christian life itself.

Attitudes about Christian care of the dead, historically, seem to have evolved through three quite different stages: hope, fear, and refusal to think about it. These are reflected in the rites themselves in various ways, some subtle and others less so. The services themselves are often crystallized attitudes about death itself.

We have no New Testament information about care of the dead and very little from the first three centuries A.D. Even *The Apostolic Tradition* tells us nothing except to indicate that there was a Christian cemetery and that the price of burial was to be kept reasonable. Tertullian indicates a funeral eucharist and a yearly eucharist on the anniversary of death ("Of the Crowns," 3). Sarapion gives us a prayer for a dead person before burial. It is mostly recital of God's acts but turns to supplication for the deceased to be at rest, for his or her final resurrection, for forgiveness of sins, for consolation of the bereaved, and ends with a petition to "give to us all a good end."[28] Augustine tells of the burial of his mother, Monica, mentioning few details except his restraint in tears and the prayers of the funeral eucharist.[29]

Several general observations can be made about early Christian care of the dead. The general atmosphere of Christian burial was that of *hope* in the resurrection. Augustine's dry-eyed statement may be an exception but not too much so. The dead Christian who had kept the faith was treated as a victor, and the funeral procession had the character of the triumph accorded a victorious general on return home. Since cemeteries, by Christian times, were outside the city walls, the carrying forth was a significant part of the rite. It was done to the accompaniment of psalms of hope and praise and shouts of "alleluia." White garments were worn, palm leaves and lights were carried, and incense was burned as the community marched to the cemetery in broad daylight (unlike the nighttime funerals of pagans). Previously, the body had been washed, anointed, and wrapped in linen at the home of the deceased while prayers were said.

At the grave, there was prayer and celebration of the eucharist. Augustine notes, "The sacrifice of our ransom was offered for her [Monica], when now the corpse was by the grave's side." After the corpse was given the final kiss of peace, it was buried with the feet toward the rising sun. An *agape* might follow immediately, and there were services on various days after death and on the anniversary of the death. For heroes of the faith such as martyrs, these anniversaries could be important occasions. The account of the second-century death of Polycarp, "The Martyrdom of Polycarp," speaks of the community's intention "to gather together in joy and gladness to celebrate the day of his martyrdom as a birthday, in memory of those athletes who have gone before, and to train and make ready those who are to come hereafter."[30]

Death, for the Christian, was a "heavenly birthday," and the saints were commemorated on their birthday *(natalis)* into eternity rather than on their mundane birthday into finite time. Chronicles of their lives and deaths were collected in **martyrologies**, a selection from which was read on each heavenly birthday (death day).

As with weddings, the church was much influenced by Roman

burial customs, although it rejected many (such as cremation). The pagan practice of commemoration of the dead by meals at the gravesite *(refrigerium)* was replaced by the eucharist, and Christian mourners gave food to the poor. The sense of continuity of the family through generations, centering on the family burial plot, is still strong in Rome.

The medieval ethos of Christian care of the dead took a different turn; that of *fear*. Burial came to be draped with the medieval imagination of hell and purgatory and the terrors of dying unprepared. The eucharist has suffered whenever it has been used for disciplinary purposes; funerals were also abused. The medieval mind tended to feel that if one could scare the hell out of people it might be possible to scare them out of hell. Death became a threat used to discipline the living. Who could ignore a prayer such as that used in the York province: "Deliver him from the cruel fire of the boiling pit"? Most medieval parish churches had graphic mural paintings of the last judgment (the doom) over the chancel arch with the torments of the damned displayed with gusto. Late medieval drama often included a hell's mouth into which unrepentant sinners were dragged. Dante shows us the whole scheme at its most sophisticated level; for others it was equally vivid and real.

The burial rites came to be permeated with awe and fear over the destination of the soul. The **office of the dead** developed out of psalms originally sung at funerals and eventually had forms to be said at vespers, matins, and lauds. Medieval burials were usually in churchyards. The body was met at the churchyard lych-gate (corpse gate), carried into the church with psalms, the eucharist was celebrated, the dead person was granted absolution, incensed, and sprinkled with holy water. Interment followed in the churchyard or beneath the church. The absolution shows the change from the early church's sense of triumphant victory. The *Dies irae* (day of wrath) chant from the twelfth or thirteenth century reflects the late medieval focus on judgment and the possibility of damnation, so different from the clear confidence of early Christians.

The Reformation did not find it easy to shake loose these attitudes, even though fear of purgatory was no longer a sanction. Luther deplored the mournful character of funerals and wanted to make them stronger expressions of hope. He condemned "popish abominations, such as vigils, masses for the dead, processions, purgatory, and all other hocus-pocus on behalf of the dead" in favor of services stressing the resurrection of the dead with "comforting hymns of the forgiveness of sins, of rest, sleep, life, and of the resurrection of departed Christians."[31] Luther left no burial rite but seems to have utilized hymns, psalms, a sermon, and simple ceremonial.

The minimum was reached in the *Westminster Directory* of 1645, which decreed that the body be "decently attended" to the cemetery but immediately buried "without any ceremony." Even funeral sermons became controversial among both the Scots and English Puritans, for they had often degenerated into eulogies of virtues real and imaginary. Some Puritans regarded burial as purely a secular matter and conducted no services. Calvin had approved of funeral sermons but never provided a liturgy for Christian burial. Usually the Reformed tradition tolerated a service of psalmody, scripture reading, sermon, and prayer after the burial.

Anglican revisions of the burial rite were more conservative, although there was a further lurch to the left in 1552. Cranmer, in 1549, condensed the office of the dead and assimilated the churchyard procession, the committal, and an optional eucharist (for which propers were given). The service might take place entirely in the graveyard or partly in the church. A conscious effort was made to stress hope through Christ and the resurrection. In 1552, reference to the eucharist disappeared and the service took place almost wholly at the graveside. The cautious prayers for the dead in 1549 had also vanished. The brief rite that remained consisted of sentences, prayers, Revelation 14:13, 1 Corinthians 15:20-58, and words of committal, while earth was cast upon the body. Subsequent history has brought expanded psalmody and more prayers. Wesley kept the 1662 *BCP* rite basically, though omitting Psalm 39, a prayer, and the committal. The great change Methodism brought was the addition of fervent hymns of hope.

Modern Christianity, all too often, has forgotten both hope and fear and *refused to think about death* as part of the Christian message. Cemeteries are now located out in the suburbs of both our cities and our consciousness. Burial customs have become largely commercialized. The seventeenth century saw the introduction of tombstones and private burial plots for ordinary people. Previously, like Hamlet's Yorick, one could occupy a bit of earth for thirty years until it was another's turn. Caskets became common for ordinary people in the nineteenth century and embalming at the time of the Civil War. The result is that moderns have become more superstitious about death than our medieval ancestors though much less colorful and imaginative. To pretend that we can preserve even our name, let alone our body, would doubtlessly have amused medieval people. Yet modern practice tries to camouflage the reality of death and ends up creating more fictions than any earlier age.

Too often, this has been the fault of the church, which has too often allowed sentimental funeral services of flowers and poetry to prevail instead of the witness of the gospel. And the church, too often, politely sidesteps mention of death in its weekly life, even during the season of Easter, the period focusing on resurrection. The teaching ministry also has neglected treating something as offensive as death.

Recent services have recaptured many of the more affirmative elements of the early Christian attitude to death. Vatican II mandated that "the rite for the burial of the dead should express more clearly the paschal character of Christian death" (CSL, par. 81). This resurrection emphasis has been largely accomplished. The visual change from black vestments to white (for Christ and resurrection) or green (for growth) marks a strong shift in emphasis. The post–Vatican II rites, which encourage the following of local custom, provide for all or parts of the service to occur at stations: in the home of the deceased, in the parish church, at the cemetery chapel, at the grave, or combinations of these. There is also a vigil service and provision for funerals of children. Many options are provided, including celebration of a funeral mass, anniversary masses, various commemorations, and prayers for the dead.

Other churches show the same emphasis on the paschal nature of the Christian understanding of death. The Presbyterian rite is entitled "The Funeral: A Service of Witness to the Resurrection," and the United Methodist rite is "A Service of Death and Resurrection." The *BCP* has two rites for the "Burial of the Dead" and an outline of a third. All three Episcopal rites contain the possibility of a eucharist as do the United Methodist, Presbyterian, and Lutheran services. Prayers for the dead are an option in the *BCP*. The greater part of these services comprises psalmody and reading of the scriptural promises.

The Lutheran, United Methodist, and Presbyterian services begin with reference to a Christian's baptism into Christ's death and resurrection, and relate baptism and burial. The United Methodist service tries to personalize the occasion by a naming and witness by those who knew the deceased best in order to commemorate his or her life. Too easily, funerals can have a generic quality without acknowledging the individual life being commemorated.

How does Christian faith understand the funeral? Its past has been a changing one. As late as the Third Lateran Council of 1179, it was possible to speak of burial of the dead as a sacrament—that is, throughout more than half of the church's history. But Christian burial never received the scholastic attention the seven did, and the failure of both Luther and Calvin to devise funeral rites shows that they had more pressing things to do. Thus the funeral has never received as much theological consideration as it deserves, although psychologists, sociologists, and popular writers have leaped in to fill the void. The Christian understanding of death has received somewhat more careful theological examination.[32]

What are the possibilities for understanding the function of Christian burial apart from the utilitarian matter of disposal of the body? Two concerns stand out: to show God's love and the community's support in consoling the bereaved and to commend the deceased to God's gracious care.

The church works best by honesty as it **consoles the bereaved**. We must beware of knowing too much about death. It remains a mystery. Efforts to probe beyond its dark veil, either in modern scientific terms or in speculative pictorial imagery, loosely based on scripture, are all unproductive undertakings. But there are two affirmations that Christian faith can make in all honesty for the benefit of the bereaved. The first of these may seem to be of little comfort, but it is vital to the course of grief and can only cause prolonged trouble if ignored. This is the reality of death itself. The Bible is clear: "We must all die; we are like water spilled on the ground, which cannot be gathered up" (2 Sam. 14:14), a far more Christian affirmation than any stone monument. For this reason, it is generally better, when possible, to have the body present at a funeral than to have a memorial service. The reality of death is not denied by a religion with the crucifixion at its heart.

But the second affirmation is the trustworthiness of God. This is not a doctrine about death (about which we know very little) but a doctrine of God's trustworthiness (about which we know a great deal). Death makes humans realize how completely dependent they are upon God when all else fails. Whatever lies beyond death is also created by God and experienced before us by Jesus Christ. Christians are not bereft of hope even in the face of death; they are comforted by the only real source of hope in the world: God's gracious love.

The Christian funeral, then, testifies to the realities of death and resurrection. The strong affirmations of scripture are far more potent than any poetry about sleep, passage, or crossing the bar. God's words in scripture and actions in sacraments are the strong medicine needed at this time, not poetry, flowers, or sentimental statements. It is important that the funeral occur in the beloved community, especially in the familiarity of the church building where words and actions of hope have been experienced on the first day of each week throughout a lifetime.

The presence of the community itself is a strong witness to God's action in love here. Other Christians being there are a visible sign of love. The community together marks the transition of the deceased to a new relationship within the church as the dead person moves to the Church Triumphant beyond the Church Militant here on earth. The role of other Christians at the funeral is to make visible by their presence the environment of love that encompasses the bereaved.

The second function of the funeral is to **commend the deceased to God**. Potentially, each of the baptized has already died and been raised with Christ in baptism (Rom. 6:3-4). Now is the time to remember that God has already shown God's acceptance of us, an acceptance first made visible in our baptism. It is only natural to wish to commend those we love to God's keeping. Concepts of purgatory are very unlikely for modern Protestants (and probably for many Roman Catholics, too, today). But the hope of resurrection in Christ is so central in Christian faith that we can hardly refrain from praying that God accomplish God's purpose for the deceased. It is most unnatural to pray for a person up to the moment of death and then be silent. God's love continues after death as well as before and carefully worded prayers can commend the dead to God's keeping without implying a belief in purgatory.

The Christian funeral, then, has two functions: ministry to the living and to the dead, although it is impossible to separate these. Both are made possible through the understanding that God acts in Christian burial, as in the sacraments, in new self-giving even at the end of life. The community of faith, entered through the waters of baptism, now for the last time again unites around one to manifest divine love made visible through the community's caring actions.

A few pastoral consequences may be briefly noted. The occasion of death is a time of a sustaining and continuing relationship for which the pastor is likely to have chief responsibility. Counseling with the family before burial and long afterward is an essential ministry. The **course of grief** cannot be rushed; the worst danger of all is when people refuse to grieve, and it catches up with them unawares. "Putting up a good front" is an invitation to catastrophe. There are few areas of greater need for pastoral sensitivity than counseling the bereaved.

Much of this ministry begins long before death in the **teaching ministry,** which helps church members understand death from a Christian perspective. Through various media, the congregation can be helped to think through the most desirable forms of funerals. None of us is fully mature until he or she knows with certainty that he or she is eventually going to die. Making plans for one's funeral is not necessarily a morbid preoccupation; it can be a witness to one's faith and a splendid way to advance in the understanding of life. Members of one retirement home weave their own funeral palls, a magnificent final affirmation.

Pastoral care does not come alone; it presupposes a flock. Others need to share with the pastor in this ministry so as to represent to the bereaved the concern and support of the community. Much can be done to enlist and train members of the congregation for ministry to those of their number who have been bereaved. They will have much to do to reintegrate the bereaved into the community. This is particularly important at great festivals of the year when the bereaved may feel most lonely. All Saints Day has become an important event in many churches to commemorate both the recently deceased and all those who have kept the faith throughout history.

The Christian funeral is worship above all else, not primarily grief therapy. It should stress the strong promises of scripture to God's trustworthiness and not rely on anything less. A service of the word seems essential to proclaim and give thanks for God's goodness. Psalmody and scripture are basic, supported by sermon, hymns, prayers, and creed. The eucharist can proclaim the continuing relationship between those in life and those in death within the Body of Christ.

The presence of the body at the funeral service and the attendance of people at the committal service are to be encouraged as ways of testifying to the reality of death. Rarely should the body be displayed. It is far better to cover the casket with a **pall**, a cloth about ten feet by six feet with a large cross embroidered or appliqued on it. It testifies far better than cut flowers to the source of our hope in Christ. The pall also cuts down on ostentatious display of coffins. Even when the body is to be given to medical research or to be cremated, it can usually be present at the funeral.

Funerals are a very personal occasion, and some means must be found in stressing that it was this particular person who died. This can be done without extravagant praise. But some form of personal identification from someone who knew the deceased well can be valuable. Sometimes mementos or photographs of things or people central in the life of the deceased may be displayed. Christians are identified by name in baptism and ought to be named as well in their funeral.

NOTES

1. What Do We Mean by "Christian Worship"?

1. George Worgul, "Ritual," *The New Dictionary of Sacramental Worship* (Collegeville. Minn.: Liturgical Press, 1990), p. 1101.

2. Gordon W. Lathrop, *Holy Things: A Liturgical Theology* (Minneapolis: Fortress Press, 1993), p. 35–79.

3. Don E. Saliers, *Worship as Theology* (Nashville: Abingdon Press, 1994), p. 166.

4. Quoted by Peter Brunner, *Worship in the Name of Jesus* (St. Louis: Concordia, 1968), p. 123. (WA 49, 588, 15-18).

5. *The Book of Concord* (Philadelphia: Fortress Press, 1959), p. 376.

6. *Institutes of the Christian Religion* (Philadelphia: Westminster Press, 1960), p. 1192.

7. Commentary on Psalm 24:7 *Commentaries* 31:248. I owe this passage to Dr. John Witvliet.

8. "Of Ceremonies," *The First and Second Prayer Books of Edward VI* (London: Dent, 1964), p. 326. Spelling modernized.

9. George Florovsky, "Worship and Every-Day Life: An Eastern Orthodox View," *Studia Liturgica* 2 (December 1963), p. 268.

10. Ibid., p. 269.

11. Nikos A. Nissiotis, "Worship, Eucharist, and 'Intercommunion': An Orthodox Reflection," *Studia Liturgica* 2 (September 1963), p. 201.

12. *Tra le sollecitudini*, in *The New Liturgy*, ed. Kevin Seasoltz, O.S.B. (New York: Herder & Herder, 1966), p. 4.

13. Godfrey Diekmann, O.S.B., *Personal Prayer and the Liturgy* (London: Geoffrey Chapman, 1969), p. 57.

14. Odo Casel, O.S.B., *The Mystery of Christian Worship* (Westminster, Md.: Newman Press, 1962), p. 141.

15. Evelyn Underhill, *Worship* (London: Nisbet & Co., 1936), pp. 84-85.

16. For a more detailed delineation of these, see James F. White, *Protestant Worship: Traditions in Transition* (Louisville: Westminster John Knox, 1989).

17. The revisions decreed by the Council of Trent appeared as the *Roman Breviary*, 1568, and the *Roman Missal*, 1570. Further work produced the *Roman*

Martyrology, 1584, the *Roman Pontifical*, 1596, *Caeremoniale episcoporum*, 1600, and the *Roman Ritual*, 1614.

18. Other books, which might be combined with these, include: the *passional* (the sufferings of the martyrs), the homily-book (excerpts from the Father's expositions of scripture), the *legenda* (accounts of the saints' lives), the responsory (with responses for use after the lessons), the *collectar* (containing the collects for the day), and an *ordo* (to show how to put it at all together for the proper day and hour).

19. These were sometimes separated as an *epistolarium* containing the Old Testament and Epistle lections and the *evangelarium* for the Gospels.

20. Separate collections of graduals, tropes, kyries, and sequences were sometimes used.

2. THE LANGUAGE OF TIME

1. Cyril Richardson, ed., *Early Christian Fathers* (Philadelphia: Westminster Press, 1953), p. 96.

2. Kirsopp Lake, trans., *The Apostolic Fathers* (Cambridge: Harvard University Press, 1965), 1:331.

3. Henry Bettenson, ed., *Documents of the Christian Church* (New York: Oxford University Press, 1952), p. 6.

4. Richardson, *Early Christian Fathers*, p. 287.

5. Kirsopp Lake, *Apostolic Fathers*, 1:397.

6. Bettenson, *Documents*, p. 27.

7. Richardson, *Early Christian Fathers*, p. 174.

8. James Donaldson, ed., *Ante-Nicene Fathers*, hereafter *ANF*, (New York: Charles Scribner's, 1899), 7:469.

9. John Chrysostom, *Baptismal Instructions*, Paul W. Harkins, trans. *Ancient Christian Writers* (Westminster, Md.: Newman, 1963), 31, p. 127.

10. Tertullian, "On Baptism," trans. S. Thelwall, *ANF*, 3:678.

11. Eusebius, *The History of the Church*, trans. G. A. Williamson (Baltimore: Penguin Books, 1965), p. 230.

12. *Egeria's Travels*, ed. and trans. John Wilkinson (London: S.P.C.K., 1971), pp. 132-33.

13. Augustine, *Letters*, trans. Wilfrid Parsons, *Fathers of the Church* (New York: Fathers of the Church, 1951), 12:283.

14. Thomas J. Talley, *The Origins of the Liturgical Year* (New York: Pueblo Publishing Co., 1986), pp. 194-203.

15. William Telfer, trans., *Cyril of Jerusalem and Nemesius of Emesa* (Philadelphia: Westminster Press, 1955), p. 68.

16. Augustine, *Letters*, 12:284-85.

17. Tertullian, "On Baptism," 3:678.

18. Eusebius, "Life of Constantine the Great," E. C. Richardson, trans., *Nicene and Post-Nicene Fathers*, herafter *NPNF*, 2nd Series (New York: Christian Literature Co., 1890), 1:557.

19. Talley, *Liturgical Year*, pp. 129-134.

20. John Chrysostom, *Opera Omnia*, ed. Bernard de Montfaucon (Paris: Gaume, 1834), 2, p. 418.

21. Ibid., 2, p. 436.

22. Cited by L. Duchesne, *Christian Worship*, 5th ed. (London: S.P.C.K., 1923), p. 260, n. 3.

23. Tertullian, "De Corona," *ANF*, 3:94.

24. Chrysostom, *Opera Omnia*, 1, p. 608.

25. Gregory Dix, *Shape of the Liturgy* (Westminster: Dacre, 1945), p. 305.

26. "Formula Missae," Bard Thompson, ed., *Liturgies of the Western Church* (Minneapolis: Fortress Press, 1961), p. 109.

27. "Book of Discipline," *John Knox's History of the Reformation in Scotland* (London: Thomas Nelson and Sons, 1949), 2, p. 281.

28. *The Westminster Directory* (Bramcote, Notts, U.K.: Grove Books, 1980), p. 32.

29. *John Wesley's Prayer Book* (Akron: OSL Publications, 1991).

30. *The Christian Year: A Suggestive Guide for the Worship of the Church*, drafted and revised by Fred Winslow Adams (New York: Committee on Worship, Federal Council of the Churches of Christ in America), 2nd ed. (rev.), 1940, p. 9.

31. *The Christian Year and Lectionary Reform* (London: SCM Press, 1958).

32. Pius Parsch, *The Church's Year of Grace* (Collegeville, Minn.: Liturgical Press, 1964-65), 5 vols.

33. *The Revised Common Lectionary* (Nashville: Abingdon Press, 1992), pp. 21-23.

34. *Preaching Through the Christian Year* (Valley Forge: Trinity Press International, 1994), 3 vols.

35. Kathy Black, *Worship Across Cultures* (Nashville: Abingdon Press, 1998).

3. The Language of Space

1. For more detail, see James F. White and Susan J. White, *Church Architecture: Building and Renovating for Christian Worship* (Akron: OSL Publications, 1998).

2. Historically, there has always been a close relationship between the artists of the book and religious expression and in no tradition has such been stronger than in Christianity. And within the context of the books arts, one of the most visible expressions of devotion through art has been in the field of bookbinding. The historic evidence is overwhelming and it is a tradition which is very much alive today. But the tradition exists now more through the support of private patrons or university libraries than from commissions from the church.

3. For a more detailed historical account, see James F. White, *Protestant Worship and Church Architecture* (New York: Oxford University Press, 1964), chaps. 3-6.

4. In these simplified floor plans, A = altar-table; C = choir; F = font; L = lectern; P = pulpit; dotted lines = balconies. Drawings are not to scale.

5. *The Letters of Stephen Gardiner*, edited by James A. Muller (New York: Macmillan, 1933), p. 355. Spelling modernized.

6. John Ruskin, *The Seven Lamps of Architecture* (London: George Allen, 1903), p. 233.

7. "Existentialist Aspects of Modern Art," *Christianity and the Existentialists*, Carl Michalson, ed. (New York: Scribner's, 1956) especially pp. 134-44.

8. Cyril Richardson, "Some Reflections on Liturgical Art," *Union Seminary Quarterly Review*, VIII (1953), pp. 24-28.

9. *The New Westminster Dictionary of Liturgy and Worship*, edited by J. G. Davies (Philadelphia: Westminster Press, 1986), pp. 521-40.

4. THE SOUNDS OF CHURCH MUSIC

1. Andrew Wilson-Dickson, *The Story of Christian Music* (Oxford: Lion Publishing, 1992), p. 44. This book and Paul Westermeyer, *Te Deum: The Church and Music* (Minneapolis: Fortress Press, 1998) are excellent general surveys.
2. Michael W. Harris, *The Rise of Gospel Blues: The Music of Thomas Dorsey in the Urban Church* (New York: Oxford University Press, 1992), pp. 185-208.
3. Edward Foley, *Foundations of Christian Music* (Nottingham: Grove Books, 1992), p. 50.
4. Ibid., p. 84.
5. This section may be more useful if read in conjunction with a recent hymnal that is indexed according to composers, translators, and authors.
6. H. J. Schroeder, *The Canons and Decrees of the Council of Trent* (Rockford: Tan Books, 1978), p. 151.
7. Anthony Garside, Jr., *Zwingli and the Arts* (New Haven: Yale University Press, 1966), pp. 7-26.
8. Andy Langford, *Transitions in Worship* (Nashville: Abingdon Press, 1999), p. 29.

5. DAILY PUBLIC PRAYER

1. *Didache*, 8, in Cyril Richardson, ed., *Early Christian Fathers*, p. 174.
2. Clement, *The Stromata or Miscellanies*, 7, 7; ANF (New York: Charles Scribner's: 1899), 2:354.
3. Tertullian, *On Fasting* 10, *On Prayer* 25; Cyprian, *On the Lord's Prayer*, 34.
4. Bernard Botte, *La Tradition apostolique de Saint Hippolyte* (Münster: Aschendorffsche, 1963) for introduction, text, notes, and French translation. English translation: Geoffrey Cuming, *Hippolytus: A Text for Students with Introduction, Translation, Commentary, and Notes* (Bramcote, Notts, U.K.: Grove Books, 1976).
5. Gregory Dix, ed., *The Treatise on the Apostolic Tradition of St. Hippolytus of Rome*, 36 (London: S.P.C.K., 1968), p. 63.
6. Dix, ed., *Apostolic Tradition*, 33, p. 60. See also 35, p. 61.
7. George Guiver introduces the latter term which seems the most appropriate. *Company of Voices* (New York: Pueblo Publishing Co., 1988), p. 53.
8. Eusebius, *Commentary on Psalm 64*, verse 10. *Patrologiae Graecae* (Paris: J. P. Migne, 1857), 23, p. 640.
9. *Apostolic Constitutions*, 2, p. 59; ANF, 7: 423; 8, p. 35, ANF, 7:496.
10. John Chrysostom, *Baptismal Instructions*, 17, trans. Paul W. Harkins, *Ancient Christian Writers* (Westminster, Md.: Newman Press, 1963) 31:126-27.
11. *Egeria's Travels*, 24, ed. and trans., John Wilkinson (London: S.P.C.K., 1971), pp. 123-24.
12. Robert Taft, *The Liturgy of the Hours in East and West* (Collegeville: Liturgical Press, 1986), p. 56.
13. Paul F. Bradshaw, *Two Ways of Praying* (Nashville: Abingdon Press, 1995), p. 70.
14. Cassian, *Institutes of the Coenobia*, 2, 3; NPNF, 2nd series (New York: Christian Literature Co.: 1890), 11:206.

15. Basil, Question 37. *Ascetical Works*, trans. Sister M. Monica Wagner, C.S.C. (New York: Fathers of the Church, 1950), pp. 309-10.

16. Chrysostom, *Homilies on First Timothy*, 14; *NPNF*, 1st series, 13:456.

17. Cassian, *Institutes*, 3, 4, *NPNF*, 2nd series, 11:215.

18. Benedict, "The Rule," *Western Asceticism* (Philadephia: Westminster, 1958), p. 327.

19. E. C. Ratcliff, "The Choir Offices," in W. K. Lowther Clarke and Charles Harris, eds. *Liturgy and Worship* (London: S.P.C.K., 1932), p. 266.

20. J. Wickham Legg, ed., *The Second Recension of the Quignon Breviary* (London: Henry Bradshaw Society, 1908), vol. 35 and J. Wickham Legg, *Liturgical Introduction with Life of Quignon* (London: Henry Bradshaw Society, 1912), vol. 42.

21. *Liturgy of the Hours: The General Instruction* (London: Geoffrey Chapman, 1971), p. 35, par. 77.

22. Taft, *The Liturgy*, p. 316.

23. Hughes Oliphant Old, "Daily Prayer in the Reformed Church of Strasbourg, 1525–1530," *Worship* 52 (1978), pp. 121-38.

24. Cf. "Formula Missae" and "Deutsche Messe," in Bard Thompson, ed. *Liturgies of the Western Church* (Minneapolis: Fortress Press, 1961), pp. 120-21 and 129-30.

25. Günther Stiller, *Johann Sebastian Bach and Liturgical Life in Leipzig* (St. Louis: Concordia, 1984), p. 55.

26. *The First and Second Prayer Books of Edward VI* (London: J. M. Dent, 1952), p. 3.

27. Ibid., p. 6.

6. THE SERVICE OF THE WORD

1. Cyril Richardson, ed., *Early Christian Fathers*, p. 287.

2. This is Anton Baumstark's famous second law, explicated in his *Comparative Liturgiology* (London: A. R. Mowbray, 1958), p. 27. The first law is that ancient elements in time tend to be duplicated by more modern items; then, when the redundancy is eventually noted, the earlier ones are eliminated (p. 23).

3. Augustine, Sermon #324, *Patrologia Latina* (Paris: J. P. Migne, 1863) 38, p. 1449.

4. Bard Thompson, ed., *Liturgies of the Western Church* (Minneapolis: Fortress Press, 1961), pp. 106-22.

5. Ibid., pp. 123-37.

6. Ibid., pp. 197-208.

7. Hughes O. Old, *The Patristic Roots of Reformed Worship* (Zurich: Theologischer Verlag, 1975), pp. 208-18.

8. Thompson, *Liturgies*, pp. 354-71.

9. Ibid., pp. 245-68.

10. Ibid., pp. 269-84.

11. *John Wesley's Prayer Book* (Akron: OSL Publications, 1995).

12. See John Knox, *Integrity of Preaching* (Nashville: Abingdon Press, 1957); Gustav Wingren, *The Living Word* (Philadelphia: Fortress Press, 1960); Karl Barth, *The Peaching of the Gospel* (Philadelphia: Westminster Press, 1963); P. T. Forsyth, *Positive Preaching and the Modern Mind* (London: Independent Press, 1960); H. H. Farmer, *Servant of the Word* (Philadelphia: Fortress Press, 1964); Fred B. Craddock,

Preaching (Nashville: Abingdon Press, 1985); David G. Buttrick, *Homiletic* (Philadelphia: Fortress Press, 1987); and Richard L. Eslinger, *A New Hearing* (Nashville: Abingdon Press, 1987).

7. God's Love Made Visible

1. "Tractus on John," 80, 3, *NPNF*, 1st series (New York: Christian Literature Co., 1890), 7:344; and John Calvin, *Institutes*, IV, xiv, 4, *Library of Christian Classics* 21, p. 1279.
2. The central thesis of E. Schillebeeckx, *Christ the Sacrament of the Encounter with God* (New York: Sheed and Ward, 1963).
3. Cf. Joachim Jeremias, *Eucharistic Words of Jesus* (New York: Scribner's, 1966), pp. 106-37.
4. Calvin, *Institutes*, IV, xvii, 32, p. 1403.
5. Text in Elizabeth Frances Rogers, *Peter Lombard and the Sacramental System* (Merrick, N.Y.: Richwood, 1976), IV, ii, 1, p. 85.
6. Ibid., IV, i, 6, p. 82.
7. Ibid., IV, i, 4, p. 80.
8. Ibid., IV, xxiii, 3, p. 221.
9. Text in Ray C. Petry, ed., *A History of Christianity* (Englewood Cliffs, N.J.: Prentice-Hall, 1962), p. 324.
10. Ibid., p. 325.
11. For an important discussion of this term and its shifting meanings cf. Piet Schoonenberg, "Transubstantiation: How Far Is This Doctrine Historically Determined?" *The Sacraments, an Ecumenical Dilemma* (New York: Paulist Press, 1966) *Concilium* 24, 78-91.
12. "Canons and Dogmatic Decrees of the Council of Trent," in Philip Schoff, ed., *The Creeds of Christendom* (Grand Rapids: Baker, n.d.), 2, 119.
13. Calvin, *Institutes*, IV, xvii, 1, p. 1361.
14. Burkhard Neunheuser, ed., *The Mystery of Christian Worship and Other Writings* (Westminster, Md.: Newman Press, 1962), p. 124.
15. See also Schillebeeckx's *The Eucharist* (New York: Sheed and Ward, 1968).
16. Calvin, *Institutes*, IV, xiv, 3, p. 1278.
17. William Temple, *Nature, Man, and God* (London: Macmillan, 1940), p. 473.
18. George Herber, "The Elixir," in *The Temple* (1633).
19. Elizabeth Barrett Browning, *Aurora Leigh*, Book 7

8. Christian Initiation

1. Mandate IV, iii, 6. Kirsopp Lake, trans., *The Apostolic Fathers* (Cambridge: Harvard, 1965), 2:85.
2. Kurt Aland, *Did the Early Church Baptize Infants?* (London: SCM Press, 1963), p. 10.
3. Oscar Cullmann, *Baptism in the New Testament* (London: SCM Press, 1950).
4. *Didache*, 9 and 7, in Cyril Richardson, ed., *Early Christian Fathers* (Philadelphia: Westminster Press, 1953), pp. 174-75.
5. *First Apology*, 61 and 65 in Richardson, *Early Christian Fathers*, pp. 282, 285.

6. Tertullian, "On Baptism," 20, *ANF* (New York: Charles Scribner's: 1899), 3:678-79.

7. Ibid., 17, *ANF*, 3:677.

8. "Of the Crowns," 3, in E. C. Whitaker, ed., *Documents of the Baptismal Liturgy* (London: S.P.C.K., 1970), p. 10.

9. Tertullian, "On Baptism," 8, *ANF*, 3:672.

10. Gregory Dix, ed., *The Treatise on The Apostolic Tradition of Saint Hippolytus* (London: S.P.C.K., 1968), p. 38.

11. R. Hugh Connolly, ed., *Didascalia Apostolorum*, 16 (Oxford: Clarendon Press, 1969), p. 147.

12. *Egeria's Travels*, 45-47, ed. and trans., John Wilkinson (London: S.P.C.K., 1974), pp. 143-46.

13. *Concerning the Sacraments*, I, 4, in Whitaker, ed., *Documents of the Baptismal Liturgy*, p. 128.

14. *Mystagogical Catechesis* 2, in Whitaker, ed., *Documents*, p. 29.

15. Ibid., pp. 40-41. See also Edward Yarnold, *The Awe-Inspiring Rites of Initiation* (London: St. Paul, 1972).

16. *Concerning the Sacraments*, III, 8, in Whitaker, *Documents*, p. 131.

17. J. D. C. Fisher, *Christian Initiation: Baptism in the Medieval West* (London: S.P.C.K., 1970), p. 148.

18. Ibid., p. 106.

19. Ulrich S. Leopold, ed., *Luther's Works* (Philadelphia: Fortress, 1965), 53, pp. 107-109.

20. Rubrics in "The Form of Prayers and . . . Manner of Administering the Sacraments," text in J. D. C. Fisher, ed., *Christian Initiation: The Reformation Period* (London: S.P.C.K., 1970), p. 117.

21. Text cited by Rollin S. Armour, *Anabaptist Baptism* (Scottdale, Pa.: Herald Press, 1966), pp. 143-44.

22. G. R. Beasley-Murray, *Baptism in the New Testament* (Exeter: Paternoster Press, 1962), p. 125.

23. Fisher, *Reformation Period*, p. 173.

24. Ibid., pp. 174-78.

25. Calvin, *Institutes*, IV, xix, 13, p. 1461.

26. For a more detailed account, see James F. White, *Sacraments as God's Self Giving* (Nashville: Abingdon, 1983), ch. 2.

27. *First Apology* 61 and 65 in Cyril Richardson, ed., *Early Christian Fathers*, pp. 282-83 and 285.

28. *Vs. Heresies*, III, xvii, 2 in Henry Bettenson, *The Early Christian Fathers* (London: Oxford University Press, 1963), p. 129.

29. *Enchiridion*, 43-52; *NPNF*, 1st Series (New York: Christian Literature Co., 1890), 3:252-54.

30. *Sentences*, IV, ii-vi, in Elizabeth Rogers, ed., *Peter Lombard and the Sacramental System*, pp. 85-116.

31. Ibid., IV, vii, 3, p. 117.

32. In Ray C. Petry, ed., *A History of Christianity* (Englewood Cliffs, N.J.: Prentice-Hall, 1962), p. 326.

33. "The Holy and Blessed Sacrament of Baptism," *Luther's Works*, 35, p. 36.

34. Ibid., p. 34.

35. "Of Baptism," G. W. Bromiley, ed., *Zwingli and Bullinger* (Philadelphia: Westminster Press, 1953), p. 156.

36. Calvin, *Institutes*, IV, xv, 1, p. 1303.

37. Menno Simons, "Foundation of Christian Doctrine," *Complete Writings*, ed., C. Wenger (Scottdale, Pa.: Herald Press, 1965), p. 120.

38. Karl Barth, *The Teaching of the Church Regarding Baptism* (London: SCM Press, 1948).

39. Oscar Cullmann, *Baptism in the New Testament* (London: SCM, 1950).

40. Joachim Jeremias, *Infant Baptism in the First Four Centuries* (Philadelphia: Westminster, 1962) and *The Origins of Infant Baptism* (Philadelphia: Westminster, 1963); Kurt Aland, *Did the Early Church Baptize Infants?* (Philadelphia: Westminster, 1963).

41. *Baptism, Eucharist, and Ministry* (Geneva: World Council of Churches, 1982), p. 4.

42. Urban T. Holmes, *Young Children and the Eucharist*, rev. ed. (New York: Seabury Press, 1982). Also Ruth Meyer, ed., *Children at the Table* (New York: Church Pub., 1995).

9. THE EUCHARIST

1. Joachim Jeremias, *Eucharistic Words of Jesus* (New York: Charles Scribner's Sons, 1966), p. 173.

2. Gregory Dix, *The Shape of the Liturgy* (Westminster: Dacre, 1945), Joseph Jungmann's *Mass of the Roman Rite* (New York: Benziger, 1951-55) 2 vols., and Yngve Brilioth's *Eucharistic Faith and Practice* (London: S.P.C.K., 1953) are modern classics of eucharistic studies. Dix's influence has been profound on almost all liturgical revision since the Church of South India rite first appeared in 1950.

3. Church of the Brethren, *Pastor's Manual* (Elgin, Ill.: Brethren Press, 1978), pp. 27-58.

4. For a résumé of this discussion, see A. J. B. Higgins, *The Lord's Supper in the New Testament* (London: SCM, 1952), pp. 13-23; also Jeremias, *Eucharistic Words*, pp. 41-84.

5. Hans Leitzmann, *Mass and Lord's Supper* (Leiden, Netherlands: E. J. Brill, 1979); also Oscar Cullmann and F. J. Leenhardt, *Essays on the Lord's Supper* (Richmond, Va.: John Knox, 1958).

6. Church of the Brethren, *Pastor's Manual*, pp. 27-58.

7. *Didache*, 9-10, 14, Cyril Richardson, ed., *Early Christian Fathers* (Philadelphia: Westminster Press, 1953), pp. 175-76 and 178.

8. *First Apology* 65, Richardson, *Early Christian Fathers*, pp. 285-86.

9. Most conveniently available in R. C. D. Jasper and G. J. Cuming, *Prayers of the Eucharist: Early and Reformed* (Collegeville: Liturgical Press, 1990), pp. 31-38. Also G. J. Cuming, *Hippolytus: A Text for Students* (Bramcote, Notts, U.K.: Grove Books, 1976), pp. 10-11. For original languages, see A. Hanggi and I. Pahl, *Prex Eucharistica* (Fribourg, Switzerland: Éditions Universitaires, 1968), pp. 80-81. These books will be most useful throughout the following pages.

10. Jasper and Cuming, *Prayers*, p. 34.

11. Bernard Botte, *La Tradition apostolique de Saint Hippolyte* (Münster, Germany: Aschendorffsche, 1963), p. 28.

12. "To the Smyrnaeans," 8, Richardson, *Early Christian Fathers*, p. 115.

13. R. J. S. Barrett-Lennard, *The Sacramentary of Sarapion of Thmuis* (Bramcote, Notts, U.K.: Grove Books, 1993), p. 27.

14. Dix, *Shape of the Liturgy*, p. 48.

15. The chronology of the most important Protestant liturgies during the five first crucial years of the effort to produce a reformed eucharist is:

1521	Andreas Karlstadt, Wittenberg Christmas Mass (German)
1522	Kaspar Kantz, "Evangelical Mass" (German)
1523	Martin Luther, *Formula Missae* (Latin)
	Thomas Müntzer, "German Evangelical Mass"
	Ulrich Zwingli, *De Canone Missae Epicheiresis* (Latin)
	John Oecolampadius, *Das Testament Jesu Christi* (German)
1524	Diobald Schwarz, *Teutsche Messe* (German)
	Guillaume Farel, *La Maniere et fasson* (French)
	"Worms Mass" (German)
	Martin Bucer, *Grund und Ursach* (German)
1525	John Oecolampadius, *Form und Gstalt* (German)
	Ulrich Zwingi, *Action oder Bruch des Nachtmals* (German)
	Döber, Mass for Nuremberg Hospital Chapel (German)
	Martin Luther, *Deutsche Messe*.

See Irmgard Pahl, ed., *Coena Domini I* (Freiburg, Switzerland: Universitätsverlag, 1983).

16. "Formula Missae," in Bard Thompson, ed., *Liturgies of the Western Church*, p. 108. This book and Jasper and Cuming, *Prayer of the Eucharist*, should be consulted for the texts of Protestant rites.

17. See Geoffrey Wainwright, *Eucharist and Eschatology* (New York: Oxford University Press, 1981).

18. *First Apology*, 65-67, Richardson, *Early Christian Fathers*, pp. 286-87.

19. *Didache*, 9, Richardson, *Early Christian Fathers*, p. 175.

20. *First Clement*, 40 and 44, Richardson, *Early Christian Fathers*, pp. 62, 64.

21. "To the Smyrnaeans" 7; Richardson, *Early Christian Fathers*, p. 114.

22. "Against Heresies" 5, 2; Richardson, *Early Christian Fathers*, p. 388.

23. Epistle 62, 13; ANF (New York: Charles Scribner's, 1899), 8:217.

24. "Mystagogical Catechesis V," *St. Cyril of Jerusalem's Lectures on the Christian Sacraments* (London: S.P.C.K., 1960), p. 74.

25. "City of God," 10, 6, NPNF, 1st series (New York: Christian Literature Co., 1890), 2:184.

26. *On the Sacraments*, IV, 14, Jasper and Cuming, *Prayers*, pp. 144-45.

27. Henry Denzinger and Adolf Schönmetzer, *Enchiridion Symbolorum*, 33rd edition (Rome: Herder, 1965), p. 260.

28. "Decree for the Armenians," Petry, ed., *A History of Christianity*, p. 328.

29. Brilioth, *Eucharistic Faith and Practice*, p. 97.

30. It is all the more ironic that Luther discarded the canon of the mass except for the words of institution which, to us, seem to use such explicitly sacrificial language.

31. Calvin, *Institutes*, IV, xvii, 7, p. 1367.

32. Ibid., IV, xvii, 38, pp. 1415-6.

33. Cyril Richardson, *Zwingli and Cranmer on the Eucharist* (Evanston, Ill.: Seabury-Western Theological Seminary, 1949), p. 48.

34. J. E. Rattenbury, *The Eucharistic Hymns of John and Charles Wesley* (London: Epworth, 1948), pp. 195-249.

35. E. Schillebeeckx, *The Eucharist* (New York: Sheed and Ward, 1968); Joseph Powers, *Eucharistic Theology* (New York: Herder & Herder, 1967).

36. *Baptism, Eucharist, and Ministry* (Geneva: World Council of Churches, 1982).

37. *Bishops' Committee on the Liturgy Newsletter*, 15 (January, 1979), p. 147.

10. OCCASIONAL SERVICES

1. See John T. McNeill and Helena M. Gamer, *Medieval Handbooks of Penance* (New York: Columbia University Press, 1938).

2. *Luther's Works* 53, pp. 116-21.

3. *Peter Lombard and the Sacramental System*, IV, 3; Rogers, ed., p. 117.

4. "Decree for the Armenians." Petry, *A History of Christianity* (Englewood Cliffs, N.J.: Prentice-Hall, 1962), p. 328.

5. Dix, ed., *Apostolic Tradition*, V, p. 10.

6. R. J. S. Barrett-Lennard, *The Sacramentary of Sarapion of Thmuis* (Bramcote, Notts, U.K.: Grove Books, 1993), p. 31. See also p. 48.

7. *Lombard*, IV, xxiii, 3, Rogers, p. 222.

8. "Decree for the Armenians," Petry, p. 329.

9. Calvin, *Institutes*, IV, xix, 18, p. 1466.

10. Ibid., IV, xvii, 39, pp. 1416-17.

11. Church of the Brethen, *Pastor's Manual*, pp. 63-71 (including a sound introduction). This rite ought to be more widely known.

12. "First Apology," pp. 65-67, Richardson, *Early Christian Fathers*, pp. 286-87.

13. "To Polycarp," 5, Richardson, *Early Christian Fathers*, p. 119.

14. *Luther's Works* (Philadelphia: Fortress Press, 1965), 53, pp. 110-15.

15. *The Celebration of Marriage* (Toronto: United Church of Canada, 1985), p. 11.

16. *A Christian Celebration of Marriage: An Ecumenical Litrugy* (Philadelphia: Fortress, Press, 1987).

17. *Lombard*, IV, xxvi, 2, Rogers, p. 243.

18. Ibid., IV, xxvi, 5, Rogers, p. 245.

19. "Decree for the Armenians," Petry, p. 329.

20. Calvin, *Institutes*, IV, xix, 34, p. 1481.

21. Dix, ed., *Apostolic Tradition*, pp. 4-19. See also Paul Bradshaw, *Ordination Rites of the Ancient Churches of East and West* (New York: Pueblo Publishing Co., 1990).

22. Bradshaw, *Ordination*, pp. 215-42.

23. *Roman Pontifical* (Washington: International Commission on English in the Liturgy, 1978).

24. *Luther's Works*, 53, pp. 124-26.

25. "Decree for the Armenians," Petry, p. 329.

26. "Babylonian Captivity," *Luther's Works*, 36, p. 116.

27. *Baptism, Eucharist, and Ministry* (Geneva: World Council of Churches, 1987), pp. 20-33.

28. *The Sacramentary of Sarapion of Thmuis*, Barrett-Lennard, p. 51.

29. "Confessions" 9, cited in Geoffrey Rowell, *The Liturgy of Christian Burial* (London: S.P.C.K., 1977), p. 24.

30. "The Martyrdom of Polycarp," V, 18, Richardson, *Early Christian Fathers*, p. 156.

31. "Preface to the Burial Hymns," *Luther's Works*, 53, p. 326.

32. For example, John Hicks, *Death and Eternal Life* (New York: Harper, 1976).

FOR FURTHER READING

1. What Do We Mean by "Christian Worship"?

Adam, Adolf. *Foundations of Liturgy*. Collegeville: Liturgical Press, 1992.

Alternative Futures for Worship, 7 vols. Collegeville: Liturgical Press, 1987.

Bouyer, Louis. *Liturgical Piety*. Notre Dame: University of Notre Dame Press, 1955.

Chupungco, Anscar, ed. *Handbook of the Liturgy*, 5 vols. Collegeville: Liturgical Press, 1997–2000.

Davies, J. G., ed. *The New Westminster Dictionary of Liturgy and Worship*. Philadelphia: Westminster Press, 1986.

Driver, Tom. *The Magic of Ritual*. San Francisco: Harper, 1991.

Duffy, Regis A. *Real Presence: Worship, Sacraments, and Commitment*. San Francisco: Harper and Row, 1982.

Forrester, Duncan, James I. H. McDonald, and Gian Tellini. *Encounter with God*. Edinburgh: T & T Clark, 1983.

Guardini, Romano. *The Church and the Catholic and the Spirit of the Liturgy*. New York: Sheed and Ward, 1935.

Hatchett, Marion J. *Sanctifying Life, Time, and Space*. New York: Seabury Press, 1976.

Jones, Cheslyn, Geoffrey Wainwright, Edward Yarnold, and Paul Bradshaw, eds. *The Study of Liturgy*, revised ed. New York: Oxford University Press, 1992.

Martimort, A. G., ed. *The Church at Prayer*, new edition, 4 vols. Collegeville: Liturgical Press, 1986–1988.

Procter-Smith, Marjorie. *Praying with Our Eyes Open*. Nashville: Abingdon Press, 1995.

Saliers, Don E. *Worship as Theology*. Nashville: Abingdon Press, 1994.

Segler, Franklin M., and Randall Bradley. *Understanding, Preparing for, & Practicing Christian Worship*, 2nd ed. Nashville: Broadman, 1996.

Senn, Frank. *Christian Liturgy: Catholic and Evangelical*. Minneapolis: Fortress Press, 1997.

Taft, Robert F. *Beyond East and West: Problems in Liturgical Understanding*. Washington, D.C.: Pastoral Press, 1984.

Wainwright, Geoffrey. *Doxology*. New York: Oxford University Press, 1980.

Webber, Robert E., ed. *The Complete Library of Christian Worship*, 7 vols. Nashville: Abbott Martin Press, 1993–94.

————. *Worship Old and New*. Grand Rapids: Zondervan Corp., 1982.

Wegman, Herman A. J. *Christian Worship in East and West*. New York: Pueblo Publishing Co., 1985.

White, James F. *Documents of Christian Worship*. Louisville: Westminster John Knox, 1992.

2. THE LANGUAGE OF TIME

Adam, Adolf. *The Liturgical Year: Its History & Its Meaning after the Reform of the Liturgy*. New York: Pueblo Publishing Co., 1981.

Bacchiocchi, Samuele. *From Sabbath to Sunday*. Rome: Pontifical Gregorian University Press, 1977.

Brown, Peter. *The Cult of the Saints: Its Rise & Function in Latin Christianity*. Chicago: University of Chicago Press, 1982.

Hickman, Hoyt L., Don E. Saliers, Laurence Hull Stookey, and James F. White, *The New Handbook of the Christian Year*. Nashville: Abingdon Press, 1992.

Johnson, Maxwell, ed. *Beyond Memory and Hope*. Collegeville, Minn.: Liturgical Press, 2000.

McArthur, A. Allan. *The Evolution of the Christian Year*. London: SCM Press, 1953.

Nocent, Adrian. *The Liturgical Year*, 4 vols. Collegeville, Minn.: Liturgical Press, 1977.

Perham, Michael, et. al., *Enriching the Christian Year*. London: S.P.C.K., 1993.

Pfatteicher, Philip E. *Festivals and Commemorations*. Minneapolis: Augsburg Publishing House, 1980.

Porter, Boone. *Keeping the Church Year*. New York: Seabury Press, 1978.

Rordorf, Willy. *Sunday*. Philadelphia: Westminster Press, 1968.

Schmidt, Leigh Eric. *Consumer Rites*. Princeton: Princeton University Press, 1995.

Stookey, Laurence Hull. *Calendar: Christ's Time for the Church*. Nashville: Abingdon Press, 1996.

Talley, Thomas J. *The Origins of the Liturgical Year*, 2nd, emended ed. New York: Pueblo Publishing Co., 1990.

Wilde, James A., ed. *At That Time*. Chicago: Litgurgy Training Publications, 1989.

3. THE LANGUAGE OF SPACE

Adams, William Seth. *Moving the Furniture*. New York: Church Publishing, 1999.

Bishops' Committee on the Liturgy. *Environment and Art in Catholic Worship*. Washington: National Conference of Catholic Bishops, 1978.

Bruggink, Donald J., and Carl H. Droppers. *Christ and Architecture*. Grand Rapids: Wm. B. Eerdmans Publishing Co., 1965.

————. *When Faith Takes Form*. Grand Rapids: Wm. B. Eerdmans Publishing, 1971.

Debuyst, Frédéric. *Modern Architecture and Christian Celebration*. Richmond, Va.: John Knox Press, 1968.

Hammond, Peter. *Liturgy and Architecture*. New York: Columbia University Press, 1961.

————, ed. *Towards a Church Architecture*. London: Architectural Press, 1962.

Huffman, Walter C., and S. Anita Stauffer. *Where We Worship*. Minneapolis: Augsburg Publishing House, 1987.

Maguire, Robert, and Keith Murray. *Modern Churches of the World*. New York: Dutton, 1965.

Mauck, Marchita. *Shaping a House for the Church*. Chicago: Liturgy Training Publications, 1990.

Meeting House Essays, 10 vols. Chicago: Liturgy Training Publications, 1991–99.

Riedel, Scott R. *Acoustics in the Worship Space*. St. Louis: Concordia, 1986.

Sövik, Edward A. *Architecture for Worship*. Minneapolis: Augsburg Publishing House, 1973.

White, James F. *The Cambridge Movement*. Cambridge: Cambridge University Press, 1962 and 1979.

————. *Protestant Worship and Church Architecture*. New York: Oxford University Press, 1964.

————, and Susan J. White. *Church Architecture: Building and Renovating for Christian Worship*. Akron: OSL Publications, 1998.

Williams, W. Peter. *Houses of God*. Urbana and Chicago: University of Illinois Press, 1997.

4. THE SOUNDS OF CHURCH MUSIC

Bishops' Committee on the Liturgy. *Music in Catholic Worship*. Washington: National Conference of Catholic Bishops, 1972.

Blume, Friedrich. *Protestant Church Music*. London: Victor Gollancz, 1975.

Cone, James H. *The Spirituals and the Blues*. New York: Seabury Press, 1972.

Day, Thomas. *Why Catholics Can't Sing*. New York: Crossroads, 1991.

Gelineau, Joseph. *Voices and Instruments in Christian Worship*. Collegeville, Minn.: Liturgical Press, 1964.

Hustad, Donald P. *Jubilate: Church Music in the Evangelical Tradition*. Carol Stream, Ill.: Hope Publishing Co., 1981.

Lawrence, Joy E., and John A. Ferguson. *A Musician's Guide to Church Music*. New York: Pilgrim Press, 1981.

Liturgical Conference. *Crisis in Church Music*. Washington: Liturgical Conference, 1967.

Lovelace, Austin, C., and William C. Rice. *Music and Worship in the Church*. Nashville: Abingdon Press, 1976.

Nelson, Gertrud Mueller. *To Dance with God*. New York: Paulist Press, 1986.

Nicholson, Sydney, H. *Quires and Places Where They Sing*. London: S.P.C.K., 1954.

Routley, Erik. *The Church and Music*. London: Duckworth, 1950.

Sizer, Sandra S. *Gospel Hymns and Social Religion*. Philadelphia: Temple University Press, 1978.

Stiller, Günther. *Johann Sebastian Bach and Liturgical Life in Leipzig*. St. Louis: Concordia, 1984.

Young, Carlton R. *My Great Redeemer's Praise*. Akron: OSL Publications, 1995.

5. DAILY PUBLIC PRAYER

Bradshaw, Paul F. *Two Ways of Praying*. Nashville: Abingdon Press, 1995.

Campbell, Stanislaus. *From Breviary to Liturgy of the Hours*. Collegeville, Minn.: Liturgical Press, 1995.

Guiver, George. *Company of Voices*. New York: Pueblo Publishing Co., 1988.

Jasper, R. C. D., ed. *The Daily Office*. London: S.P.C.K. and Epworth, 1968.

Liturgy of the Hours: The General Instruction with commentary by A. M. Roguet, O.P.; Peter Coughlan and Peter Purdue, trans. London: Geoffrey Chapman, 1971.

Mateos, Juan. "The Origins of the Divine Office," *Worship* 41 (October 1967): 477-85.

———. "The Morning and Evening Office," *Worship* 42 (January 1968): 31-47.

Old, Hughes Oliphant, "Matthew Henry and the Puritan Discipline of Family Prayer," Privately printed, 1978.

———. "Daily Prayer in the Reformed Church of Strasbourg," *Worship* 52 (1978): 121-38.

Salmon, Pierre. *The Breviary Through the Centuries*. Collegeville, Minn.: Liturgical Press, 1962.

Scotto, Dominic F. *The Liturgy of the Hours*. Petersham, Mass.: St. Bede's Publications, 1987.

Storey, William G. "The Liturgy of the Hours: Cathedral vs. Monastery," *Worship* 50 (1976): 50-70.

Taft, Robert. *The Liturgy of the Hours in East and West*. Collegeville, Minn.: Liturgical Press, 1986.

6. THE SERVICE OF THE WORD

Brightman, F. E. *The English Rite*, 2 vols. London: Rivingtons, 1921.

Cabié, Robert. *The Church at Prayer*, Vol. 2, *The Eucharist*. Collegeville: Liturgical Press, 1986.

Cuming, G. J. *A History of Anglican Liturgy*, 2nd ed. London: Macmillan, 1982.

Davies, Horton. *The Worship of the English Puritans*. Westminster: Dacre Press, 1948.

Dix, Gregory. *The Shape of the Liturgy*. Westminster: Dacre, 1945.

Hageman, Howard G. *Pulpit and Table*. Richmond, Va.: John Knox Press, 1962.

Jungmann, Joseph A. *The Mass of the Roman Rite*, 2 vols. New York: Benziger Brothers, 1951–1955.

———. *The Liturgy of the Word*. Collegeville, Minn.: Liturgical Press, 1966.

———. *Pastoral Liturgy*. London: Challoner, 1962.

Old, Hughes Oliphant. *The Reading and Preaching of the Scriptures*, 7 vols. Grand Rapids: Wm. B. Eerdmans Publishing Co., 1998.

———. *Worship That Is Reformed According to Scripture*. Atlanta: John Knox, 1984.

Reed, Luther D. *The Lutheran Liturgy*. Philadelphia: Fortress Press, 1960.

Van Dijk, S. J. P., and J. H. Walker. *The Origins of the Modern Roman Liturgy*. London: Darton, Longman, and Todd, 1960.

White, James F. *Protestant Worship*. Louisville: Westminster John Knox, 1989.

7. GOD'S LOVE MADE VISIBLE

Baillie, Donald. *Theology of the Sacraments*. New York: Charles Scribner's Sons, 1957.

Browning, Robert L., and Roy A. Reed. *The Sacraments in Religious Education and Liturgy: An Ecumenical Model*. Birmingham: Religious Education Press, 1985.

Cooke, Bernard J. *Sacraments and Sacramentality*. Mystic, Conn.: Twenty-Third Publications, 1983.

Fink, Peter, ed. *The New Dictionary of Sacramental Worship*. Collegeville, Minn.: Liturgical Press, 1990.

Hellwig, Monika. *The Meaning of the Sacraments*. Dayton: Pflaum/Standard, 1972.

Jenson, Robert. *Visible Words*. Philadelphia: Fortress Press, 1978.

Leeming, Bernard. *Principles of Sacramental Theology*. London: Longmans, 1960.

Macquarrie, John. *A Guide to the Sacraments*. New York: Continuum, 1998.

Martos, Joseph. *Doors to the Sacred*. New York: Doubleday, 1981.

Osborne, Kenan B. *Sacramental Theology: A General Introduction*. New York: Paulist Press, 1989.

Powers, Joseph. *Spirit and Sacrament*. New York: Seabury Press, 1973.

Rahner, Karl. *The Church and the Sacraments*. London: Burns & Oates, 1963.

Schmemann, Alexander. *Of Water and the Spirit*. London: S.P.C.K., 1976.

Segundo, Juan Luis. *The Sacraments Today*. Maryknoll, N.Y.: Orbis Books, 1974.

Senn, Frank C. *A Stewardship of the Mysteries*. New York: Paulist Press, 1999.

Staples, Rob. *Outward Sign and Inward Grace*. Kansas City: Beacon Hill Press, 1991.

Vorgrimler, Herbert. *Sacramental Theology*. Collegeville, Minn.: Liturgical Press, 1992.

White, James F. *Sacraments as God's Self Giving*. Nashville: Abingdon Press, 1983.

————. *The Sacraments in Protestant Practice and Faith*. Nashville: Abingdon Press, 1999.

Worden, T., ed. *Sacraments in Scripture*. London: Geoffrey Chapman, 1966.

8. CHRISTIAN INITIATION

Austin, Gerard. *Anointing with the Spirit: The Rite of Confirmation: The Use of Oil & Chrism*. Collegeville, Minn.: Liturgical Press, 1992.

Baptism in the New Testament. Baltimore: Helicon Press, 1964.

Beasley-Murray, G. R. *Baptism in the New Testament*. London: Macmillan, 1962.

Burnish, Raymond. *The Meaning of Baptism*. London: Alcuin Club/S.P.C.K., 1985.

Cully, Kendig Brubaker, ed. *Confirmation: History, Doctrine, and Practice*. Greenwich, Conn.: Seabury, 1962.

Duffy, Regis A. *On Becoming a Catholic*. San Francisco: Harper & Row, 1984.

Fisher, J. D. C. *Confirmation Then and Now*. London: S.P.C.K., 1978.

Gilmore, Alec, ed. *Christian Baptism*. London: Lutterworth, 1959.

Johnson, Maxwell, ed. *Living Water, Sealing Spirit*. Collegeville, Minn.: Liturgical Press, 1995.

————. *The Rites of Christian Initiation*. Collegeville, Minn.: Liturgical Press, 1999.

Kavanagh, Aidan. *The Shape of Baptism: The Rite of Christian Initiation*. New York: Pueblo Publishing Co., 1978.

Made, Not Born. Notre Dame: University of Notre Dame Press, 1976.

Marsh, Thomas A. *Gift of Community: Baptism and Confirmation.* Wilmington: Michael Glazier, Inc., 1984.

Neunheuser, Burkhard. *Baptism and Confirmation.* New York: Herder & Herder, 1964.

Riley, Hugh. *Christian Initiation.* Washington: Catholic University Press, 1974.

Schnackenburg, Rudolf. *Baptism in the Thought of St. Paul.* Oxford: Blackwell, 1964.

Searle, Mark. *Christening: The Making of Christians.* Collegeville, Minn.: Liturgical Press, 1980.

Stevick, Daniel B. *Baptismal Moments: Baptismal Meanings.* New York: Church Publishing, 1987.

Stookey, Laurence H. *Baptism: Christ's Act in the Church.* Nashville: Abingdon Press, 1982.

Turner, Paul. *Confirmation: The Baby in Solomon's Court.* New York: Paulist Press, 1993.

———. *Sources of Confirmation.* Collegeville, Minn.: Liturgical Press, 1993.

Yarnold, Edward, *The Awe-Inspiring Rites of Initiation*, 2nd ed. Collegeville, Minn.: Liturgical Press, 1994.

9. THE EUCHARIST

Bouyer, Louis. *Eucharist.* Notre Dame: University of Notre Dame Press, 1968.

Bradshaw, Paul. F. *The Search for the Origins of Christian Worship.* New York: Oxford University Press, 1992.

Cabié, Robert. *The Church at Prayer,* Vol. 2, *The Eucharist.* Collegeville: Liturgical Press, 1986.

Davies, Horton. *Bread of Life and Cup of Joy.* Grand Rapids: Wm. B. Eerdmans Publishing Co., 1993.

Foley, Edward. *From Age to Age.* Chicago: Liturgy Training Publications, 1991.

Jasper, R. C. D., and Geoffrey Cuming. *Prayers of the Eucharist,* 3rd ed. New York: Pueblo Publishing Co., 1987.

Jungmann, Joseph. *Mass of the Roman Rite,* 2 vols. New York: Benziger, 1951–1955.

Klauser, Theodor. *A Short History of the Western Liturgy.* London: Oxford University Press, 1969.

Macy, Gray. *The Banquet's Wisdom.* New York: Paulist Press, 1992.

Mazza, Enrico. *The Celebration of the Eucharist.* Collegeville, Minn.: Liturgical Press, 1999.

Ratcliff, E. C. *Liturgical Studies.* London: S.P.C.K., 1976.

Rordorf, Willy, et al. *The Eucharist of the Early Christians.* New York: Pueblo Publishing Co., 1978.

Schmemann, Alexander. *The Eucharist: Sacrament of the Kingdom.* Crestwood, N.Y.: St. Vladimirs, 1988.

Senn, Frank, ed. *New Eucharistic Prayers.* New York: Paulist Press, 1987.

Stookey, Laurence H. *Eucharist: Christ's Feast with the Church.* Nashville: Abingdon Press, 1993.

Vagaggini, C. *The Canon of the Mass and Liturgical Reform.* London: Geoffrey Chapman, 1967.

Watkins, Keith. *The Feast of Joy.* St. Louis: Bethany Press, 1977.

Welker, Michael. *What Happens in Holy Communion?* Grand Rapids: Eerdmans, 2000.

10. OCCASIONAL SERVICES

Bradshaw, Paul F. *The Anglican Ordinal.* London: S.P.C.K., 1971.

Cooke, Bernard. *Ministry to Word and Sacraments: History and Theology.* Philadelphia: Fortress Press, 1980.

————. *Reconciled Sinners: Healing Human Brokenness.* Mystic, Conn.: Twenty-Third Publications, 1986.

Cope, Gilbert, ed. *Dying, Death, and Disposal.* London: S.P.C.K., 1970.

Dallen, James. *The Reconciling Community: The Rite of Penance.* New York: Pueblo Publishing Co., 1986.

Empereur, James L. *Prophetic Anointing.* Wilmington: Michael Glazier, Inc., 1982.

Gusmer, Charles W. *And You Visited Me: Sacramental Ministry to the Sick and Dying.* New York: Pueblo Publishing Co., 1984.

Irion, Paul E. *The Funeral: Vestige or Value?* Nashville: Abingdon Press, 1966.

Jennings, Theodore W., Jr. *The Liturgy of Liberation: The Confession and Forgiveness of Sins.* Nashville: Abingdon Press, 1988.

Kelsey, Morton. *Healing and Christianity.* New York: Harper & Row, 1973.

Knauber, Adolf. *Pastoral Theology of the Anointing of the Sick.* Collegeville, Minn.: Liturgical Press, 1975.

Mackin, Theodore. *The Martial Sacrament.* New York: Paulist Press, 1989.

McNeill, John T. *A History of the Cure of Souls.* New York: Harper & Row, 1977.

Palmer, Paul F. "Christian Marriage: Contract or Covenant?" *Theological Studies* 33 (December 1972): 617-65.

Power, David N. *Gifts That Differ: Lay Ministries Established and Unestablished.* New York: Pueblo Publishing Co., 1980.

Power, David, and Luis Maldonado, eds. *Liturgy and Human Passage.* New York: Seabury Press, 1979.

Rowell, Geoffrey. *The Liturgy of Christian Burial.* London: Alcuin/S.P.C.K., 1977.

Rutherford, Richard, and Tony Barr. *The Death of a Christian: The Rite of Funerals,* revised ed. Collegeville, Minn.: Liturgical Press, 1990.

Scott, Kieran, and Michael Warren. *Perspectives on Marriage.* New York: Oxford University Press, 1993.

Searle, Mark, and Kenneth W. Stevenson. *Documents of the Marriage Liturgy.* Collegeville, Minn.: Liturgical Press, 1992.

Stevenson, Kenneth. *Nuptial Blessing.* London: Alcuin/S.P.C.K., 1982.

Vos, Wiebe, and Geoffrey Wainwright, eds. *Ordination Rites.* Rotterdam, Netherlands: Liturgical Ecumenical Trust, 1980.

Willimon, William. *Worship as Pastoral Care.* Nashville: Abingdon Press, 1979.

INDEX